THE THEATRES OF MOLIÈRE

Molière's plays are the cornerstone of French Classical dramatic repertoire. Adapted and exploited in his day by dramatists of the English Restoration, they are now again growing in popularity in the English-speaking theatre.

In this detailed volume, Gerry McCarthy examines the practice and method of possibly the greatest actor-dramatist in the Western tradition. From the rough farces of Molière's days on the road to the creation of the diverse and spectacular court entertainments on his return to Paris, McCarthy sheds new light on the dramatic intelligence and theatrical understanding of Molière's writing for the actor.

Drawing on Molière's own brief discussions of performance and the contemporary evidence of his practice, this is a crucial addition to the debate on style and method in classical acting and on the staging of classical plays on the contemporary stage.

Gerry McCarthy is Professor of Theatre Studies at the University of Ulster. He has taught and directed in Canada, France and the UK, and his previous publications include *Edward Albee* (1987).

THEATRE PRODUCTION STUDIES
General Editor: John Russell Brown

'[This series] … will be welcomed by students and teachers alike.' –
New Theatre Quarterly

'To progress today's theatre into tomorrow's, we need to understand
yesterday's, and John Russell Brown's admirable detective series …
continues reconstructing what it was like to go to the theatre in the
past.' – *Cue*

Designed to span Western theatre from the Greeks to the present
day, each book in this path-breaking series explores a period or genre,
drawing together aspects of production from staging, wardrobe, and
acting styles, to the management of a theatre, its artistic team, and
technical crew. Each volume focuses on several texts of exceptional
achievement, and is well illustrated with contemporary material.

Already published and available:

SHAKESPEARE'S THEATRE
Peter Thomson

JACOBEAN PUBLIC THEATRE
Alexander Leggatt

BROADWAY THEATRE
Andrew Harris

GREEK TRAGIC THEATRE
Rush Rehm

MOSCOW ART THEATRE
Nick Worrall

AMERICAN AVANT-GARDE THEATRE
Arnold Aronson

THE THEATRES OF MOLIÈRE
Gerry McCarthy

THE THEATRES OF MOLIÈRE

Gerry McCarthy

London and New York

First published 2002
by Routledge
11 New Fetter Lane, London EC4P 4EE

Simultaneously published in the USA and Canada
by Routledge
29 West 35th Street, New York, NY 10001

Typeset in Garamond 3 by GreenGate Publishing Services,
Tonbridge, Kent
Printed and bound in Great Britain by Biddles, Ltd, Guildford and Kings Lynn

British Library Cataloguing in Publication Data
A catalogue record for this book is available from the British Library

Library of Congress Cataloging in Publication Data
McCarthy, Gerry.
The theatres of Molière / Gerry McCarthy.
p. cm.
Includes bibliographical references and index.
1. Molière, 1622-1673–Stage history. 2. Molière, 1622-1673–Dramatic production. I. Title.

PQ1871 .M37 2002
792.9'5'094409032–dc21
2001057000

ISBN 0415033497 (hbk)
ISBN 0415259479 (pbk)

FOR REBECCA, BEN AND JOE

CONTENTS

CONTENTS

FIGURES

ACKNOWLEDGEMENTS

I am grateful for permission to reproduce copyright material in the possession of the Bibliothèque nationale, Paris, the Nationalmuseum, Stockholm, the National Gallery of Art in Washington and the Ashmolean Museum in Oxford. I would also add my thanks to the staff in these institutions, who dealt efficiently and courteously with my requests for assistance.

I cannot overstate the debt I owe to John Russell Brown as both an indefatigable general editor and the source of energy, amusement and friendship over the period of this book's composition. I thank my students at the University of Birmingham and the University of Ulster and my friends in the theatre who have supported productions of Molière, without which this book would have been impossible for me to contemplate. I remember them all with gratitude if I do not name them individually here. I particularly thank Jacques Fournier and the actors of L'Embarcadère at Besançon, where I was invited to direct English classic plays, and came to know better another tradition of seventeenth-century performance. Finally, I gratefully thank my friend and colleague John Reddick for his many insights and suggestions at various points in the writing of this book, whose typescript he read with his characteristic care and concern.

PREFACE

A half-century ago W.G. Moore observed in his *Molière: A New Criticism*[1] that 'perhaps the most obvious thing to say about Molière is just that he was an actor', and he called for studies that would start from such a straightforward viewpoint. He went on to cite another actor, Louis Jouvet, who remarked in the theatre an insensitivity to Molière's text as a script for performance, and identified in his Conservatoire students[2] a characteristic neglect of the text and the substitution of spurious 'interpretations' of the roles. At the same time, Jouvet complained that Molière was dead in the universities, a victim of the theories of the *professeurs barbus*, who overlooked the practice of drama and the stage. Moore provokingly cited Jouvet's assertion that despite so much research, study, and, he might have said, performance, the student of Molière was left in a state of 'bewilderment' when facing his work.

It is to the credit of the universities that there has been a radical effort to research the history of Molière's theatre and establish the documents upon which an assessment may be made of his theatre practice. We are now in possession of a repertoire of documents and an iconography of Molière and his seventeenth-century context without which any study such as this would have been impossible. The scrupulous archival research of Jurgens and Maxfield-Miller[3], and the compilation and analysis by Mongrédien of a repertoire of contemporary texts and documents[4], now place precious materials conveniently in our hands, while Chevalley[5] has similarly assembled the images of Molière and his theatrical and social environment. These and other efforts have paralleled an increased critical curiosity as to the significance of performance in the understanding of Molière and the moral and intellectual structures which are undeniably apparent in his texts. We may still enquire whether, armed as we are with documentation of the history of the stage in Molière's age, we are in a position to explain the nature of performance itself as it was learned and practised by Molière. Most vexingly of all it is questionable whether academic research has made it possible to learn from our study of Molière those crucial perceptions of the phenomena of performance, in particular acting, which the work of the greatest actor–dramatist may afford.

When Bray, writing some five years after Moore, famously asked the question 'Molière pense-t-il?', his objective was hardly to argue that Molière's works are thoughtless, but that they embrace thought in a medium which is peculiarly social and collective in its operation. He opposed a tendency to see in Molière a moralist arguing a proposition, or satirising the manners of his age, and using theatre as the means of criticism. Such opposition does not deny the experience of the spectator, nor indeed of the sensitive reader, engaging with moral questions, but asserts the primacy of an experience of the actual practices of the stage. This is the complex enjoyment which the dramatist set out to procure, and to hypothesize what he 'thought' in any other terms is to ascribe intellectual positions and social purposes which are secondary to the living nature of the performance. Moore must have had as much in mind earlier when he considered the evidence for Molière's acting and concluded that 'the physical is everywhere and is very often symbolical of the moral'.[6] Citing Gustave Lanson writing at the beginning of his century,[7] Moore accepted the importance of the tradition of farce to Molière and alerted us to the moral significance of the knockabout moments which abound in the plays: Harpagon, the miser, accusing his audience of theft, or the servant Sganarelle taking a tumble as he attempts to baffle with his philosophy his sceptical master Dom Juan. Such moments, which Moore saw as 'mime', somehow encapsulate the proposition of the comedy, and offer a snapshot of the forces at work in the drama, but I fancy that Moore meant us to probe further the fundamental nature of physicalization in the processes of acting and audience response. We might also accept his suggestion that Jouvet's remarks, founded on experience of acting, may serve as a pointer.[8]

This book re-examines Molière, the man of the theatre, in the context of his profession, his education and the views of behaviour he might have held in common with his contemporaries. It also looks to Molière as a supremely conscious artist who explicitly discussed the nature of the medium in which he performed, and, in an extraordinary and imaginative output, embraced and developed its fundamental characteristics. Molière set out to follow the fashionable new tragedy of his day and spoke the alexendrines of Corneille and his contemporaries, Tristan l'Hermite and Du Ryer, but he achieved his mastery in exploiting the forms of the old popular comedy. Education and taste on one hand met energy, sensuality and the plain common sense of the street on the other. Molière's shrewd recognition of the power of the actor and his relationship with his audience unites the two.

There is a tendency in all ages to take for granted the art of the actor, and this is heightened further where the actor is to be despised or proscribed. He is seen as being guilty of an excessive and unseemly display, and he unnerves his temperate critic. While the person of the actor attracts attention, the art he professes is examined less curiously. Molière the actor could be described as 'dangerous', and even as a 'demon', and some of his plays resonated contemporary ideas in a fashion that some found subversive. But ultimately it was the power of acting that his enemies understood and feared. In the present time it is almost unthinkable that a fine actor could be found dangerous in this way. Our conception of acting scarcely encompasses subversion, although it may comprehend scandal. For us today, actors are remarkable for their power to move rather than persuade us; they may live dangerously on the stage, but we feel the excitement of unpredictability or outrage in our immediate presence, not in the context of society as a whole. The resonance of acting within the larger context of the social world depends on recognition. The audience must participate in the playhouse and in its amusements, and this demands an embodied understanding. It demands active participation in thinking. In studying plays from a tradition in which acting is at the forefront, we need to see the opportunities for playing that the surviving texts reveal, but also we need to be alert to what we learn as we make our discoveries. Molière, carefully studied, may afford us insights into the nature of acting itself.

Molière is treated in this book as the actor–dramatist he was, and his innovative approach to theatre presentation is important for what it tells us about theatre and drama in general, some of it at variance with our predispositions today. We will be most concerned with the way in which his writing and staging of plays absorbed the methods of the day and interacted with a stage which was rapidly evolving in the types of entertainment offered to the audience, and in the magnificence of the staging which could be procured. At a moment when the illusions of the scenic stage were beginning to enchant the French theatre, an actor appeared who was capable of creating drama out of the simple materials that are the human body and the rough platform stage of the street performer. His art was analytical and it was creative. For all that he was seen as the imitator of society, he was the creator with his audience of a shared pleasure, abstracted into a world of mind and fantasy. As an actor he offered and played a creative hypothesis in which recognition of life played a crucial part, but where the processes of life and thought were stretched to absurd and telling extremes. The strength of his method was in tune with the sometimes vulgar realism of his material, and was naturally born of his experience in popular comedy. This poor stage was rich, however, in its abstract possibilities, and its limited space accommodated a striking density of information to be juggled in the minds of the spectator.

We will very often draw attention to the banal fact of the stage and its importance to the actor: it sets the bounds of the actual space within which the actor can negotiate the terms of his performance, or beyond which can be placed other virtual spaces in which actions are presumed to play upon the exchanges witnessed on the platform itself. In considering the actor on this stage we are clear that space is for the human species as for any other animal species the condition for interactivity, and for the actor it is the most powerful determining factor in social relationships. Of all the senses at work in the 'live' theatre perhaps the sense of touch is the least remarked, yet tactility and proximity are strongly interlinked.

Beyond the sensual immediacy of this vital space in which the actual tactility of the performer is known and experienced throughout the playhouse, there lies the virtual space of the mental constructions which are symbolized in the actions and evocations of the performance. We often speak of the 'world of the play' or the 'imaginative space' of the action, and pass on to consider the representations which are presented in that world. These rapidly become in much current performance theory 'representations of' a world of everyday social and cultural experience, and we discover a set of parameters within which social and cultural critical 'discourses' can be applied. In this book we will note the way in which Molière the actor–dramatist arrests the mind on the creative boundary between the means of representation and the possibilities of recognition which lie beyond the performance.

In his few critical writings Molière occasionally argues the value of comedy in evoking moral problems and behaviours which may serve as examples of the pitfalls which attach to our everyday life in society. He also stresses, repeatedly, pleasure. He was expected by those hostile to the theatre to attempt a justification of the dangers of that pleasure and that justification was sought in the common-place that the moral effect of the stage was aversive. However, we will see that, far from teaching the way of the world, Molière was concerned with the creative power of the stage over the ways of the mind. He talked accurately of particular functions in performance and play-going, but also of the general value of recognition in the playhouse. Although in his day he was accused of satire, he answered that his mockery always remained part of the *thèse générale* which comedy proposed.

Molière's plays reveal an extraordinary mind and talent at work in a medium capable of taking a general thesis and developing it in the shared thought of actors and audience assembled in a given place and time, and unified in the physical forms and rhythms of the perfor-mance. When Molière speaks of the pleasure of the occasion he does so with an almost guarded wonder, above all in the undertaking of dramatic comedy, aimed at the amusement of good society. Lest this be thought to be some sort of sycophancy he made it quite clear that, as a whole, the audience that appreciated comedy, and certainly his comedy, possessed the best of intellectual qualities: *le sens commun.*

INTRODUCTION

This book considers the achievement of a seventeenth-century Parisian actor who entered the business of theatre and learned to exploit presentation and performance as none of his contemporaries ever did. He created theatre events and set up stages wherever an audience might be assembled and could be induced to patronize his company. He may well have commenced his career playing with street performers; he knew failure and success in the public play-houses he occupied at different periods of his career, and he responded to the astonishing opportunities and demands of a court where theatre was to be created as and where the sovereign required it. His was the imagination of the practitioner, for whom the carpen-ter's contract and the playwright's script are equally necessary to the entertainment he provides, and it was in fulfilment of the necessities of a company that he turned to the adaptation and writing of plays, and ultimately became the dramatist we know today as Molière.

Molière has rightly been seen by scholars and critics as a drama-tist who was also, crucially, *un homme de théâtre*, a viewpoint pioneered by René Bray's forthright study of 1954.[1] He worked within the forms of theatre of his day, but out of that experience created entertainments which suited his own acting and that of a remarkably stable and versatile company. The way in which Molière brought the elements of performance and presentation together will be our particular concern, as will the way in which his drama promotes the exercise of human capacities in both player and audience. It is always illuminating to discover a dramatist writing for the individual characteristics of particular actors, and there are instances of this in Molière's work. Much more important is the ability of the dramatist to write for the general function of acting (or dance or musical performance), with an understanding of how human life is experienced in the playhouse in the excitation

1

and engagement of human beings as participants in a remarkable exchange.

The circumstances of Molière's years of apprenticeship in the theatre and of his steadily maturing practice are important, even when one allows that the plays demonstrate the flowering of a remarkable genius. The society into which Molière was born experienced the excitement of a modern world of sophistication in manners and conversation, where intellectual and social stimuli abounded and there was leisure enough for the privileged sections of society to indulge its curiosity, and display its intellectual and cultural awareness. The theatre, although rooted in rough, popular entertainment, provided a revitalized medium in which the audience could recognize the breadth of its own concerns, and experience the refinement of its own manners and morals. We must suppose an audience which was considerably more conscious of the nature of the medium of drama, and more practised in music and dance, than we are today. Above all, we must conceive of an awareness in this audience of performance as a mobilization of different human capacities in the service of play and imagination, and not, as might be the case today, as the reproduction of behaviours and sensitivities appropriate to individualized concepts we term 'characters'. Our view of 'acting' and 'drama' betrays a certain unease, for while we generally seek and applaud states of feeling in the actor which secure our sympathy, we retain the sense that acting is pretence, and that its images of life remain superficial. This may be linked to the tendency, even in specialized academic analysis, to subsume 'acting' into 'performance' and 'drama' into 'theatre', as if to elude a certain prejudice which attaches to either. In discussing Molière and his theatres in this book, we will be anxious to see acting as a medium of performance beside lyric and choreographic performances, and to see theatre as the term which embraces the many different occasions of entertainment, inside and outside the playhouses we now call 'theatres', and which admits the organization of different physical spaces bringing together performer and audience. By speaking of 'theatres' in the plural, we refer to the varied occasions of Molière's professional activity, with radically different locations for his often temporary stages and for the varied performances which were shared with significantly different types of assembly. When we speak of 'theatre', we do not abuse the term to somehow sanitize 'drama', or 'comedy' or 'play'.

In 1643, when the twenty-one-year-old Jean-Baptiste Poquelin and a dozen or so associates contracted together to form a theatre company, we may well imagine a shared enthusiasm for a new and fashionable performance art. We must also see a business undertaking, aiming to compete with the two established Paris playhouses at the Hôtel de Bourgogne and the Théâtre du Marais. Theatre had become profitable in a capital city which had seen considerable economic expansion through the early decades of the century, and must have promised much to a group of middle-class Parisians, predominantly young, and able to look elsewhere for advancement in the world. The difficulty which faced Poquelin and his fellows was to come as a second wave after the actors and writers of the 1630s who had created a Parisian audience, and educated its taste. In creating a new company, *L'Illustre Théâtre*, they offered the novelty of personnel but not of method, and lacked some attraction, ultimately to come after an initial failure and more than a decade of provincial touring, when they returned to the capital and established themselves in a new genre, modern comedy, under the leadership of Poquelin now calling himself Molière.

Some of the first references to Molière and his company reflect the sorry beginnings of the troupe and the importance of the group of actors with whom he would share a life-long association, above all the Béjarts: Joseph, Madeleine and Geneviève and their much younger sister Armande-Grésinde, Molière's future wife. Tallement des Réaux chattily sums up what was the view of Madeleine Béjart's place in Molière's company:

> We come last to la Béjart. I never saw her play; but it is said she is the best actress of all. She is in a provincial troupe; she has played in Paris, but that was in a third company which was there only a short time [the *Illustre Théâtre*]. Her masterpiece was the character of Épicharis, tortured by Nero [in *La Mort de Sénèque*, by Tristan l'Hermite].[2]

Tallement adds a note to the evocation of Madeleine's appeal:

> A boy by the name of Molière left the benches of the Sorbonne to follow her; he was long in love with her, wrote music for the troupe{?}, and at length joined it and married her. He composes plays where there is some wit. He is not a wonderful actor, save for the comical. His plays are performed only by his own troupe; they are comic.[3]

Molière had indeed studied law, albeit at Orléans, and the young Jean-Baptiste Poquelin may well have been confirmed in his theatrical vocation by his attraction to Madeleine Béjart. There seems little doubt that she was subsequently his mistress, and the relationship must have been sufficiently comradely to ensure that his much later marriage to her sister, Armande-Grésinde, did not disrupt the life of the company, where Madeleine remained until at least 1669, at which time she played Dorine in *Tartuffe*. Tallement's acerbic remarks on Molière's acting recognize his success in comedy, but also how individual he must have seemed: despite the custom of the day where the printed play was available to any who wished to perform it, no-one challenged Molière in the performance of his own works.

The years that Molière shared with Madeleine Béjart touring the provinces were vital to his professional development. Every actor begins as a spectator, and in the ensemble which Molière led, his experience of the performances he had seen on the streets and in the playhouses of Paris was transmuted into an improvised comedy driven by the imagination of an emerging dramatist. This was the beginning of the career which is well known in literary history, but which was founded on fifteen earlier years of experience as a professional player. That experience and the continued practice of theatre presentation were intrinsic to the theatrical and dramatic forms and works that Molière would create. Fashioned by the theatre, he would prove one of its most extraordinary innovators. He would also be an inspirational exponent of its arts of performance, and an acute observer of the nature of theatrical pleasure.

Molière's career came to its premature end just as the technology of theatre presentation was asserting its potential to overwhelm the performer, above all the actor, and drama was being assimilated to lyric performance in the new French opera, which could marshall singing and dancing to fill the ever more elaborate stagings of the Italian scenic theatre. His theatrical imagination was such that he had been able to centre his own entertainments in the deeply human experience of the actor, conceiving the means of imaginative life out of the bare skeleton of words and action which is the play.

Part 1

LE PREMIER FARCEUR DE FRANCE

1

STREET AND STAGE

The importance of public display in seventeenth-century Paris is attested by the diplomatic and political spectacles which from time to time marked the life of the capital and, indeed, by the planning of the open spaces which were required for such events.[1] But if Peter Burke is correct in describing Louis XIV's France as a 'theatre state', the term is justified beyond the court in the forms of daily life, trade and amusement. Molière would have known the display and performance in the market place, where the show was offered in its own right on the trestle stage put up on the Place Dauphine, or the Pont Neuf, or in the booths of the town's two ancient fairs. For most of the population, it must be remembered, theatre meant theatre of the street.

For Molière the example of street theatre could have been inspirational, and he would have had every opportunity to see the players of a living tradition of popular French and Italian farce. The paintings and engravings of the early part of the century depict a range of performers, stages and the trade that accompanied performance. Such actors worked close to the public and addressed their audiences directly in the market place or the fairground. Their stages were set up beside the other sellers of wares in public places already pressured by the influx of commerce and the circulation of goods. The impact of these traders was resisted by the municipality, but without effect. In 1666 Gui Patin, the Parisian physician, was writing about the inadequacy of the legislation that restricted them:

> They are beginning to put into effect the previously agreed policy against the sellers, dealers and cobblers who encumber the public way, because they want to clean up the streets of Paris; the king has said that he wants to do to Paris what Augustus did to Rome.[2]

Throughout the century measures were introduced to improve the physical state of the city, increasing paving, and regulating the street as a place of exchange.

If the peddler represented for the authorities an irregular and dubious trader, likely to gull the innocent and misrepresent his wares, this was because entertainment was all too natural a part of his function. Commodities never change hands without a flow of information, and in the seventeenth century market presentation was at a premium. In everyday life the market place was the principal vehicle for the exchange not only of goods but of news. Pea-shellers, for example, were notorious gossips, like the present-day taxi-driver or hairdresser, delivering a service which could be supplied only in the presence of the customer.

The passage of information depended on public space. In an age where a relatively small proportion of the population could read, effective widespread publication depended upon human presence and the human voice. Town criers were part of Parisian street life and, although official announcements were made via a system of posters, *affiches*, or, for royal legislation, *placards*, placed at appointed sites, they were confirmed *viva voce* by the *juré-crieurs du Roi*, heralded at stopping places by three *juré-trompettes*. Only then was legislation binding. At particular sites, posters, including those for theatre performances, were displayed, and discussed for the benefit of those who could not read, but might consequently be all the more willing to attend. A quasi-theatrical display aided daily exchange and intercourse in the city. The pictorial sign, and the live presentation of events, far outweighed the printed word. Movement about the city was negotiated by means of landmarks and signs: churches indicated parishes, and if the correct parish could be found and the street discovered by enquiry, the individual house might be identified by its painted sign. (Molière was born at the *pavillon des singes*, named after the sculpted and painted pole at the doorway.) So important and widespread was the trade sign to the merchant or artisan that an attempt had to be made ultimately to regulate its size and positioning.

Another form of advertisement was the creation of the events through performances, particularly associated with the street seller's wares. The dialogue between trader and public grows into that of the seller and his assistant: a cross-talk act still familiar today with market and fairground traders. A development of this is the professional entertainer, and then the small company, standing alongside the salesman, showing in a living drama the nature and effects of the products on sale. The chief instance of this is the sale of medicines, where the miraculous powers of the nostrum can be demonstrated by the players. Through the first half of the century, the engravers' workshops were active producing images of celebrated *opérateurs* who entertained and sold, aided by their band of players. The most considerable among them maintained a small acting company, including players who went back and forth between street theatre and the drama of the playhouses. Italian *commedia dell'arte* players are evident on the stages of mountebanks in Italy, France and the Low Countries, and French players could surely find similar employment should the need arise. When the theatres were closed in Lent, street theatre escaped regulation, and at all times it offered low overheads and a guaranteed audience.

Street performance figures notably in the career of the *farceur*, Guillot-Gorju, famous in the 1620s, and from whose widow, it was later maliciously rumoured, Molière had purchased the secrets of his success. Having first qualified in medicine, he performed with a charlatan, but was then recruited to the *comédiens du roi* at the Hôtel de Bourgogne. After a period of some years, it is said, he resumed his career in medicine. The actor Des Lauriers played as the *farceur* Bruscambille at the Bourgogne, where his speciality was to deliver comic addresses to the crowd at the beginning of the performance, while at other times he worked in the street with the *opérateur* Jean Farine. His act was popular enough to be published in 1658 (or possibly it was the name which was capable of selling the material).

Figure 1.1   Street theatre: l'Orviétan, the seller of remedies. *Courtesy of the Bibliothèque nationale, Paris*

Figure 1.2 The company of Gilles le Niais. *Courtesy of the Bibliothèque nationale, Paris*

Similarly the actor working with the *opérateur* Desiderio Descombes published a volume in the guise of his stage character: *Les Rencontres, fantaisies et coqs-à-l'âne facétieux du Baron Grattelard*.

The miracle remedy, *orviétan*, is so famous that it gives its name to the seller, *L'Orviétan*, seen in a popular print (Figure 1.1) accompanied by at least two characters from his native Italian *commedia*: a Polchinelle, and a Brigantin, whose appearance suggests a relationship to Trivelin or Harlequin. A third character, l'Aveugle, seems more appropriate to native taste. The show is lively and full of movement: l'Aveugle is bated in some way while l'Orviétan controls the audience reaction. The setting is simple but, as the artist makes clear, solid. A closed, covered set stands on a substantial trestle stage, with space for a small group of privileged spectators, while the passing public stops below in the street, or goes on its way. In the engraving of Gilles le Niais (Figure 1.2), the setting goes as far as a scenic drop, and one may see, thanks to the artist, the heavy timber construction of the staging. Again the acting is rendered in lively fashion, with the stupid Gilles, wearing his characteristic closely fitting cap, following intently the progress of a card game.

In most cases the prints of street theatre insert into the composition some brief verse explaining the fun, often in the form of a street wall-poster. It would appear that not only were these theatres substantial semi-permanent structures attracting the casual passer-by, but they also promoted themselves by means of publicity.

The classic engraving of the famous company of Tabarin and Mondor playing the Place Dauphine (Figure 1.3) shows a simple trestle stage with a curtain serving as backdrop and discovery space. In a double act the star actor Tabarin enlivens the *opérateur* Mondor's presentation of a product for which ambitious claims have to be communicated. His name, 'mount of gold', reflects the exquisite action of the nostrum, which might promise gold in drinkable form as an ingredient. Tabarin, for his part, accompanied by his small troupe, including three musicians and an obvious pair of lovers, drew an audience to a show which included music and dancing. His talent for dramatic narrative was famous: working in large spaces to considerable audiences, he had the routine of pummelling his vast hat into different forms for the characters he played.

The stand-up act is particularly suited to such performance conditions, where direct address allows a performer to feel the rhythm of audience attention and develop his action accordingly. This can explain the power of apparently crude writing which emerges from this kind of popular street performance, and which finds an echo in the early play attributed to Molière, *La Jalousie du Barbouillé*. This opens with the 'sell', a monologue discovering to the audience the narrative basis of the play, and sharing with them the viewpoint of the actor.

Figure 1.3   Tabarin playing the Place Dauphine. *Courtesy of the Bibliothèque nationale, Paris*

Il faut avouer que je suis le plus malheureux de tous les hommes. J'ai une femme qui me fait enrager: au lieu de me donner du soulagement et de faire les choses à mon souhait, elle me fait donner au diable vingt fois le jour; au lieu de se tenir à la maison elle aime la promenade, la bonne chère, et fréquente je ne sais quelle sorte de gens, ... [etc.]

(Sc. i)[3]

I must confess that I am the most unfortunate of men. I have a wife who drives me crazy: instead of comforting me, and doing little things that I desire, she tells me twenty times a day to go to the devil; instead of staying at home, she prefers parading in public, good food, and keeps company with God knows what sort of people ... {etc.}

Not only are the robust techniques of the street theatre imported into the playhouse, but the best known of the charlatans, *opérateurs* and street players find their way into plays for the conventional stage. Molière himself included l'Orviétan in the interludes of his *L'Amour médecin*:

SGANARELLE

Holà, Monsieur, je vous prie de me donner une boîte de votre orviétan, que je m'en vais vous payer.

L'ORVIÉTAN *chantant*

L'or de tous les climats qu'entoure l'Océan,
Peut-il jamais payer ce secret d'importance?
Mon remède guérit, par sa rare excellence,
Plus de maux qu'on peut nombrer dans tout un an;
La gale,
La rogne,
La tigne,
La fièvre,
La peste,
La goutte,
Vérole,
Descente,
Rougeole,
O grande puissance de l'orviétan!

(II, vii)[4]

SGANARELLE

Hey! Good sir, I pray you give me a box of your orviétan, and I will pay you for it.

THE ORVIÉTAN singing

The gold from all the shores washed by the sea,
Would it ever buy this precious secret?
My remedy can cure, with its rare and excellent power,
More ills than one could number in a year
Scabies
Itch
Mange
The fever
The plague
The gout
The pox,
Hernia
Measles.
O, the mighty power of orviétan!

According to the satire, *Élomire hypocondre*, written for the rival Hôtel de Bourgogne and published in 1670, Molière's interest in the mountebanks was closer still. This rambling piece shows a hypochondriacal Élomire, Molière, enraging his family with his search for a remedy to his imagined ills. At one point the *opérateurs* Bary and l'Orviétan appear and discuss with Élomire the secrets of the art of *bouffonnerie*, of clowning or farce-playing:

BARY

Apprenez mes illustre confrères
Que tout notre art consiste en deux points nécessaires:
Le premier, c'est d'apprendre à grimacer des mieux;
L'autre, de bien débiter ces grands charmes des yeux,
Ces gestes contrefaits, cette grimace affreuse,
Dont on fait toujours rire une troupe nombreuse.[5]

BARY

Learn, my illustrious brothers
That all our art consists of two necessary points:
The first, is that one learns to grimace with the best;
The other, to employ well, to charm the watching eyes,
Those fake gestures, that horrid grimace,
With which one always makes a great assembly laugh.

Later in the work the melancholic Élomire is offered a form of art therapy: a play, depicting a private quarrel between a company of actors and their *chef de troupe*, Molière himself. Here the rebellious actors dispute the account that Élomire gives of his distinction and accomplishment as their star attraction. While he cites his excellent professional training at college (Molière was at the Collège de Clermont) and in Orléans (where indeed he took his law degree), the actors, led by Angélique (Madeleine Béjart), protest: he profited little from education, bought his degrees, and learned his trade from the charlatans l'Orviétan and Bary.

ANGÉLIQUE

En quarante, ou fort peu de temps auparavant,
Il sortit du collège, âne comme devant;
Mais son père ayant su que, moyennant finance,
Dans Orléans un âne peut avoir sa licence,
Il y mena le sien; c'est à dire ce fieux
Que vous voyez ici, ce rogue audacieux.
Il l'endoctora donc, moyennant pécune,
Et croyant qu'au barreau ce fils ferait fortune,
Il le fit avocat, ainsi qu'il vous a dit,
Et le para d'habits qu'il fit faire à crédit.
Mais, de grace, admirez l'étrange ingratitude!
Au lieu de se donner tout à fait à l'étude,
Pour plaire à ce bon père et plaider doctement,
Il ne fut au palais qu'une fois seulement.
Cependant, savez-vous ce que faisait le drôle?
Chez deux grands charlatans, il apprenait un rôle,
Chez ces originaux, l'Orviétan et Bary,
Dont le fat se croyait déjà le favori.[6]

ANGÉLIQUE

In 'forty, or shortly before,
He quit the college, as much an ass as ever;
But since his father knew that, by means of cash,
In Orléans an ass can have his degree,
He took his own there; that is to say this wretch
That you see here, this bare-faced rogue.
He doctored him then, by means of graft,
And believing that at the bar this son could make his way,
He made him an advocate, just as he has said,
And dressed him up in clothes that he ordered on credit.

14

But, for pity's sake, wonder at the strange ingratitude!
Instead of committing himself entirely to his studies,
To please his good father, and plead learnedly in the court,
He went there but one single time.
However, do you know what he did, this clown?
In the company of the two great mountebanks he learned a part,
In company with these models, l'Orviétan and Bary
Whose favourite the fool thought himself.

The satire goes on to allege that not only did Molière learn his art from the charlatans, but, gullible as he was, he allowed himself to be poisoned in the service of Bary, where he played the role of the patient miraculously saved from snakebite by the antidotes of his master:

ÉLOMIRE

Pour l'Orviétan, d'accord; mais pour Bary je nie
D'avoir jamais brigué place en sa compagnie.

ANGÉLIQUE

Tu briguas chez Bary le quatrième emploi:
Bary t'en refusa, tu t'en plaignis à moi;
Et je me souviens bien qu'en ce temps-là, mes frères
T'en gaussaient, t'appelant le mangeur de vipères;
Car tu fus si privé de sens et de raison,
Et si persuadé de son contrepoison,
Que tu t'offris à lui pour faire ses épreuves,
Quoiqu'en notre quartier nous connussions les veuves
De six fameux bouffons crevés dans cet emploi.[7]

ÉLOMIRE

As to l'Orviétan, I grant you; but for Bary, I deny
Ever having plotted to get into his company.

ANGÉLIQUE

You plotted there to get the fourth casting;
Bary refused it to you, and you complained to me about it;
And I remember well that in those days, my brothers
Mocked you for it, calling you the viper-eater;
For you were so short of sense and reason,
And so convinced of his antidotes,
That you offered yourself to him as a guinea-pig,
For all that, in our parish, we were acquainted with the widows
Of six famous clowns who died playing that part.

Figure 1.4   Charlatans selling at the fair, one handling a snake. Jacques Callot: *The Fair at Impruneta* (detail). *Courtesy of the National Gallery of Art, Washington*

Cruelly attributing Molière's pallor to the effects of snakebites suffered as the gullible assistant of a charlatan, the satire suggests that the street was indeed where he started his career as an actor (see Figure 1.4). The grain of truth always makes mockery more trenchant, and there is no reason entirely to discount the idea that a young man addicted to the theatre should try his hand with the professionals on the streets and squares of Paris.[8]

Street entertainers were naturally attracted to the crowded squares and to the Pont Neuf, both a crossing point and market place. More important still were the two permanent fairs of the capital, the Foire Saint-Germain situated hard by the Abbey church on which it depended, and the Foire Saint-Laurent on the site of the present-day Gare de l'Est. These combined the appeal of the market place with a permanent arrangement of vendors' stalls and entertainers' stages, at least some of which were closed so that admission could be charged. The latter catered for the popular taste for acrobats, puppeteers and rope-dancers, as well as farce-players, dancers, singers and musicians. English visitors were struck by the French enthusiasm for dice and gaming:

The fair of Saint-Germain begins the 3rd of February and holds all the Lent; the place where the fair is kept in, is a large square house with six or seven rows of shops, where the customers play at dice when they come to buy things; the commodity is first bought, and then they play who shall pay for it. After candle-lighting is the greatest gaming, sometimes the King comes and dices.[9]

Most companies would learn in the conditions of the fairground, as did Molière's *Illustre Théâtre* playing the Rouen fair in the autumn of 1643, or, between 1645 and 1658, touring the assortment of venues that were to be found in the provinces.

The engagement of supernumerary performers for the *Illustre Théâtre* shows how, like the popular players of the street, a spread of skills was required. Musicians were to play for the 'ballet', in which the company would dance, but where the addition of a professional dancer could augment their efforts. In June 1644 the *Illustre Théâtre* engaged the *danseur* Daniel Mallet 'in plays as well as dances',[10] at half the retainer again of the musicians, 30 sous daily. The agreement makes reference to some professional discords in which the *Illustre Théâtre* had been of service to the dancer, who was being pursued by one Cardelin, *voltigeateur ordinaire du Roi*, who may have wished to retain Mallet as a rope-dancer. He is styled *opérateur du Roi*, an entertainer, and had worked as a *voltigeateur*, a tumbler and rope-dancer.

The vogue for these French performers was widespread. Mallet may not have performed on the rope for Molière's company, but he bridged the gap between the entertainments of the street and those of the playhouse. The rope-dancer or the tumbler was an attraction at the fair, and succeeded at court where his specialized skills were required in grotesque or comic episodes in the *ballet de cour*.[11] Mallet's engagement brought to the troupe the breadth of performance skill displayed in the street or at the fair, but also at court. It should never be forgotten that in thirty years of theatre activity Molière, the would-be tragedian, worked shoulder to shoulder with entertainers in almost every medium of performance. The appeal of popular performance was something that he learned in his first years, and remembered still when he played before the King some of the repertoire which he had refined before a popular audience.

2

EDUCATION:

Jean-Baptiste Poquelin at the Collège de Clermont

Actors in seventeenth-century France were not (save in a possible early instance) apprenticed, the normal means by which a craft was learned. A parent might place a likely boy as apprentice to a *maître joueur d'instruments*, and an adult might engage the same musician to teach him the violin, or act as his *maître de danse*. No Parisian bourgeois would seek to train a child in a profession which was socially dubious, and proscribed by the church. On the other hand, seventeenth-century education in general favoured accomplishments that might be developed and refined for the theatre, the very least of which was the ability to read.

The Parisian bourgeoisie had access to education, if only to parish classes for the children of the poor. For those of moderate means the *petites écoles* taught the rudiments of reading and writing, beyond which the wealthier could proceed to the *collège*, opening the way to the lettered professions. In the *petites écoles*, the recitation of the lesson from memory was a key part of the pedagogy. Abraham Bosse's engraving of the teacher, working in his own room, shows a small group of boys who present themselves, elegantly if apprehensively, for the performance of their lesson (see Figure 2.1). We see the respectful approach, the hat held as advised by de Lauze in the *Apologie de la Danse* of 1623:

> in front of the busk of the pourpoint with the left arm, but always with a negligent air; a too precise manner now lacking gentility.[1]

The body is carried forward with a similar *négligence*, emphasising the leg turn-out prescribed by the dancing manuals:

> I will have a Master (of dancing) to teach a Gentleman how to keep his body in a good posture when he stands, sitteth or

walketh, how to come in or go out of a Chamber where is
Company; he must be taught how to carry his head, his
hands, and his toes out, all in the best way, and with the
handsome presence. A master teaches the steps, but the
Grace, the carriage, and the free motion of the body must
chiefly come with use.[2]

'Use' is apparent in the second pupil advancing to the master's desk,
while a third waits in the background, his hat on his head, ready to
advance and make his salutations. The first seems to have lost his
aplomb at the sight of the master's birch. While the boys are generally occupied with books, the girls engage in some more domestic
occupation. The lesson is a semi-public performance, in a society sensitive to the presentation of the self. Two men at the doorway view
the way in which the young adult, costumed as such from the age of
seven, executes the memorized lesson. Molière would forget none of
this in the catechising of Agnès in his *L'École des femmes*. Here the
master sits, and the pupil approaches, to be corrected, first, in her
deportment. The symbolism of the chair and the physical positions is
both socially explicit, and theatrically expressive. Molière was adept
at the use of a chair on stage.

Figure 2.1 Abraham Bosse: *The Schoolmaster. Courtesy of the Ashmolean Museum,
Oxford*

19

ARNOLPHE *(assis)*
Agnès, pour m'écouter, laissez là votre ouvrage.
Levez un peu la tête et tournez le visage:
Là, regardez-moi là durant cet entretien,
Et jusqu'au moindre mot imprimez-le-vous bien.
Je vous épouse Agnès …

(III, ii)[3]

ARNOLPHE (seated)
Agnès, to hear me, set aside there your handwork.
Raise your head a trifle, and turn your face:
Here, look at me here during our conversation,
And make sure you mark every last word.
Agnès, I shall marry you …

Arnolphe's insistence on the deportment of his 'pupil' conforms to an educational practice which prescribed detailed movements and physical attitudes appropriate to the various occupations of the day, and moulds mind and body even in the fine skill of writing:

> That the body may be held correctly, the master will himself place the scholar in the posture that he must adopt, and dispose each limb in the place where it must be, and when he shall see any change in posture, he will take care to put it once more in place.[4]

At the end of the famous lesson which Agnès must 'dévorer du coeur', Arnolphe requires her to curtsey, and turns to mental exercise, handing her what is to be her catechism, the *Maximes du mariage ou devoirs de la femme mariée avec son exercise journalier*. Like manuals of devotion, these require exercises to be undertaken regularly and learned by heart. The scene takes educational practice and sets it on the stage, as a performance within a performance:

ARNOLPHE
Faites la révérence. Ainsi qu'une novice
Par coeur dans le couvent doit savoir son office,
Entrant au mariage il en faut faire autant;
Et voici dans ma poche un écrit important
(Il se lève)
Qui vous enseignera l'office de la femme.[5]

ARNOLPHE

You may curtsey. Just as a novice
In the convent must know by heart her duties,
Entering upon marriage's estate one must do as much;
And here in my pocket is a weighty text
(He rises)
Which will instruct you in the duties of the wife.

This was the scene which Chaveau engraved as the frontispiece for the edition of the play published in 1663, preserving, presumably, a notable moment in the performance. Molière strains his plotting here by having Agnès capable of reading and writing despite the ignorance Arnolphe has procured. However, through her reading, like any other performer, Agnès, played by Mademoiselle de Brie, can adopt new roles, perhaps even that of the dutiful wife. When she writes, Molière makes Agnès brilliantly tentative, searching out another role entirely.

When the young Jean-Baptiste was sent to school, the Poquelin family enrolled him with the Jesuits at the Collège de Clermont, ensuring that he received the most progressive and fashionable education in Paris, patronized by the nobility as well as the upper bourgeoisie. Molière could have known the Prince de Conti (the younger brother of the Grand Condé), later his patron and then his censor, although the Prince was seven years his junior. The presence of a scion of one of France's greatest families among the pupils gives an indication of the social spectrum Molière would have seen, and a glimpse of the world of hereditary power to which he, and many of his fellows, would win access.

The educational philosophy of the Jesuits was pragmatic, and reconciled the Christian life with the world of government and the professions. They were training these young men for roles in a society where most communication was live, and demanded effective presentation and performance. The rewards of this training are beguilingly expressed by Père Richeome:

It is humanely divine and divinely human to know how worthily to manage a topic with wit and tongue, to conceive it in the mind with fair and judicious thoughts, to arrange one's thoughts in wise order, to clothe them in rich terms and to bring them to the listener's ear with a sound memory, a lively ringing voice, sweetly penetrating; and with a like address in the whole body, to make oneself heard to good effect; to plant new opinions and new desires in men's hearts

and to uproot the old; to sway and bend stiff wills, to brace
up and stiffen the twisted and the weak; and victoriously to
persuade and dissuade at one's will.[6]

Performances of this power ensured the reputations of preachers such
as Bossuet and Bourdaloue, and troubled those, less worldly than the
Jesuits, who deplored the aesthetic pleasures of even the sermon. No
pupil in the colleges could be ignorant of the debate on the perils
and delights of fine and persuasive speech, and Molière's training
would have equipped him to exploit the abuse of rhetoric in a gallery
of roles found in the tradition of popular farce. He himself sometimes
played the arch-abuser of language, the pedantic *docteur* in a
grotesque parody of rhetorical practice, interrupting or delaying any
business in hand with a rigmarole of proofs or illustrations. In *Le
Dépit amoureux*, the elaborations of the learned Métaphraste enrage
Albert who finally erupts at the pedant's Latin tags:

> ALBERT
> Maître, en discourant ensemble,
> Ce jargon n'est pas fort nécessaire, me semble.
> Je vous crois grand latin et grand docteur juré:
> Je m'en rapporte à ceux qui m'en ont assuré;
> Mais dans un entretien qu'avec vous je destine
> N'allez point déployer toute votre doctrine,
> Faire le pédagogue, et cent mots me cracher,
> Comme si vous étiez en chaire pour prêcher.
>
> (II, vi)[7]

> *ALBERT*
> *Master, for our conversation*
> *This jargon is hardly necessary, I think.*
> *You are a great Latinist and sworn Doctor:*
> *I have the word of those who tell me so;*
> *But in the chat that I intend to have with you*
> *There is no call to unfold all of your scholarship,*
> *To act the professor, and spit out the dictionary,*
> *As though you were preaching in the pulpit.*

The comedy rests on the contrast of learned nonsense and ignorant
commonsense. The preoccupation of Métaphraste with literary
quotation (he is particularly fond of Virgil) and rhetorical ornaments prevents the consideration of actual questions and answers.

22

More substantial pleasures are involved with the practice of rhetoric in *Tartuffe*, where words subtly portray sensual pleasures in the language of devotion, and arguments are marshalled to excuse the impermissible. Tartuffe's rhetoric is the same casuistry Molière's tutors were held to practise, and denounced famously by Pascal in his *Lettres provinciales*. The playwright was an apt pupil.

TARTUFFE

L'amour qui nous attache aux beautés éternelles
N'étouffe pas en nous l'amour des temporelles;
Nos sens facilement peuvent être charmés
Des ouvrages parfaits que le Ciel a formés.

(III, iii, ll. 933–936)[8]

TARTUFFE

The love which binds us to those eternal beauties
Does not stifle that we bear to those more temporal
Our senses easily may be enchanted
By heaven's perfect handiwork.

Richeome's art of 'planting new opinions and desires in the heart of another' is expertly employed in the *faux dévot*. Condemning the immorality of the play, Molière's detractors protested that such rhetoric was indeed capable of planting such ideas in the lady's mind, while Molière in the *Lettre sur l'imposteur* stresses the effect of comedy in highlighting the *ridicule* of such language. Classroom training in argument perfected a method which was adaptable, even to the dangerous scenes between Elmire and Tartuffe:

ELMIRE

La déclaration est tout à fait galante,
Mais elle est, à vrai dire, un peu bien surprenante.
Vous deviez, à ce me semble, armer mieux votre sein,
Et raisonner un peu sur un pareil dessein.
Un dévot comme vous, et que partout on nomme …

TARTUFFE

Ah! pour être dévot, je n'en suis pas moins homme;
Et lorsqu'on vient à voir vos célestes appas,
Un coeur se laisse prendre, et ne raisonne pas.
Je sais qu'un tel discours de moi paraît étrange;
Mais, Madame, après tout, je ne suis pas un ange …

(III, iii, ll. 961–970)[9]

ELMIRE

The declaration is most gallant,
But, I declare, somewhat astonishing.
You should, it seems to me, better arm your breast,
And ponder a little such a plan
A pious man like you, whom everywhere people speak of as ...

TARTUFFE

Ah! pious I may be, but nonetheless a man;
And when one comes to see your heavenly attractions,
The heart gives in, and entertains no reasons.
I know such words from me seem strange;
But, madam, after all, I'm not an angel ...

Tartuffe does in fact 'raisonner', and debates the theme which Elmire sets him. The play found its subject and its style close to the roots of Molière's training with the Jesuits, perhaps echoed in Elmire's response to Tartuffe:

TARTUFFE

Le soin que nous prenons de notre renommée
Répond de toute chose à la personne aimée,
Et c'est en nous qu'on trouve, acceptant notre coeur,
De l'amour sans scandale et du plaisir sans peur.

ELMIRE

Je vous écoute dire, et votre rhétorique
En termes assez forts à mon âme s'explique.

(III, iii, ll. 997–1002)[10]

TARTUFFE

The care we take to guard our reputation
Answers in all occasions to the one we love
And only with us may you find, accepting our heart's devotion,
Love without scandal, and pleasure without fear.

ELMIRE

I have heard you out, and your rhetoric
Addresses my soul in pretty urgent terms.

In their Christian ministry the Jesuits were on the side of art, and taught fine speech as a legitimate and enjoyable means to worthy ends. So the Collège de Clermont concerned itself with extended training in those parts of rhetoric which attach to the delivery of speeches: *elocutio*, *pronuntiatio* and *memoria*.

24

Elocutio, the part of rhetoric which governed style, led on naturally to *pronuntiatio*, the effective delivery of speech. This meant pleasing presentation, both in terms of audibility, vocal quality and variety; and also a free and flexible personal response to the language used. The happy cultivation of style and presentation was vain if the delivery was not sustained by *memoria*, a fluent recall. If these elements of the performance of the speech cohered, one could then expect a natural physical engagement in the speaker, *actio*, and the liberation of moral and emotional response in the speaker. This is linked practically to persuasion by *ethos*, the moral character of the speaker and his known qualification for his views.

The parts of rhetoric which concerned delivery are also those fundamental to the actor, a fact the Fathers recognized in extending classroom exercises into the fully staged world of the theatre. From the writing of a speech to be delivered in the class, to the periodic staging of full performances, the Jesuits of the Collège de Clermont led the way in the use of theatre as a cultural and educational tool. In 1636, at which time Molière must have been a pupil, the Father Provincial, Père Binet, argued that the practice had gone too far:

> Exercises in speaking are transformed to veritable plays to the detriment of study … Oratory is neglected in favour of tragedy.[11]

Throughout Europe the Jesuits were notable for this slide into an erudite but engaging type of theatre. At the Collège de Clermont an enthusiastic public had to be checked by setting the number of productions at two per year: the rhetoric class performed on the occasion of the distribution of the King's prizes, and another, shorter performance was given, possibly at *carnaval*, by the boys in *seconde* a year below. Plays were extensively rehearsed and expensively produced, and appealed to an audience absolved of the taint associated with theatre elsewhere, by the spirit of moral probity and social élitism which prevailed. The pleasure of the audience subsequently became a factor in the substitution of French for the Latin required by the grammarian. In 1685, when the King's enthusiasm for acting had begun to wane under the influence of Madame de Maintenon,[12] and when one might have expected smaller public interest, Père Jouvancy was still protesting against a drift into popularity. Plays should not be given in French:

> In this form of work we are normally clumsy and laughable. Besides, our rule forbids it and commands that our exercises

serve to perfect youth in the Latin tongue. Our shows should not create any manner of pleasure, but pleasure worthy of learned men and spectators of quality. The wondrous creations of art debase themselves when the poet concerns himself with flattering the taste of the ignorant multitude.[13]

The Latin text would have been a handicap for many, particularly women, but its use would not have seemed inappropriate. The eccentric journalist Loret is not abashed by his own difficulties:

> Les Écoliers des Jésuites,
> Dont les personnes sont instruites
> Aux sciences, soir et matin,
> Représentèrent en latin,
> Sur un théâtre magnifique,
> D'Égeric, l'histoire tragique,
> Dont les vers, à ce que m'ont dit
> Des gens d'esprit et de crédit,
> (Et me l'ont dit en conscience)
> Sont pleins d'art et d'intelligence …[14]

> *The pupils of the Jesuits*
> *Who are well versed*
> *In learning, night and day,*
> *Gave lately, in the Latin tongue,*
> *Upon a magnificent stage*
> *Égeric, a tragic story*
> *Whose verses, by the report*
> *Of persons of wit and credit*
> *(And told to me in earnest truth)*
> *Are full of art and understanding …*

Loret was something of a gadfly, and if his attention were not secured he would not necessarily remain in his place. The good Fathers saw him walking out on the 1659 performance when he had been supplied with 'neither stool nor chair' but in the following year, aided by the hospitality shown him:

> Pour moy, créature rampante,
> La pièce me parut charmante,
> Mes yeux furent souvent ravis,
> Et, commodément, je la vis

Sans aucun accident sinistre,
Grâce au sage Père ministre,
Autrement, le Père Gelé,
Par qui je fus là, régalé
De vin, de fruits, en abondance,
Et d'une place d'importance.[15]

As for me, poor lowly creature,
The play appeared enchanting,
Often my eyes were delighted,
And, comfortably, I beheld the sight,
With no untimely misfortune,
Thanks to the wise Father-minister,
Otherwise known as Father Gelé,
By whom I was furnished
With wine, fruits, most liberally,
And seated in a place of distinction.

In the provinces college plays attracted large crowds and a town might often support the production from the public purse, or turn to the Fathers for the organization of extraordinary celebrations, such as the reception of royalty. They knew the theatrical culture of Italy and the advances in staging which were being made there, in addition to the new fashions for entertainments which brought together elements of music, dancing and speech. If the public coveted admission to entertainments staged at the Collège de Clermont, it was because of the splendour and variety of the entertainment, and chief among the attractions was the element that required the theatrical resources they possessed: the ballet.

Most surprising perhaps to us today is the Jesuits' belief in a training in dance and the performance of ballets. Payments were made to dancing masters for the instruction of the pupils, and also to consorts of musicians employed to provide accompaniment. By the end of the century the colleges would retain these teachers permanently. One example is of particular interest. In 1638 the Collège de Clermont celebrated the birth of the Dauphin Louis with a three-day festivity:

There was no religious house which did not adorn its walls with candles. The Jesuits, after their public and private devotions, besides lining their walls with thousands of lights on the 5th and the 6th, gave on the 7th a curious fire-work display in their courtyard which was lighted by a

dolphin, among two thousand other lights, which lit a ballet and a comedy on the same subject, played in masterly
fashion by their pupils.[16]

The review points out not only the quality of the acting and dancing
but also the professionalism of the entire display. The combination of
dancing and light, culminating in a fireworks display, was designed
to appeal to current taste, and would have found favour in any court
divertissement. Indeed costumes and other materials were obtained
from the court on occasion. The *Mercure françois* records the elaborate
scenery of the 1638 production being hired in for the occasion.[17]
Charles Sorel, while satirizing his tutors in his *Histoire comique de
Francion*, describes a college performance early in the century where
confusion arises from the similarity of costumes which were all
adapted from 'cast-offs from a ballet of the King's'.

The concern in the *Ratio studiorum* for the dignity of tragedy and
comedy affected the role that dance came to play in the Jesuit theatre. The Jesuits were impelled by the limited currency of the
language of performance, Latin, to comment on the actions through
the medium of dance, which, in turn, as was customary with the *ballet de cour*, involved recitations in French and the setting of words to
music. At the end of the century this practice was recognized:

> At the Collège de Clermont, where there is given each year a
> great tragedy, they link most often the subject of the ballet
> to that of the tragedy. Thus at the tragedy whose subject was
> The Ruin of the Assyrian Empire, there was chosen for the
> subject of the ballet The Dreams, for this ruin had been pre
> dicted by several dreams ...[18]

The acts of the play and the ballet *intermèdes* are interleaved in such a
way that le père Lejay can explain the dance as part of an integrated
work with choreography conveying the sense of the play.

> It is not sufficient that these movements and these gestures
> are composed, elegant, harmonious, agreeable to the eye; if
> they have not a determined sense, a precise meaning, they
> will offer only a vain and futile dance, and will not deserve
> the name of dramatic ballet, whose end is imitation. The
> gestures and the steps must be the representation of the
> actions which are interpreted [in the play] and display these
> to the spectators, in such a manner that the latter have no

need of explanatory commentary and understand the mute language of the dancers.[19]

It is a theme of the time that merit can go unrecognized if it is not presented in polite society.[20] Among the exercises the Fathers taught, dance gives support to the physical presentation of the person, idealized in a social practice of movement. The training of the body and the resolution of tensions, according to the manuals of dance, accommodated the individual to the social world. He might achieve through the exercise of dance a naturalness and balance in his movements which extend to the entire personality. Experience of education and observation of the world suggested to the Jesuits the power of physical form in coordinating the individual with the group, and explained the function of dance as a means of knowing the world:

> ... [dancing] goes so far as to express the nature of things, and the habits of the soul, which cannot be seized by the senses save through movements.[21]

The linking of rhetoric and dance opens a perspective on the Jesuits' training and its importance to the actor. The forms of behaviour which he was expected to demonstrate on stage in their very perfection were acquired by close study and by exercise. 'Natural' behaviour could be discussed only when its components had been minutely dissected out for examination. The lessons of these analyses were prescriptions for performance in everyday life. They organized the forms of thought, gesture and bodily movement and sustained the presentation of the self. The instinctive regard for the dance can be seen as the sense of integration prevailing in an atmosphere of analysis and codification. In the debate over *Tartuffe* Molière advanced ideas which derive from a similar insight: that meanings are embodied in physical performances.

Educational practice was a determining factor both of acting styles, and, inevitably, of the works which were written for performance. Whatever the theory of *le naturel*, the balanced performance aimed to please and persuade. The rhetorical stance is concerned with the structures of thought, urged and encouraged by stick and carrot of passion and pleasure. But the very processes of rhetorical thought are systematic, at a remove from the flux of particular experiences. A training of this sort could result in affectation or pedantry, present in the desiccated thought and persons of some of Molière's entertaining pedants, but equally, the Jesuits understood how performance might assemble abstract forms artfully so that they may create the illusion of natural life.

The Jesuits helped fashion Parisian theatre culture of the first half of the seventeenth century, equipping both actors and writers for the creation of a modern theatre with a literature of its own. An actor who had been in their hands would have learned before a fashionable public the physical and mental disciplines governing the presentation of speech and movement. His experience would show how works of moral and philosophical complexity could be written and played for an audience drawn from the dominant religious or social élite. Such an actor, and Molière was one, would have seen in the new modern repertoire of the Jesuit-trained Corneille and his contemporaries, the secular image of the theatre they had known at college. In entering the theatre, Molière intended to succeed in tragedy.

3

FARCEURS:

Old French Farce and *commedia dell'arte*

The farceurs of the Hôtel de Bourgogne

The theatre of the Jesuits contrasted sharply with a tradition dependent almost entirely on the art of the actor and which, in Molière's childhood, reflected the tastes of another public. This was the popular farce, a world away from the discreet and intensified concerns of the martyrs and heroes of both college and professional stages. The Old French Farce, conserving a tradition going back to the medieval stage, was still played by a celebrated company of *farceurs* at the Hôtel de Bourgogne, the sole licensed theatre of the capital. Despite the achievement of the resident *troupe royale* in encouraging a new audience for serious drama, the actors were perhaps better known in the early part of the century for their performances under the comic mask. In this they were rivalled only by the Italian *commedia dell'arte* actors, with whom they occasionally shared the theatre. With new repertoire the respectable audience grew through the 1630s, but the farce continued strongly, and contemporaries recount how Molière's grandfather took him to see the French *farceurs*, and possibly the Italians too, playing at the Bourgogne or at the Louvre. Italian and French traditions interacted, greatly to the advantage of the latter. The *commedia dell'arte* showed the value of physical mastery in the playing of a simple scenario or *canevas*, particularly where the language of performance was unfamiliar, even to many at court. French *farceurs*, for all the advantage of language, did not develop any form of extended text, but relied also on improvisation.[1] Illustrations of their scenes and their characters show, as in the *commedia*, episodes of cuckoldry, gluttony and theft, with a distinctly popular appeal. At a time when the nuances of social life preoccupied the well-to-do, the *farceurs* must have offended as much by their naïvety as by the indelicacy of their material.

Figure 3.1 The farce-players of the Hôtel de Bourgogne in the 1620s and 1630s. Left to right: Le Capitaine Fracasse, Turlupin, Gros-Guillame, Gaultier-Garguille. *Courtesy of the Bibliothèque nationale, Paris*

The *comédiens du roi* played farce with a basic company of some six to eight players, all active in tragedy. Several were well known under their farce names: Turlupin, Guillot-Gorju, Gros-Guillaume, Gaultier-Garguille and le Capitaine Fracasse. The lovers, like their counterparts the *innamorati* in the *commedia dell'arte*, hardly warranted a stage name. The lover in Bosse's engraving (Figure 3.3) may

Figure 3.2 Farce scene at the Hôtel de Bourgogne. *Courtesy of the Bibliothèque nationale, Paris*

be Charles Lenoir, transferred to the Bourgogne from the Marais by order of Louis XIII, but he is indicated merely as 'L'Amant'.[2] The detail of these engravings shows the style of playing as well as the staging employed. Actors are depicted in lively exchanges, their bodies caught in strong attitudes with a clear focus of attention. Sometimes the actor looks out at the spectator, a gaze we naturally return, enjoying the shared intelligence which operates between actor and audience. The setting encourages this complicity, with some vantage point for the actor to observe the scene and engage in a privileged exchange with the spectator. In most cases there is a simple stage with wings and two practicable doors. Above are windows, as in Bosse, where Jannequin observes the scene or, as in the frontispiece to the *Nouvelles Chansons de Gaultier-Garguille*, from which Turlupin and Gros-Guillaume look out above the old man to the audience. This tiny illustration reduces the stage to its simplest scheme, compressed to draw attention to a few key spatial relationships. Where the setting is indicated more fully, there may be a painted backcloth, or upstage a curtain is sometimes rigged (see Figure 3.1), providing a hiding place. The set may well conceal the decor of another play, or incorporate some of its elements.[3] In all cases we see how the simple set promotes a free exchange of information between players and spectators.

The masks and costumes of the farce are reminiscent of the *commedia dell'arte*. The roles of captain and doctor are common to the two traditions, as is the old husband or father played by a Gaultier-Garguille or a Pantalone. Turlupin and Jodelet have the vivid

Figure 3.3   The farce-players of the Hôtel de Bourgogne c.1635: Guillot-Gorju centre, l'Amant stage right, and Jodelet left. Jaquemin observes from above. *Courtesy of the Nationalmuseum, Stockholm*

costume of the Italian players and, while Gros-Guillaume appears to be cast in a French mould, given the accent on his size and gourmandise, there is nevertheless a hint of the *commedia* Brighella about the stripes to be seen on the costume. Street dress is worn by the Lovers alone, and where it is adopted by the Capitaine, Docteur, or Gaultier-Garguille, the stage costume is achieved by emphasising some aspect of the everyday, either a superfluity of grandeur, ludicrous old-fashionedness or academic black. In the Bosse engravings we see concealed or exiting the figure of the Capitaine, who displays something of the magnificence and cowardice of his Italian and Roman ancestors. Perhaps for political reasons, Capitaine Fracasse was played Spanish, and in Figure 3.1 is illustrated carrying, besides his magnificent and underused sword, a tress of onions. The leading farceurs have an element of the fantastic about them, and their costume and mask identify them as the purest of theatrical constructs.

Figure 3.4   Turlupin. *Courtesy of the Nationalmuseum, Stockholm*

Turlupin, created by Henri Legrand, wears a loosely fitting costume with baggy trousers and an ample soft hat (see Figure 3.4). There is no recollection of any particular street costume: the cloth is light-coloured, and jacket and trousers bear a green stripe down the arms and leg, reminiscent of the Brighella from which he may have been derived. His costume is made more flexible by the addition of a cloak which in the Bosse engraving is pulled round him (see Figure 3.3). Doubtless it could be used to indicate the playing of indoor and outdoor scenes, and also when the demands of the plot required, it could hide his face, half-masked above his beard and moustache. His costume is completed by his belt and an obvious wooden sword. Appropriately enough it is this which is drawn in the farce scene depicted, while his master has his hand only upon the hilt of his own. The *emploi*[4] of Turlupin must have been the resourceful servant, or the trickster when working on his own account. Above all he is credited with a brilliant use of language, one of the essential skills in a company elaborating plays based on a succession of stratagems and devices. The name of Turlupin became synonymous with the artful pun, and years after his death such witticisms could be decried as Turlupinades, a term Molière would employ for the nonsense of his affected *petit marquis*.

The legacy of the Old French Farce is most apparent in Gros-Guillaume (Robert Guérin, Lafleur in serious plays) and in the old men, Gaultier-Garguille and Guillot-Gorju. It is possible that Gros-Guillaume derived from the miller figure in the old plays, and his floured face and ample proportions would suggest as much (see Figures 3.1 and 3.2). Unmistakable in his loose striped costume which does nothing to disguise his impressive girth, he played, unusually, without a mask. The tradition of playing *enfariné*, white-faced using flour, or *barbouillé*, red-faced with wine lees, survived into the seventeenth century alongside the masks of other roles. Gaultier-Garguille (Hughes Guéru) was again a masked actor (see Figures 3.1 and 3.2) playing the old bourgeois in farces based on cuckoldry and marital intrigue, and perhaps *docteur* roles as well. He is depicted in his old-fashioned costume with a prominent purse and stick; both essential props for his *emploi*. Guillot-Gorju (Bertrand Haudoin de St Jacques) trained as a physician and played *docteur* roles at the Bourgogne. It is possible that he was Dean of the Faculty of Medicine at some stage which would have added spice to his pedantry. However, he was equally fitted to follow Gaultier-Garguille into the roles that Pantalone would have taken in the *commedia dell'arte*.

The illustrations of the actors at work convey the style of their improvised comedy and its strong physical presentation to the audience. The strengths of the *farceurs* are acknowledged, against the grain, by criticism of the stage which deplored its depravity. From another point of view, the defenders of the theatre looked down on the farce as evidence of the vulgarity which had been purged with the advent of a literary drama. Nonetheless as the appeal of the farce diminished its acting was not entirely rejected. Corneille, successful in a new light comedy in recognisably contemporary social style, carried his experiments into the hybrid *Illusion Comique* (1637) in which one of the acts is dominated by the extravagance of Matamore, the Spanish captain at the Marais. The company was identified with new writing, but the audience was still drawn by the farce actors, among them Julien Bédeau, who played as Jodelet, depicted at the time of Bosse's engraving among the Bourgogne *farceurs* (see Figure 3.3). He seems to play *enfariné* like Gros-Guillaume, in a striped costume similar to that of Turlupin, with a closely fitting light-coloured cap, and in all illustrations, the set of his moustaches giving a characteristic wide-mouthed expression. He returned to the Marais troupe in 1641 and in a popular print of him saving himself from the flames when the theatre burned down in January 1644, he is depicted as the greatest treasure of the company.

Jodelet's acting was important enough to beget a series of plays by Scarron written in the early 1640s (one is punningly entitled *Le Mâitre Valet*), but still reflecting the more literary taste of the day. Scarron, like Corneille, exploited the skills of a performer with an accumulated technique and a well worked relationship with his audience. Farce and literary drama combined around a performer, as would happen again when Jodelet joined the company of another actor who had perfected himself in the farce. When, briefly, these two actors came together, Molière created *Les Précieuses ridicules*, the play that amalgamated old and new tastes in entertainment, and revealed the potential of the farce actor in the hands of the dramatist.

Commedia dell'arte

Old French Farce, charged with indecency and contaminated by popular appeal, was also rivalled by a similar tradition of improvised playing under the mask, the Italian *commedia dell'arte*. Its long popularity and influence on Parisian theatre was in part the fruit of Italian influence and taste at court, particularly after the marriage of Henri IV to Marie de Médicis in 1600. Through various changes and permutations of personnel and company, the Italian actors remained in the capital, acting literary drama as well as their own farce which, for all its elegance, was no more decent than that of the street. The companies played regularly for the Parisian public, whether at the Hôtel de Bourgogne or effectively beneath the royal roof at the Petit-Bourbon.

The great company of *I Gelosi* under the direction of Flaminio Scala was first summoned by Henri III in 1576 to play at Blois, where they were also given royal permission to play for the public in the *Salle des États*. In Paris they outdid the four best preachers in the city in their attendances, and were soon at odds with the magistrature, who refused to accept the royal letters-patent permitting them to perform.

> Notwithstanding the said prohibition they commenced their performances again the following September in the Hôtel de Bourbon as before, by the express command of the King. For the corruption of the time was such that players in farces, buffoons, prostitutes, and mignons, had all the credit they wished from the King.[5]

The troupe later disbanded, but a number of the actors appeared again in France in the *Comici Fedeli*, favoured by the regent Marie de Médicis and her son Louis XIII. This company comprised G.B. Andreini, playing Harlequin and Lelio the first Lover; a second Lover, Leandro; then Pantalone, Pedrolino, the Capitano Rinoceronte and the Dottore Graziano. It was completed by two Innamorata. The Queen's correspondence with G.B. Adreini shows the interest generated by acting and the different masks of the company:

> … hasten then, as quickly as you may upon this my assurance and dispose yourselves to maintain the high reputation of Harlequin and his troupe, together with the other good roles which you have recently added to it. The King, my son, and I await the pleasure and diversion that you always provide.[6]

Most significant for Molière and his playing was the company, headed probably by Giuseppe Bianchi, which was invited to Paris by Louis XIII in 1639, where it remained until the troubles of the

Fronde in 1648. In 1653 they were reconstituted under the leadership of their Harlequin, Domenico Biancolelli, and Scaramouche, Tiberio Fiorilli. This was the company which established the *théâtre italien* as a permanent feature of the Parisian scene, and familiarized its audience with the masks of Pantalone, the Dottore, Capitano, and, most delightfully, Arlecchino, Scaramuccia and Trivelino. Fiorilli and his fellow actors were also skilled dancers and musicians, and would perform in opera, the mixed entertainment with music and danced interludes, which was introduced at the French court in the 1640s. However the *commedia dell'arte* players remained supreme in the scenarios of their old comedies, which depended on the capacity of the actor improvising on the basis of an extensive technique. As late as 1728 the Italian Riccoboni, writing the *Histoire du théâtre italien*, considered the improvised technique to be the glory of the tradition:

> Impromptu comedy throws the whole weight of the performance on the acting, with the result that the same scenario may be treated in various ways and seems to be a different play each time. The actor who improvises, plays in a much livelier and more natural manner than one who learns his rôle by heart. People feel better, and therefore say better, what they invent than what they borrow from others with the aid of memory.[7]

Despite their virtuosity, the epithet the actors earn over and over again is 'natural'. Although by the early eighteenth century the acting style may have been more in tune with the delicacy and sentiment of the age, the improvised technique suggests a stark contrast with the rigidity of the French, presumably described here in tragedy:

> Their style may suffer from this method of playing à *l'impromptu*, but at the same time the action gains in naturalness and vividness. There is always a happy blend of gesture and inflection with the discourse, and the actors come and go, speak, and act as informally as in ordinary life. Their acting gives a far different effect of naturalness and truth from what one sees in the French theatre, where four or five actors stand in a line like a bas-relief, at the front of the stage, and each declaims his speech in turn.[8]

Riccoboni describes an aspect of acting which is visible in improvisation, and elusive when a performance is composed on the basis of a written text. What is meant by 'natural' in the Italian performance? Riccoboni notes a blend of language and movement, and the absence in the 'natural' performance of formal delivery. The context of the everyday is evoked in explaining the pleasing quality of this acting, but at the same time the everyday equates with liveliness, vivacity and truth. There is more than an echo here of Molière's picture of the stiffness of the Bourgogne tragedian meeting the young provincial actor in *L'Impromptu de Versailles*. In both cases the artificiality of acting stems from undue deliberation in language and gesture. Molière mocks the actor who speaks 'with emphasis' to make points clear and win applause, the claptrap of the Restoration actor. He would have seen in the Italians the spontaneity which came from improvisation, and the ability, noted by Riccoboni, to embody harmoniously the various skills of mind and body which taken together constitute the natural or unself-conscious action. This is acting which, whatever its conventional theatrical appearance, achieves the integration of the human system, so well understood by Molière's Jesuit teachers.

We can see in a scenario played by Scaramouche and Arlequin how the artful improviser builds a scene out of the meeting of body and mind in the creation of spontaneous thought on the stage. Here the absence of the language which concretizes such a moment is the source of the comedy: two actors play through the shared moments of physical balance to create a pseudo-thought. As the audience engages with the process, the climaxes come and go, and it enjoys a physical identification with what is done. It is a species of isomorphism that the comic actor naturally understands, out of which comes the shared rhythm of actor and audience. The liveliness of the procedure is due to the control which is exercised through the disciplined inventions of the body. The gag lies in the fact that there is no shared idea between performers and audience whatever, only the physical form of shared intelligence.

OCTAVE, SCARAMOUCHE, then HARLEQUIN
(OCTAVE, who has just arranged a meeting-place with the beautiful ANGÉLIQUE, wishes to give her an agreeable surprise. He asks SCARAMOUCHE to find a means of doing so, and leaves. SCARAMOUCHE, alone upon the stage, ponders deeply. HARLEQUIN comes in, and SCARAMOUCHE, without telling him the reason for his request, sets him thinking about ways and means.

*They walk up and down the stage without speaking, wrapped in
thought.
Now and again they go up to each other and say:)*
Egad, I have it!
(They begin the same business again, saying:)
No, that won't do.
(Once more they begin the same business. HARLEQUIN *turns round
and faces* SCARAMOUCHE, *who says:)*
Oh, that is sure to do the trick!
(And they both leave the stage without a word of explanation.)[9]

The improvisational skills of the *commedia dell'arte* companies were
grounded on such a base. They were admired for the sheer range of
their talents, being acrobats, tumblers, rope-walkers, dancers and
musicians. It is not in the least surprising that they should have pen-
etrated to the heart of Parisian theatre, and were to be found
wherever plays could be performed: in the street or the fair, the public playhouse, or at the court. It was a city where these talents were
appreciated. On Molière's return to Paris, the ground was prepared.

4

COUNTRY MANNERS

On 24 October 1658, the troupe [Molière's] began to appear before their Majesties and all the Court, upon a stage which the king had caused to be erected in the Guard Room of the Old Louvre; *Nicomède*, the tragedy of Corneille the Elder, was the play they chose for this splendid debut. These new actors did not displease, and people were greatly satisfied above all by the attractions and the acting of the women. The renowned actors who at the time distinguished the Hôtel de Bourgogne were present at this performance. When the play was over, Monsieur de Molière came on to the stage and, having thanked His Majesty, in the most modest terms, for the benevolence with which he had excused his faults and those of his troupe, which had appeared only trembling before so august an assembly, he said to him that the eagerness they felt to have the honour of entertaining the greatest king in the world had made them forget that His Majesty had in his service excellent originals, of which they were but wretched copies; but that since he had been willing to tolerate their country manners, he begged very humbly that it might please if he gave one of the little entertainments which had earned him some reputation and with which he pleased the provinces. This compliment, whose substance alone we report, was so agreeably turned and so favourably received that all the Court applauded, and even more so at the little play, which was The Lovesick Doctor [...]. M. de Molière played the doctor, and the fashion in which he acquitted himself of this character brought him in such great esteem that His Majesty gave orders that he establish his troupe in Paris. The hall of the Petit-Bourbon was granted him, to play there alternating with the Italian actors.[1]

The return to Paris was well managed. After its early failure, the company may have played from time to time in the capital, but certainly it had somewhere earned a reputation sufficient to arouse expectations at court. The performances of tragedy commanded by the twenty-year-old Louis XIV, and the presence of the actresses, earned the particular approval of a court where *agrément*, the satisfaction of the eye and judgement of the onlooker, mattered in the conduct of its affairs, and in its involvement in the theatre, not least in its dance performances led by Louis himself. At the same time, Molière offered the 'greatest king in the world' country pleasures. No contemporary suggested this was foolish, perhaps because at court the taste for improvised comedy was alive. Grimarest, Molière's first biographer, writing with hindsight in 1705, affirms that Molière meant to challenge the Bourgogne, which no longer had its great players of farce.

> Their debut was fortunate; and the actresses above all were judged to be good. But as Molière felt that his troupe would not triumph over that of the Bourgogne in serious acting, after the play he came forward on the stage and gave his thanks to His Majesty, and asked him to approve one of the little entertainments which had acquired him a little reputation in the provinces. In which he counted on success, because he had accustomed his troupe to play little comedies extempore, after the manner of the Italians.[2]

However, besides the introduction at court, Molière had a lease on the Marais playhouse, where the resident company had experienced difficulties. There he might have hoped to secure a new play from Thomas, the younger Corneille, whose *Timocrate* had been played in the winter of 1656–1657, and was the longest-running success of its day.[3] He was still looking to the town, and to tragedy, for his success. These 'country' plays represented an outmoded and vulgar form, but Grimarest likens the company's acting to that of the Italians, who were far from unfashionable. They, rather than the actors of the Marais, were to become Molière's colleagues.

The shared tenancy at the Petit-Bourbon, adjoining the Louvre, granted Molière a residency in a royal theatre, fitted for Italian staging, alongside actors who had been favourites of the King since his childhood. The Italians had played in scenic spectaculars such as *La Finta Pazza* (1645, revived 1657), and must have inherited the décors of Torelli,[4] but above all they were masters of improvised comedy. The newcomers were granted the *jours extraordinaires*, Wednesday, Thursday and Saturday, when the Italians did not play. To recompense their hosts they paid the sum of 1,500 *livres* in recognition of investment already made in equipment. The arrangement was advantageous, and incited later envious allegations that Molière had filched the secrets of his comic acting from Tiberio Fiorilli, the leader and Scaramouche of the Italian company. The frontispiece of the satire *Élomire hypocondre* shows Élomire (Molière), mirror in hand, being coached by Fiorilli, who, for his part, readies the whip (see Figure 4.1).

We gain an impression of the farces offered to the court in two texts attributed to Molière, *La Jalousie du Barbouillé* and *Le Médecin volant*, but most are lost. Molière, according to La Grange, played the *docteur* in the lost *Docteur amoureux*, and probably took the same role in *La Jalousie du Barbouillé*. In *Le Médecin volant* he played Sganarelle, the ingenious servant whose thinking he would exploit the better

Figure 4.1   Molière 'apprenticed' to Scaramouche, according to a contemporary satire, *Élomire hypocondre. Courtesy of the Bibliothèque nationale, Paris*

once it became entangled with moral and metaphysical questions. The Louvre saw also his Mascarille, the ingenious valet of *L'Étourdi*,[5] the mask under which he would play alongside Jodelet in a new town farce, *Les Précieuses ridicules*, the following year. Molière was not anxious to publish these early farces: there was no need, nor any evident commercial advantage for the booksellers of the Galérie du Palais. Only the vogue of *Les Précieuses ridicules* obliged him to publish, or see his success pirated. However, he protested, the affected ladies of the title were designed to be seen strictly by the flattering light of the theatre's candles:

> Mais comme une grande partie des grâces qu'on y a trouvées dépendent de l'action et du ton de voix, il m'importait qu'on ne les dépoullât pas de ces ornements. J'avais résolu, dis-je, de ne les faire voir qu'à la chandelle [...] et je ne voulais pas qu'elles sautassent du théâtre de Bourbon dans la galérie du Palais.[6]

> *But as a large part of the graces which have been found in them (the Précieuses) depend on the action and the tone of the voice, it was a matter of importance to me that they be not stripped of these embellishments. I had resolved, I say, to have them seen only by candlelight, {...} and I had no wish that they should leap from the theatre in the Bourbon to the galérie du Palais.*

Certain plays were to be seen and not read, he remarked, as with his *divertissement*, *L'Amour Médecin*: 'Il n'est pas nécessaire de vous avertir qu'il y a beaucoup de choses qui dépendent de l'action. (*It is not necessary to warn you that there are many things which are dependent on the action*).'[7] The caveat applies to more than slapstick. Even the dramatist, writing in the controlled measures of verse, can never render tone of voice or the particular playing of actions, and sanctions the freedom of the actor. While the farce builds immediacy and invention, and reinforces play, shared between actor and audience, Molière's text will support a more nuanced but still physically charged style of acting, responsive to the actor's unfolding experience in the play. Molière's own 'masks', Mascarille and then Sganarelle, are both *commedia* characters, apt in the simple intrigues of the little farce, but also with a potential life in the rhyming verse of *L'Étourdi*, or *Le Cocu imaginaire*.

La Jalousie du Barbouillé

The idea for the play could have come to Molière from a story in Boccaccio, but more likely the *commedia dell'arte* transmitted it as a dramatic scenario. It is designed to secure attention and to reward an audience quickly with a comic pay-off: thirteen scenes follow a rudimentary intrigue, to be resolved by a deception. Le Barbouillé is tormented by his young wife, Angélique, fonder of amusement than her wifely duties. He seeks enlightenment from Le Docteur who replies only with pedantry. Angélique appeals for support to her father Gorgibus, characterizing her husband as a drunkard. When she leaves at night for an assignation, Le Barbouillé locks her out. On her return, she pleads to be admitted, but her triumphant husband refuses, and declares that he will shame her before the world. When she feigns death, Le Barbouillé comes to the door, she slips inside, and locks him out. With the tables turned, Angélique summons her family to complain of her husband's drunkenness and neglect.

The speed of the play demands frank exposition. The internal states of characters are confided rapidly by actor to audience, and the dramatic problem is stated almost as the *quod est demonstrandum* of a geometrical proof, a challenge to the imagination of the audience. An actor, crudely characterized by his costume and red-faced make-up, presents the problem of marriage in terms of space. His wife likes to 'courir', to run around. How may he keep her at home or prove her absences to persons whom she must respect, her family and relatives?

Il faut pourtant la punir. Si je la tuais …. L'invention ne vaut rien, car tu serais pendu. Si tu la faisais mettre en prison …. La carogne en sortirait avec son passe-partout. Que diable faire donc?

(Sc. i)[8]

She must be punished. If I could kill her …. That idea is no good, for you would be hanged. If you could have her thrown into gaol …. The wretch would get out of it with her pass-key. What the devil is to be done?

The space for the performance can be supplied by a platform stage with practicable wing flats and a second level behind. The art lay in the animation of this space, which comes to embrace the dangerously public world where Angélique entertains the handsome Valère, and from which she departs to enjoy the pleasures of any society but that of her unappealing husband. It is also where her guilt may be proved should she be found there when she should be 'at home', within the inner, off-stage, space of the theatre. The stage is the board in a game, where the pieces must move to satisfactory positions or the game is lost. An essential player is also the audience, alerted by the actors:

ANGÉLIQUE

Cependant que mon mari n'y est pas, je vais faire un tour à un bal que donne une de mes voisines. Je serai revenue auparavant lui, car il est quelque part au cabaret: il ne s'apercevra pas que je suis sortie. Ce maroufle-là me laisse toute seule à la maison, comme si j'étais son chien.

(Sc. viii)[9]

ANGÉLIQUE

While my husband is gone, I am going to spend a while at a ball which one of my neighbours is giving. I shall be back before him, for he is at the inn somewhere: he won't be able to see that I have gone out. That rogue leaves me all alone at home, as though I were his dog.

The up-stage curtain or painted drop bounds both Angélique's uncomfortable domesticity, and her place of safety. When the door is shut and her husband within, the crux of the plot is reached. The positions of the players express the moral balance of the play, with the plain boorish husband within, and the guilty wife left marooned in the open 'public' space of the stage. The dramatic challenge is to invert the positions:

LE BARBOUILLÉ

… Comment, diable! être toute seule à l'heure qu'il est! Je ne sais si c'est imagination, mais mon front m'en paraît plus rude de moitié.

ANGÉLIQUE

Hé bien!, pour être toute seule, qu'en veux-tu dire? Tu me querelles quand je suis en compagnie: comment faut-il faire?

LE BARBOUILLÉ

Il faut être retiré à la maison, donner ordre au souper, avoir soin du ménage, des enfants; mais sans tant de discours inutiles, adieu, bonsoir, va t'en au diable et me laisse en repos.

ANGÉLIQUE

Tu ne veux pas m'ouvrir?

(Sc. xi)[10]

LE BARBOUILLÉ

... What the devil! Out alone at this time of night! It may be my imagination, but my forehead doesn't half seem lumpy.

ANGÉLIQUE

Well! As for being out alone, what are you going to say about that? You quarrel with me when I am out in company: what am I to do?

LE BARBOUILLÉ

You should stay quietly in the house, give orders for supper, see to the housework and the children; but that's enough of this useless talk, goodbye, good evening, go to the devil and leave me in peace.

ANGÉLIQUE

You won't let me in?

The comic effect is governed by the actor's handling of each simple action, and the swift succession of alternatives; a cajoling plea is followed instantly by a furious demand, and as abruptly by a plaintive question:

ANGÉLIQUE

Hé! mon pauvre petit mari, je t'en prie, ouvre-moi, mon cher petit coeur!

LE BARBOUILLÉ

Ah, crocodile! ah, serpent dangereux! tu me caresses pour me trahir.

ANGÉLIQUE

Ouvre, ouvre donc!

LE BARBOUILLÉ

Adieu! *Vade retro, Satanas.*

ANGÉLIQUE

Quoi? Tu n'as point de pitié de ta femme, qui t'aime tant?

(Sc. xi)[11]

ANGÉLIQUE

Ah! my poor little husband, I beg you, open up, my dear sweetheart!

> LE BARBOUILLÉ
>
> *Ah, crocodile! ah, deadly snake! You caress me only to betray me.*
>
> ANGÉLIQUE
>
> *Open up, open the door!*
>
> LE BARBOUILLÉ
>
> *Good-night!* Vade retro, Satanas.
>
> ANGÉLIQUE
>
> *What? You won't have pity on your wife, who loves you so much?*

The device of Angélique's 'suicide' is sufficient to produce the inversion of positions. The 'death' is treated in perfunctory fashion: the important question is the change of space:

> LE BARBOUILLÉ
>
> Serait-elle bien assez sotte pour avoir fait ce coup-là? Il faut que je descende avec la chandelle pour aller voir.
>
> ANGÉLIQUE
>
> Il faut que je t'attrape. Si je peux entrer dans la maison subtilement, cependant que tu me chercheras, chacun aura bien son tour.
>
> (Sc. xi)[12]

> LE BARBOUILLÉ
>
> *She wouldn't be stupid enough to have done something like that? I had better go down with the candle just to see.*
>
> ANGÉLIQUE
>
> *I have to catch you out. If I can slip into the house while you are looking for me, then we shall be quits.*

The vigour of this procedure is reproduced across the span of Molière's output, as when the fundamentals of *La Jalousie du Barbouillé* are exploited in *George Dandin*, and derives from the freedom conferred paradoxically by the slender resources and the low-brow demands of the form. Molière naturally inherits characteristics of the popular stage, with its age-old problems of sex and money, and youth and age. The husband who fears cuckoldry, and the father who wishes to govern his daughter's affections, are perennial subjects, structured essentially in time and space, with little refinement of ideas or language. However the farce player cannot long sustain his simplified action without the encounter with creative obstacles.[13] These can derive from inventions within the plot, but frequently they are interventions of verbose characters, who come equipped for any eventuality. They speak, but do not need a writer. *La Jalousie du Barbouillé* incorporates set speeches and set *lazzi* to obstruct the action and energize the playing. The Docteur ignores essentials in favour of his erudition and the formalities of the schoolroom:

LE BARBOUILLÉ

Je m'en allais vous chercher pour vous faire une prière sur une chose qui m'est d'importance.

LE DOCTEUR

Il faut que tu sois bien mal appris, bien lourdaud, et bien mal morigéné, mon ami, puisque tu m'abordes sans ôter ton chapeau, sans observer *rationem loci, temporis et personae*. Quoi, débuter d'abord par un discours mal digéré, au lieu de dire: *Salve, vel Salvus sis, Doctor Doctorum eruditissime*! Hé! pour qui me prends-tu mon ami?

(Sc. ii)[14]

LE BARBOUILLÉ

I was on my way to look for you to make a request concerning a matter of great importance to me.

LE DOCTEUR

You must be badly instructed, a great dullard, and very badly brought up, my friend, since you approach me without removing your hat, without observing rationem loci, temporis et personae. *What, to begin, straight off, with a speech which is badly conceived, instead of saying:* Salve, vel Salvus sis, Doctor Doctorum eruditissime! *Ah! Who do you take me for, my friend?*

This resistance is remarked in popular prints of the seventeenth century which stress the delight of his rambling and irrelevant speeches. The Docteur Balouarde appears in an illustration which carries the legend:

When the Doctor speaks, who can tell
If he speaks Latin or low Breton
And often the one who listens to him
Interrupts him with a beating.[15]

The Docteur is restrained in a different manner by Le Barbouillé, who hauls him off by his foot. Physical action and verbal obstruction reappear constantly throughout the work of Molière, and the root in farce may be easy to identify, as in *Le Mariage forcé*, whose pair of contrasted *docteur* roles is used to procure a virtuosic beating. The essence of the encounter is fundamental to the experience of drama: physical life and mental abstraction are brought together in a shared creative proposition.

Le Médecin volant

This little play shows Molière using traditional *dottore* routines that he would continue to exploit throughout his career. The roles of pedant and physician are variously part of the emploi of the *docteur*. In *Le Médecin volant* he follows traditional practice in contriving a disguising, whereby the valet assumes the functions of a physician and is required, according to the learned practices of the profession, to make a display of his art.[16]

GORGIBUS

Très humble serviteur à Monsieur le Médecin! Je vous envoie quérir pour voir ma fille, qui est malade; je mets toute mon espérance en vous.

SGANARELLE

Hippocrate dit, et Galien par vives raisons persuade qu'une personne ne se porte bien quand elle est malade. Vous avez raison de mettre votre espérance en moi; car je suis le plus grand, le plus habile, le plus docte médecin qui soit dans la faculté végétale, sensitive et minérale.

GORGIBUS

J'en suis fort ravi.

SGANARELLE

Ne vous imaginez pas que je sois un médecin du commun. Tous les autres médecins ne sont, à mon égard, que des avortons de médecine. J'ai des talents particuliers, j'ai des secrets. *Salamalec, salamalec. 'Rodrigue, as-tu du coeur?'* Signor, si; segnor, non. *Per omnia saecula saeculorum.* Mais encore, voyons un peu.

SABINE

Hé! ce n'est pas lui qui est malade, c'est sa fille.

SGANARELLE

Il n'importe: le sang du père et de la fille ne sont qu'une même chose.

(Sc. iv)[17]

GORGIBUS

Doctor, your most humble servant! I sent for you to see my daughter, who is ill; I place all my hopes in you.

SGANARELLE

Hippocrates says, and Galen by excellent reasons persuades us, that a person does not feel well when she is ill. You are right to put your hopes in my hands; for I am the greatest, the most clever, the most learned physician in all in the Faculty of Animal, Vegetable and Mineral.

GORGIBUS

I am delighted to hear it.

SGANARELLE

Do not imagine that I am some commonplace physician. All other physicians are no more, in comparison to me, than abortions of the art. I have special talents, I have secrets. Salamalec, salamalec. 'Rodrigue, as-tu du coeur?' Signor, si; segnor, non. Per omnia saecula saeculorum. *But now, let us see the patient.*

SABINE

Hey! he's not the one who is ill, it's his daughter.

SGANARELLE

No matter: the blood of the father and the daughter are one and the same thing.

It is an important part of the fun to have the valet's learning challenged, composed as it is of scraps of church Latin, theatrical quotation (from *Le Cid*) and hocus pocus. Molière swiftly introduces a second *docteur* figure, L'Avocat, who, learning of the eminence of the physician, begs a few moments' conversation, which he stuffs with pedantry, while Sganarelle utters a mouthful of nonsensical 'Latin'. L'Avocat, greatly satisfied by such an exchange, withdraws, with an indication in the text of the usual *ad libitum* of the role.

Subsequent mock-doctors in Molière employ the same sort of *lazzo* of fanciful language in the creation of the role-within-a-role. Another Sganarelle in *Le Médecin malgré lui* does so, and the disguised Toinette in *Le Malade imaginaire* can dupe her 'patient' and master Argan in a preposterous display:

TOINETTE (*en médecin*)

Je suis médecin passager, qui vais de ville en ville, de province en province, de royaume en royaume, pour chercher

d'illustre matières à ma capacité, pour trouver des malades
dignes de m'occuper, capables d'exercer les grands et beaux
secrets que j'ai trouvés dans la médecine. Je dédaigne de m'a-
muser à ce menufatras de maladies ordinaires, à ces bagatelles
de rhumatismes et défluxions, à ces fièvrottes, à ces vapeurs,
et a ces migraines. Je veux des maladies d'importance: de
bonnes fièvres continues avec des transports au cerveau, de
bonnes fièvres pourpres, de bonnes pestes, de bonnes hydrop-
sies formées, de bonne pleurisies avec des inflammations de la
poitrine: c'est là que je me plais ...

(III, x)[18]

TOINETTE *(dressed as a doctor)*
*I am a travelling physician, going from town to town, from province to
province, from kingdom to kingdom, to seek out illustrious cases for my
skills, to find diseases fit for my interest, capable of exercising the great
and beautiful secrets that I have discovered in medicine. I do not deign
to amuse myself with piffling everyday maladies, with bagatelles like
rheumatism and defluxions, with passing fevers, vapours and
migraines. I desire important maladies: fine chronic fevers with brain-
storms, good purpural fevers, good plagues, good solid dropsies, good
pleurisies with inflammation of the chest: that is what pleases me ...*

The patient is the creation of his own delusions, and occupies a virtual
or imaginative 'space' where Toinette plays her traditional lazzo. In *Le
Médecin volant*, Lucile chooses the position of the patient to escape her
father Gorgibus, and occupies a place in actual stage space in which the
attention of the audience moves creatively from one focus to another:

SGANARELLE
... Mais encore, voyons un peu.

SABINE
Hé! ce n'est pas lui qui est malade, c'est sa fille.

SGANARELLE
Il n'importe ...

(Sc. iv)[19]

SGANARELLE
... But now, let's see.

SABINE
Hey! It's not him who is ill, it's his daughter.

No matter ...

The text records the shifts very clearly. From the vacuous demonstrations of his nonsense 'learning', Sganarelle turns to the business in hand, 'Mais encore', and heads off towards the father. His attention is drawn by Sabine: 'Hé!'. He must move towards her and she must prompt him to turn his attention to the off-stage daughter: 'c'est sa fille'. Sganarelle triumphantly overcomes the gaffe with the farce actor's simple play on words: they are of one blood. He modifies his approach to Gorgibus, and asks for a sample of the patient's urine. This he goes on to drink copiously. The imagined illness is developed with a wild and irreverent candour:

SGANARELLE

Voilà de l'urine qui marque grande chaleur, grande inflammation dans les intestins: elle n'est pas tant mauvaise pourtant.

GORGIBUS

Hé quoi? Monsieur, vous l'avalez?

SGANARELLE

Ne vous étonnez pas de cela: les médecins, d'ordinaire, se contentent de la regarder; mais mois, qui suis un médecin hors du commun, je l'avale, parce qu'avec le goût je discerne mieux la cause de la maladie. Mais à vous dire la vérité, il y en avait trop peu pour asseoir un bon jugement: qu'on la fasse encore pisser.

(Sc. v)[20]

SGANARELLE

This urine indicates great heat, a great inflammation of the intestines: but it's not so bad, however.

GORGIBUS

Hey, what this? Sir, are you swallowing it?

SGANARELLE

Do not be amazed at this: doctors, ordinarily, are content with looking at it, but I, who am a doctor above the common herd, I swallow it, because with taste I discern better the cause of the illness. To tell you the truth there was too little to determine a good opinion; let her piss some more.

The delight of this lies in the theatricality of both the device, wine as urine, and the rampaging performance of the disguised valet. A play is performed within the play, but unlike *Le Malade imaginaire* it is so unsubtle a play that it risks going off the rails, and has to be 'directed' by the exasperated Sabine.

In *Le Malade imaginaire* Molière places the acting problem in a new dimension. The roles are internally governed by a more complex awareness in the performers: Toinette judges her own performance, and modulates it with skill. Argan's imaginary illness is first and foremost a mental construct, a delusion, created by the operations of mind in the actor, rather than an illusion created by the play of others. (Molière does not abandon this cruder sort of comedy entirely in the play, happily to say.) Illness as a given circumstance of the drama becomes an ethical question which only subsequently is played upon by the intriguing Toinette and Cléante. The 'physician' must operate on the delusions of the character Argan, which are placed in the mind rather than in theatrical space. Moreover, the texture of the play is more closely woven by the delusional characters of the actual physicians who come to attend the patient, and whose practices are grounded in the traditional pedantry of the *docteur* roles.

But even in Molière's final play the joy of role and travesty are manifest: Toinette is given the device first used in *Le Médecin volant* of a 'brother' whom she remarkably resembles. As she moves rapidly in and out of her disguise, the actress creates two characters as did the actor in the earlier play. The performer diverts the mind with a problem of philosophical and geometrical beauty: being in two 'places' at once.

The early *Médecin volant* was, as the title indicates, celebrated by the *tour de force* of the conclusion where Sganarelle 'invents' a dastardly twin brother when surprised by Gorgibus in his valet's clothes, and plays a series of scenes where one or other of the characters is placed inside the house. The playing depends (like *La Jalousie du Barbouillé*) on the disposition of the theatrical space of the simple farce stage. Gorgibus goes into the house by the door to find the 'brother Narcisse' and to reconcile him to the physician who is waiting 'below':

GORGIBUS (*à la fenêtre*)
Voilà votre frère qui vous attend: il m'a promis qu'il fera tout ce que je voudrai.

SGANARELLE (*à la fenêtre*)
Monsieur Gorgibus, je vous prie de le faire venir ici: je vous conjure que ce soit en particulier que je lui demande pardon,

parce que sans doute il me ferait cent hontes et cent oppro-
bres devant tout le monde.
(*Gorgibus sort de la maison par la porte, et Sganarelle par la
fenêtre.*)

GORGIBUS

Oui-da, je m'en vais lui dire. Monsieur, il dit qu'il est hon-
teux, et qu'il vous prie d'entrer, afin qu'il vous demande
pardon en particulier. Voilà la clef, vous pouvez entrer; je
vous supplie de ne pas me refuser et de m'en donner ce con-
tentement.

SGANARELLE

Il n'y a rien que je ne fasse pour votre satisfaction: vous allez
entendre de quelle manière je le vais traiter. (*A la fenêtre.*)
Ah! te voilà, coquin. – Monsieur mon frère, je vous demande
pardon, je vous promets qu'il n'y a point de ma faute. – Il
n'y a point de ta faute, pilier de débauche, coquin? Va, je
t'apprendrai à vivre. Avoir la hardiesse d'importuner M.
Gorgibus, de lui rompre la tête avec tes sottises![21]

GORGIBUS (at the window)
*There is your brother, waiting for you; he has promised me he will
do everything that I wish.*

SGANARELLE (at the window)
*Monsieur Gorgibus, I beg you to make him come here: I beg of you
that I may ask his pardon in private, because without doubt he will
shame me a hundred times and reproach me a hundred more before
everyone.*
(Gorgibus leaves the house by the door, and Sganarelle by
the window.)

GORGIBUS
*Yes indeed, I will go and tell him. Monsieur, he says that he is
ashamed, and he asks you to go in, so that he may ask your pardon
in private. Here is the key, you may enter; I implore you not to refuse
me and to content me in this matter.*

SGANARELLE
*There is nothing I would not do to give you satisfaction. You shall
hear how I use him.* (At the window.)
*Ah! there you are, you rogue. — My dear brother, I beg your par-
don, I promise you that it is not at all my fault. — Not your fault,*

monument of debauchery, rogue? Go on, I will teach you how to live. To have the effrontery to annoy M. Gorgibus, to wear him out with your foolishness!

This is in itself a tall order for any actor, and a delight to an audience as the performer pits himself against the demands of the illusion. Molière caps the effect by introducing Gros-René who has watched the whole performance unconvinced, and who urges Gorgibus to call them both to the window. Sganarelle as Narcisse duly ends a scene of reconciliation by embracing the hat and the ruff of the physician 'which he has placed on his elbow'. Gros-René puts it down to witchcraft, but it is craft of another sort.

The particular attraction of these *petites comédies* lay in the strength and indeed the naïvety of their theatrical effects, and *Le Médecin volant* shows perhaps even more clearly the roots of Molière's acting genius burrowing into the soil of traditional drama. The play was not original and reproduced ideas present in earlier *commedia dell'arte* scenarios, but for that matter it would be followed almost immediately by another Italian *Medico volante*, owing a debt to Molière, and Boursault would write a rival play for the actors at the Hôtel de Bourgogne. The cult of originality is foreign to the age, and Molière is as accustomed to reworking his own material as he is that of other dramatists. The more closely one looks at the range of plays on medicine that mark the progress of Molière's career, the more one sees the repertoire of acting effects progressively refined.

Les Précieuses ridicules

This appealing satire of contemporary affectation supplies matter to a pair of masked actors in the traditional intrigue of the valet disguised to dupe the adversaries of the master. As in the old farce, the castings are revealed in the names of the characters, with La Grange and du Croisy under their own names. Magdelon and Cathos echo Madeleine Béjart and Catherine de Brie, while Marotte, a diminutive of Marie, suggests Marie Ragueneau, daughter of the poet and pastrycook, and future wife of La Grange. With a Gorgibus, Molière in his farce role of Mascarille and the celebrated Jodelet there can be no mistaking the style. Here are actors prepared for the strong playing and perfunctory characters of farce. When farce comes to town, it changes its clothes and brushes up its accent, but the playing remains the same: the resolution of simple dramatic problems with a brilliant use of theatrical resources. Molière's title announces a daring notion: fashion turned to ridicule, a delicate undertaking that Molière justified, affirming that '… les plus excellentes choses peuvent être copiées par de mauvais singes, qui méritent d'être bernés' (… *the most excellent things can be aped by wretched persons, who deserve to be mocked*)'.[22] Molière, newly up from the country, delights in the behaviour of persons of quality. The fakes are always the more interesting, expressing, as falsehood does, the grotesque understanding of true propriety. In a similar way, as Molière's contemporary La Rochefoucauld would say, hypocrisy is the homage that vice pays to virtue.

Molière's town farce depended on language even more than the traditional interventions of the pedant or the physician. The new rhetoric of the salons was fresher and more dangerously close to the audience and its acquaintance. Communication was by both speech and ceremony, and eschewed the least vulgarity: 'le beau style … les belles manières … la bonne façon'. The subject of the play, preciosity, showed language at odds with the realities of everyday life, which creep in at every point in the performance of the *farceurs*. The very entrance which brings a sedan chair and porters on-stage is an extravagant intrusion of the Parisian streets into the salon, only possible in the imagination of the farce. Fashionable dress was best protected from the mud by the use of coach or chair, but porters, the audience knew, were notoriously difficult to deal with, and they did not belong in a salon, or on a stage.

The farce invades the world of affectation, whose rhetoric, characters, manners and private mythology are appropriated by the clowns. Thus costume, make-up, deportment and manners bring the unlikely quartet of players together. Cathos and Magdelon make up according to the fashions of the town:

MAROTTE

Que désirez-vous, monsieur?

GORGIBUS

Où sont vos maîtresses?

MAROTTE

Dans leur cabinet.

GORGIBUS

Que font-elles?

MAROTTE

De la pommade pour les lèvres.

GORGIBUS

C'est trop pommadé. Dîtes-leur qu'elles descendent. Ces pendardes-là, avec leur pommade, ont, je pense, envie de me ruiner. Je ne vois partout que les blancs d'oeufs, lait virginal, et mille autres brimborions que je ne connais point. Elles ont usé, depuis que nous sommes ici, le lard d'une douzaine de cochons, pour le moins, et quatres valets vivraient tous les jours des pieds de mouton qu'elles emploient.[23]

MAROTTE

What do you desire, Sir?

GORGIBUS

Where are your mistresses?

MAROTTE

In their boudoir.

GORGIBUS

And what are they concocting?

MAROTTE

Pomade for their lips.

GORGIBUS

There is too much of this pomade. Tell them to come down. These baggages with their pomade have, I believe, determined to ruin me. Everywhere I see nothing but white of egg, virgin milk, and a thousand other concoctions that I can't recognize. They have used up, since we arrived here, the lard from a dozen pigs, and four valets would live, day in, day out, off the sheep's feet they have used.

The excesses of fashionable make-up translate, as with Congreve's Lady Wishfort, easily to the stage. Overdone salon fashion (always one of Molière's targets) combines with the fantastic appearance of the masked servants in the borrowed costume of the masters. Jodelet's *enfariné* make-up is so well known that Molière cannot resist a visual pun:

MASCARILLE

Ne vous étonnez pas de voir le vicomte de la sorte: il ne fait que sortir d'une maladie qui lui a rendu le visage pâle comme vous le voyez.[24]

MASCARILLE
*Do not be astonished to see the viscount thus, he has just escaped an
illness which has left his face pale as you see it.*

This awareness of the player is typical of the theatre of Molière. It is
a matter of style whether such attention to performance applies to
acting in general, or is attached to the capacities and techniques, or
even the idiosyncrasies, of the individual member of the company.
The farce can assume the characteristics of the player or the playing,
and expects that the role will sit happily with the accumulated technique and imagination of the player.

These plays concentrate on the raw elements of performance: space
and time shared with the audience through thought, physical presence and action, creating a rhythm of experience. Molière's friend
Boileau-Despréaux sensed the appeal of the early farce, despite his
later disapproval of the dramatist's return to the form with *Les
Fourberies de Scapin*:

> Monsieur Despréaux never tired in his admiration of
> Molière, whom he always called the Contemplator. He
> would say that nature seemed to have revealed to him all her
> secrets, at least as far as it concerned the manners and char-
> acter of men. He greatly regretted that the little comedy of
> *The Lovesick Doctor* had been lost, because there is always
> something outstanding and instructive in his least works. In
> his view, Molière thought truly but did not always write
> truly, because he followed too swiftly the flight of his first
> inspiration, and he found it impossible to correct his
> works.[25]

5

L'ÉCOLE DES FEMMES AND THE FORM OF COMEDY

L'École des femmes was first played at the Palais Royal on 26 December 1662 for the town audience. Molière's company and the Italians had moved to the new theatre after the demolition of the Petit-Bourbon had commenced late in 1660, and Louis' concern that the troupes be adequately rehoused suggests the extent to which Molière's company had succeeded with the court. *Les Fâcheux*, created in the summer of 1661 for the entertainment of the King at Vaux-le-Vicomte, further established Molière in the royal favour, but its success pointed too obviously, and expensively, in the direction of music and dance for it to set the pattern of the repertoire at the Palais Royal.[1] This was a work which would be frequently revived, despite higher ticket prices, *au double*, to cover the expense of production, but could not be regarded as a staple in the diet of the town audience.

Substantial new plays were required for the acting company, with music by only a small band. *Dom Garcie de Navarre ou Le Prince jaloux*, Molière's Cornelian drama, should have fulfilled such a need. First performed on 4 February 1661, it took scarcely enough money to pay the author's fee of 550 *livres*, and when it was withdrawn on the 17th it took only 70 *livres*.[2] Molière created a serious play with dignified characters in the manner of *Don Sanche d'Aragon*, Corneille's *comédie héroique*, substantially a continuation of the romanesque *tragi-comédie* which had flourished in the 1640s.

Molière was schooled in Corneille and learned much from the example. He could appreciate the sustaining idealism of Corneille's writing, but his own genius was probably too sceptical ever to create a work in a like spirit. Moreover, for all his ambition as a tragedian, the role of Dom Garcie did not suit his playing, and a contemporary account alleges that he withdrew from the cast even before the play failed and closed.[3] Nevertheless, Molière's experience of tragic acting would encourage a 'serious' five-act work, but one which would have a different, lighter tone. It would lead, in *L'École des femmes*, to the creation of a modern comedy with an intellectual and moral complexity unimaginable to his contemporaries. It was a form which would initially both delight and puzzle its audience.

The new play annexed Corneille's tragic scene to the popular stage of *Sganarelle* or *Le Médecin volant*. The audience of these plays enjoyed the progress of action about the scenic space, and understood the play of misinterpretation and mistaken identity, procured by virtuoso acting aided by costume or properties. The 'serious' actor in Molière now found in some of the resources of the Cornelian stage a means of developing comic playing into areas of moral and intellectual concern as considerable as those of tragedy.[4] The audience now watched the progress of an idea.

The success of the tragic actor requires extended rhythms shared with the audience to sustain the affective and moral experience of the action over extended periods of time. Comedy depends upon unexpected shifts of attention and perception, controlled by the lively mental and physical rhythms of the comic actor. For Molière's spectator this meant above all the sharp, sometimes violent, contrasts of popular comedy,[5] employing wit and ingenuity, and far from the moral and intellectual range of tragedy. The fashioning of *L'École des femmes* reflects the forms of the Cornelian drama, with a central figure embroiled in a powerful moral dilemma opposing private and public affairs, set against a semi-abstract staging, and with an astonishing outcome revealing the moral power and possibly the identity of the tragic figure. To this Molière brought his own incisive vision of what his age termed *le ridicule*: incoherence in apparently sustained and imperious social performances. It was an understanding of life which was abroad in the streets, but most evident in the salon.

L'École des femmes has been seen as a burlesque of Cornelian heroics, with bourgeois domestic tyranny adopting the absolute attitudes of aristocratic heroes.[6] Molière had much to say about the acting of tragedy, and he said it as part of the famous quarrel which followed *L'École des femmes*, but he was preoccupied by acting rather than literature, and *L'École des femmes* was a vehicle for an actor. The Cornelian echo in his play was appropriate for the comic style he was developing and the story of power which he had decided to treat.

L'École des femmes can be imagined as a play in the manner of *La Jalousie du Barbouillé*, and in other circumstances Molière might have developed into an efficient little farce Paul Scarron's story *La Précaution inutile*, with its series of attempts by a jealous husband to sequester his young bride during his absences. The subject can be

reduced to an ancient formula, enlivened by the novelty of the innocence or simplicity of the girl. We know that, later, *Tartuffe* would
start life in a three-act form, and the comparison of *La Jalousie du
Barbouillé* and the expanded *George Dandin* shows how Molière's plays
can be rooted in the farce. Molière's genius could be seen in *Les
Précieuses ridicules*, but the full power of his performance needed five
acts brought to bear on a set of ideas. If some saw him only as a
farceur,[7] Molière was to refine his comic acting into a flexible realist
style capable of recognisably reflecting contemporary social life. This
was to redouble the risks of farce. *La Jalousie du Barbouillé*, which
sketched rapidly the intrigues of a lusty young wife, seemed innocent beside the obvious contemporary relevance and considerable
moral development of *L'École des femmes*.

Molière's new play had an unfamiliar look. There was no trace of
the stock farce roles of the company, and above all he himself abandoned the theatrical characters of Mascarille or Sganarelle to play a
recognisable bourgeois, Arnolphe. The issue the play presented was
consistent with the sobriety of the role Molière adopted: the virtue of
one's wife in liberal society. Arnolphe on one hand is willing to lend
an ear to the gossip of the town, and to ridicule its cuckolds, but on
the other, taking the name of Monsieur de la Souche, he imprisons a
young woman, Agnès, as part of a master plan to secure a stupid, and
therefore faithful, wife. When he meets the son of an old friend he is
happy to encourage him in his sentimental adventures until he learns
that the young man, Horace, has discovered an adorable girl, shut
away nearby in the house of a Monsieur de la Souche. Trapped in his
masculine role of back-slapping encouragement, Arnolphe must listen to the accounts of Horace's pursuit of the future Madame de la
Souche.

The most evident link with the earlier repertoire was in the title
of the play, recalling the successful *L'École des maris*, with its 'lessons'
on conduct in marriage. The chief reminiscence of earlier acting lay
in the hearty roles of Alain and Georgette, the servants who incom-
petently discharge the instructions of Monsieur de la Souche as he
tries to safeguard Agnès against equally incompetent pursuit by
Horace. The development was chiefly one of style. Roles were now
instantly recognized by contemporaries, who proceeded to debate
Molière's success in rendering believable characters. The dramatic
action was developed in an unusually interesting way, given a revo-
lutionary new range in the acting, and the play brought into focus
topical and exciting questions regarding the status of women and
the nature of marriage. Whereas *L'École des maris* has a simple,

uncontentious symmetry in its moral organization, here the action probed deeper. In the earlier play the scheme requires that the girl who is given her head behaves properly and marries her ageing suitor, while the one who is supervised finds the means to deceive hers. Agnès in *L'École des femmes* is given more developed circumstances, a character history and detailed employments around the house. As her two relationships, with Arnolphe and with Horace, develop, Molière deftly makes one inform the other as the 'wife' is schooled by her two suitors. The intrigue itself is transformed as a source of interest in that it is constantly revealed to Arnolphe as he listens to the explanation of how his *alter ego* Monsieur de la Souche will be defeated.

The innovation of the play lies in the manipulation of dramatic information. Once the initial premises are established, Molière creates a flow of changing circumstances which depend upon mental representations entertained by the actor as opposed to observable scenic interactions. The split role of Arnolphe–Monsieur de la Souche, drawn as it is from the simple disguises of the farce, as the means of baffling an adversary, requires a new virtuosity in the playing, far beyond the tricks of *Le Médecin volant*. With *L'École des femmes* Molière applies the double structure throughout a play to a substantial ethical purpose, ultimately to baffle the protagonist himself.

So great was the success of *L'École des femmes* that criticism inevitably followed, animated above all by professional envy. The quarrel that resulted can be followed in a series of polemics by both Molière and his detractors. Prominent among the latter was at this time Donneau de Visé, allied to the rival company at the Hôtel de Bourgogne, who contributed four separate works to a vicious war which raged from December 1662 to March 1664. His *Nouvelles nouvelles* included in February 1663 a lengthy discussion of *L'École des femmes* to which the journalist–critic returned after Molière's *La Critique de l'École des femmes* was performed in August. His play, *Zélinde*, possibly staged at the Bourgogne, has Molière criticized and attacked by a merchant in the rue Saint-Denis, and his fashionable clientele. On the other hand, the rival theatre certainly played Boursault's polemic: *Le Portrait du peintre ou la Contre-critique de l'École des femmes*,[8] where Molière and Madeleine Béjart were subjected to personal abuse; and the actor Montfleury *père* denounced Molière to the king as having married the 'daughter' of his former mistress Madeleine[9] with the obvious implication of incest. Molière alludes to these bitter matters in *L'Impromptu de Versailles*, but refuses to follow Madeleine's urgings to reply.[10]

Disputes of taste escalated rapidly in the conditions of seventeenth-century theatrical and literary life. Plays were read aloud by their authors in fashionable salons, and the judgements of influential 'connoisseurs' and patrons are disingenuously welcomed in many a preface to a published work. Moreover the town was comparatively small and in good society a play could rapidly become generally familiar. The exercise of judgement was then an aspect of both playgoing and the literary life of salons, and there are frequent echoes of this in the plays of Molière himself.

Neo-Aristotelian orthodoxy, which could be seized by a formulaic mind and applied as *les règles*, was always bound to encounter difficulties when literature was at the mercy of live performance. Donneau de Visé's objections to *L'École des femmes* were that it was defective as a play, indecent in its matter, and ignorant of the taste of town. In damning the alleged excesses of the performance, he permits an estimate to be made of its effectiveness, in particular the acting of Molière, evolving rapidly from the farce. Donneau de Visé demands a rational Arnolphe if the confidence between him and Horace is to be convincing. Molière played the confusion of the victim.

> The latter should adopt a better countenance, and, pretending to be of service to him {Horace}, give him advice of a kind to defeat him, or at least put fear into his heart: tell him that he is being spied upon, and give reasons for him to abandon Agnès. This is what needed to be done to justify the confidences exchanged: this is what the stage required, and this is what would have been done by any other than Arnolphe, who is content to turn aside and pull faces.[11]

De Visé gives a lively indication of the physical style of Molière's performance, and its associated intellectual purpose. Where the critic wishes the ambivalent attitudes of the dramatic character to be concealed so as to be invisible within the dramatic action, Molière the actor turns out towards the audience to reveal them. The series of scenes in which Horace informs Arnolphe of the steps he has taken to gain access to Agnès were greatly debated, as were Molière's acting and 'grimaces', a mark of his lack of discretion. The force of the acting could be doubly denounced by calling attention to the defective dramaturgy of the *récits*, the speeches where Horace delivers to the anguished Arnolphe the frequent bulletins revealing his amorous progress. Here the very success of Molière's acting exposed him to the censure of the critics. In his dramatized defence of the play, *La*

Critique de l'École des femmes, Molière's Uranie declares that, far from being defective, these scenes are the heart of the play:

> Pour moi, je trouve que la beauté du sujet de *L'École des femmes* consiste dans cette confidence perpétuelle; et ce qui me paraît assez plaisant, c'est qu'un homme qui a de l'esprit, et qui est averti de tout par une innocente qui est sa maîtresse, et par un jeune étourdi qui est son rival, ne puisse avec cela éviter ce qui lui arrive.[12]

> *For my part, I find that the beauty of the subject of* The School for Wives *lies in that perpetual confidence; and what to me seems rather amusing is that a man who has wit, and who is warned of everything by an innocent who is his mistress, and by a young fool who is his rival, cannot, with all that, avoid what happens to him.*

This *confidence perpétuelle* is indeed delightful. It invokes a rational but energetic style of performance, constraining together divergent aspects of action and response. The characteristics of the playing are well recorded in contemporary attacks, and Molière himself boldly repeats the criticisms in the *Critique de l'École des femmes*:

> Et ce Monsieur de la Souche enfin, qu'on nous fait un homme d'esprit, et qui paraît si sérieux en tant d'endroits. Ne descend-t-il point dans quelque chose de trop comique et de trop outré au cinquième acte, lorsqu'il explique à Agnès la violence de son amour, avec ces roulements d'yeux extravagants, ces soupirs ridicules, et ces larmes niaises qui font rire tout le monde?[13]

> *And after all, this Monsieur de la Souche, who is made out to be a man of sense, and who appears so serious in so many respects, does he not fall into something too comical and exaggerated in the fifth act, when he explains to Agnès the violence of his love, with those absurd rolling eyes, those ridiculous sighs and those foolish tears which make everyone laugh?*

The debate over Molière's grimaces is an indication of how his writing and playing calculated a physical rhythm. As listener, Molière's Arnolphe experiences a series of propositions which are in tension with his inner reflections as undeclared victim. Horace's insistence on approval produces another level of tension. His account of Agnès, instructed by Monsieur de la Souche, throwing a stone at him, implies a series of natural physical responses, for which no text is supplied. Yet his half-dozen questions are to be answered in both bodily attitude and facial strain.

HORACE

Cette pierre ou ce grès dont vous vous étonniez
Avec un mot de lettre est tombée à mes pieds;
Et j'admire de voir cette lettre ajustée
Avec le sens des mots et de la pierre jetée.
D'une telle action n'êtes-vous pas surpris?
L'amour sait-il pas l'art d'aiguiser les esprits?
Et peut-on me nier que ses flammes puissantes
Ne fassent dans un coeur des choses étonnantes?
Que dites-vous du tour et de ce mot d'écrit?
Trouvez-vous pas plaisant de voir quel personnage
A joué mon jaloux dans tout ce badinage?
Dites.

ARNOLPHE

Oui, fort plaisant.

HORACE

Riez-en donc un peu.
(*Arnolphe rit d'un ris forcé.*)

(III, iv, ll. 914–926)[14]

HORACE

This stone or rock that so surprised you
Fell at my feet, but with a little letter;
And I am amazed to find this letter explains
The meaning of her words and the stone she'd thrown.
Aren't you surprised she'd do such a thing?
Does not love sharpen people's wits?
And can anyone tell me that it's not the power of love
That can accomplish in her heart such amazing things?
What do you say to her trick and the word she sent?
Are you not amused to see the role
Played by my jealous rival in these goings-on?
Tell me.

ARNOLPHE

Yes, highly amused.

HORACE

Then laugh a little
(Arnolphe laughs with forced laugh.)

The procedure is clear, and artificial. Life is rarely as clear-cut in its oppositions, and the play could be criticized as a description of how matters fall out in the world. In the theatre, however, the abstract proposition can be given life in an integrated physical performance, arousing the curiosity of an audience and exciting its speculation and its energy.

The physical score for the actor in *L'École des femmes* and the texture of thought it supported were quite new, and must have delighted an audience whose manners and social sense were highly developed. Molière's performance appealed to thinking and judgment, to understanding of words and their effect, and an appreciation of the life of tacit meanings in the playing. The physical method is quasi-algebraic, with physical attitude standing for the discursive explanations of speech. What is unsaid in the role of Arnolphe is there to be played in the body of the actor. The play was memorable for the 'Ouf!' of Molière's exit.

The stage works, then, as an imaginative analogue rather than a reconstruction of daily life, albeit that the medium employs the everyday material of the human body and the human personality. Molière's use of the performer makes clear the analogical value of this performance, which artistically transforms the actor into something conveniently less than the intricate 'being' he is otherwise, and which achieves a structuring of experience and an ordering of reality in appropriate and stimulating terms for his audience. The abstract and analogical quality of the stage emerges in the domestic scenes between Arnolphe and, first, Alain and Georgette, and then Agnès. Reference is made to the inner space of the house, but Arnolphe calls for a chair in the public square. Given the decor, Molière inevitably draws attention to the clash of abstract and figurative space. The figurative value of seventeenth-century stage space is very limited (even the changing décors of *Dom Juan* stress artifice rather than the nature of places which are represented). Nevertheless Molière laid himself open to criticism when he had Arnolphe call Agnès 'outside'. Such a disregard for place was seen as a misunderstanding of the probable actions of a man jealous of his intended wife. It was actually the error of a *farceur* using the stage to present actors.

Zélinde shows the collision of Molière's theatrical imagination with the naïve realism of the critic. '*L'incident du grès*'[15] provokes an extended discussion between the merchant Argimont and his customer of the weight of stone a woman could wield, the likely damage it would inflict, and the probability of the victim examining the stone for any attached letter. The discussion is fastidious, and the evidence carefully examined lest Molière should claim a smaller stone was meant than seemed apparent. In another example in II, ii, Argimont acknowledges the theatrical effect of the performance, albeit grudgingly, as dazzling but contrary to all probability, as Alain and Georgette, fall, simultaneously, to their knees so many times. Presumably the unreasonableness of the procedure is doubly damnable since it is amusing. The critic notices despite himself the symmetry of the acting, a term which normally is not employed to demean an effect:

> The scene played by Arnolphe with Alain and Georgette, when he asks them how it is that Horace has got into his house, is a piece of stage business which dazzles, since it is not true to life that the same two persons fall to their knees, as many as six or seven times, symmetrically on either side of their master. I admit that fear may make them kneel, but it is impossible that this should happen so often, and it is not a natural action.[16]

The later scene between the servants with its comparison of women and soup betrays too obviously the wit of the dramatist rather than the slow mind of the peasant. The disagreeable comments of the critic make clear the value of the acting: physically patterned and intellectually energetic. While here criticized for lack of verisimilitude, Molière, seen below in Argimont's shop, is described as some sort of magician, capable of conjuring up the very image, words and aspect of the people he observes.

> *He had his eyes glued to three or four persons of quality who were buying their lace, he appeared attentive to their words, and it seemed, from the motion of his eyes, that he was peering into the very depths of their souls to see there what they did not say; I even think that he had writing tablets, and that behind his coat he wrote down, without being noticed, the most noteworthy things they said.*
>
> ORIANE
> *{...} Perhaps he had a pencil, and was drawing their grimaces, so as to represent them to the life on his stage.*

ARGIMONT
{...} If he did not draw them on his tablets, I have no doubt that
he printed them on his imagination. He is a dangerous person ...[17]

Donneau de Visé's attacks draw attention to a physical power in the
acting of Molière: to its supposed incoherence or exaggeration or to
its dangerous accuracy. His grimaces are overdone; or are the very
'portraits' of examples in life, which the public was anxious to identify. What is the balance, then, between these judgements? Absurd
overacting, or dangerous, vindictive imitation? The evidence is that
Molière took his acting performance a step forward in the role of
Arnolphe, and set himself a task which was more carefully structured
than anything he had yet attempted, combining the strength and
exaggeration of farce with a range of social reference, and a new ethical awareness.

The contrast with *L'École des maris* of 1661 shows the advance.
Sganarelle is conceived in terms which could well apply to a
Pantalone in the Italian *commedia dell'arte*. Molière has the first lines,
and presents the eccentric character to the audience:

SGANARELLE
Mon frère, s'il vous plaît, ne discourons point tant,
Et que chacun de nous vive comme il l'entend. [...]
Que j'ai pour tout conseil ma fantaisie à suivre,
Et me trouve fort bien de ma façon de vivre.

(I, i, ll. 1–8)[18]

SGANARELLE
If you please, my brother, not so many speeches,
And let each of us lead the life he means to. {...}
The only counsel that I'll follow is my fancy,
And I am well pleased with my way of life.

The opposition is between two characters, each clearly presented.
Molière's Sganarelle declares his peculiarity: the affectation of old-
fashioned dress and manners. The style permits an energetic and
simplified performance: he will follow fancy as his guide. The principle is set out frankly in all its absurdity. Like any farce, the stage
presentation stresses strong characteristics, here typified in the out-
landish costume. Sganarelle's brother is twenty years older, but
conforms to the manners and dress of the day, whereas Sganarelle
himself affects the fashions of twenty years earlier. With *L'École des*

femmes the approach is quite different: a proposition is reiterated in the first line of the play and confirmed by Arnolphe. Molière is dressed *en habit de ville* and, as the accounts reveal, is perfectly serious in aspect. Arnolphe is every inch the bourgeois, and the audience can scarcely have imagined that this would be the central role of the comedy.

CHRYSALDE

Vous venez, dites-vous, pour lui donner la main?

ARNOLPHE

Oui, je veux terminer la chose dès demain.

CHRYSALDE

Nous sommes ici seuls; et l'on peut, ce me semble,
Sans craindre d'être ouïs, y discourir ensemble:
Voulez-vous qu'en ami je vous ouvre mon coeur?

(I, i, ll. 1–2)[19]

CHRYSALDE

You say you have come to give her your hand?

ARNOLPHE

Yes, I will finish the matter by tomorrow.

CHRYSALDE

*We are alone here; and we might, it seems to me,
Talk it over together without fear of eavesdroppers:
Do you wish me, as your friend, to be open with you?*

Nothing in the scene conveys the problem which will shortly emerge. The gentlemanly appearance of Molière in the role was much remarked, contrary to expectations of the farce. Here was a play where the manners of the world were adopted in the most natural of ways. Where is the familiar 'extravagance' of the acting?

To understand the aberrant aspects of the role of Arnolphe, the audience required more than the evidence of their eyes. They had to think through a proposition. Chrysalde fears for him should he proceed with a marriage, given his former mockery of cuckolded husbands. The question is developed progressively with an easy acceptance of the views one of another.

CHRYSALDE

Prendre femme est à vous un coup bien téméraire.

70

ARNOLPHE

Il est vrai, notre ami …

[…]

Fort bien …

[…] Mon Dieu, notre ami, ne vous tourmentez point …

(I, i, ll. 8–73)[20]

CHRYSALDE

Taking a wife is a bold move for you.

ARNOLPHE

True, my friend …

{…}

Very well …

{…}

Heavens, my friend, don't bother yourself at all …

In an entertaining discussion of an age-old problem, the speakers defer properly one to another, and the tone remains well within the bounds of friendly debate. The acting style here exaggerates nothing. On the contrary, Arnolphe's role advances an argument which is at least plausible and might have been accepted in broad terms by many members of the audience. It is also in Molière the heart of the role. For the actor it is the idea which counts. Without an adequate intellectual focus the basic integration of the performance cannot proceed. As Molière plays this first scene, he achieves what did indeed seem paradoxical at the time: a shared imaginative proposition about social life, given form in thinking and action, which was at the same time both convincing and absurd. Arnolphe's arguments walk a fine line between prudence and inhuman obsession:

Épouser une sotte est pour n'être point sot.
Je crois en bon chrétien, votre moitié fort sage;
Mais une femme habile est un mauvais présage …

(I, i, ll. 82–85)[21]

To marry a fool is to avoid being foolish.
I believe, as I am a good Christian, that your wife is quite blameless;
But a clever wife is a bad omen …

Here the forms of everyday life were adapted to the stage to grace with dress and deportment purposes which were close enough to current social concerns as to be entertained by the audience.

The opening scene unfolds Arnolphe's purpose and the means he has employed to secure it, and delivers a reasoned response to the risk of failure he has derided in others. The argument is based on experience, and Molière takes the audience through a recreation of the scenes he alleges recur throughout the town. The presentation is imaginative, but asks the audience to consider propositions which are close to home.

ARNOLPHE

Fort bien: est-il au monde une autre ville aussi
Où l'on ait des maris si patients qu'ici?

(I, i, ll. 21–22)[22]

ARNOLPHE

Wonderful: is there anywhere another town
Where husbands are as tolerant as here?

The performance now places examples in the imaginative playing space, the 'town' of the play, which is a creation of shared thought between actor and audience. The examples demand a sense of place and life conferred by the actor and are set up as a series of balanced alternatives:

L'un amasse du bien, dont sa femme fait part
À ceux qui prennent soin de le faire cornard;
L'autre un peu plus heureux, mais non pas moins infâme,
Voit faire tous les jours des présents à sa femme,
Et d'aucun soin jaloux n'a l'esprit combattu,
Parce qu'elle lui dit que c'est pour sa vertu.
L'un fait beaucoup de bruit qui ne lui sert de guère;
L'autre ...

(I, i, ll. 25–31)[23]

One heaps up wealth, which his wife shares
With those who take care to give him horns;
Another a little happier, but no less shamed,
Sees every day presents made to his wife,
And yet no jealous thought disturbs his mind,
Because she says that they are for her virtue.

One protests out loud, to hardly any effect;
Another ...

This method is abstract, but manifest in terms of acting and stage space. The examples are typical but not specific. They are here and there, generally in the life of the town, and lie naturally to one hand or the other of the actor and his audience.

Enfin, ce sont partout des sujets de satire;
Et comme spectateur ne puis-je pas en rire?

(I, i, ll. 43–44)[24]

After all, everywhere there are subjects for satire,
And should I not be the spectator, and laugh at them?

The contrast with Molière's earlier roles must have been striking: the actor takes the worldly attitude of the habitué of the town and reviews its follies and eccentricities. Even in *Les Fâcheux* some months before, Molière had given himself the part of one of the grotesque bores, not the long-suffering gentleman Eraste, which he left to the young La Grange. All Molière's roles to this point were characterized by some exaggeration or manifest absurdity. The debate recalls that the criticism of Molière leaned heavily on the perception of an *Arnolphe ... honnête homme*. A gentleman could not be absurd.

Arnolphe adopted a view of society which the house could not but enjoy: satirical, and even unkind, but sharp-edged and witty. The fashion in which the equally civilized Chrysalde counters with a different and more patient view of men and women, only adds to the effect. The audience is drawn into, first, the observation of the town, and then into another prospect: not what can be 'seen' as the shared experience of actor and audience, but a hypothesis. Arnolphe proposes a solution to the problem of fidelity in marriage in the figure of a stupid wife. Morally the proposition is monstrous; emotionally and personally dubious. Within the terms of the discussion, and in the space of the abstract town where the actor builds his world, it is particularly piquant, with the hypothesis now located with greater specificity in the minds of actor and audience. The stupid wife-to-be is particularized in terms of her parentage and upbringing outside the town. She is then located within the stage space, *'dans cette autre maison'*. She is 'within', in the house indicated by the decor.

In the playing of the role there is a clear effort made to achieve precision, not peculiarity. Any absurdity or exaggeration will be perceived by the audience judging the basic equation of social prudence and private sensual felicity.

ARNOLPHE

Vous me direz: Pourquoi cette narration?
C'est pour vous rendre instruit de ma précaution.
Le résultat de tout est qu'en ami fidèle
Ce soir je vous invite à souper avec elle;
Je veux que vous puissiez un peu l'examiner,
Et voir si de mon choix on doit me condamner.

(I, i, ll. 149–154)[25]

You will say to me: why this account?
It is so I may acquaint you with my precaution
The result of that is that as a faithful friend
I can invite you this evening to dine with her;
I want you to be able to form some opinion of her,
And see if any would condemn me for my choice.

The key terms are almost mathematical: *instruit, résultat, examiner, choix*. Arnolphe even gives Chrysalde leave to doubt his proposition until he has met the girl herself. This cool rationalism begins to break down as abstractions come closer and closer to the material world in which formulae must be submitted to empirical examination. Chrysalde questions a curious detail: Arnolphe is no longer to be known in this vicinity as Arnolphe, but as Monsieur de la Souche, taking the name of a *tronc pourri*,[26] a 'rotten tree stump'.

Mais enfin de la Souche est le nom que je porte:
J'y vois la raison, j'y trouve des appas;
Et m'appeler de l'autre est ne m'obliger pas.

(I, i, ll. 184–185)[27]

When all's said, Monsieur de la Souche is the name I bear:
I see the reason for it and I understand the appeal,
And otherwise to address me is to displease me.

The term *appas*, or 'attractions', is cunningly selected from the *galant* lexicon, and assorts ill with the *raison* Arnolphe otherwise claims. Arnolphe's philosophy of control breaks down at the point where human emotion intrudes. Chrysalde finds him 'fou de toutes les manières' (*quite mad*).[28]

Intellectual power combined with the disturbance of passion was entirely new in French acting. In tragedies, rhetoric procured an agreeable and rational flow of emotion, couched in a role which never risked real disorder, still less breakdown. The term *beau désordre* describes the way in which such a display was to be seen. With the physical and intellectual resources of the *farceur*, Molière could employ the violence of emotional performance, yet discipline it within precise physical forms. These are then examined from the 'philosophical' position adopted by Arnolphe:

ARNOLPHE

Comme il faut devant lui [Horace] que je me mortifie!
Quelle peine à cacher mon déplaisir cuisant!
Quoi? pour une innocente un esprit si présent!
Elle a feint d'être telle à mes yeux, la traîtresse,
Ou le diable à son âme a soufflé cette adresse.
Enfin me voilà mort par ce funeste écrit.
Je vois qu'il a, le traître, empaumé son esprit,
Qu'à ma supression il est ancré chez elle;
Et c'est mon désespoir et ma peine mortelle.
Je souffre doublement dans le vol de son coeur,
Et l'amour y pâtit aussi bien que l'honneur,
J'enrage de trouver cette place usurpée,
Et j'enrage de voir ma prudence trompée.
[...]
Ciel! puisque pour un choix j'ai tant philosophé
Faut-il de ses appas m'être si fort coiffé!...
[...]
Sot, n'as-tu pas de honte? Ah! je crève, j'enrage,
Et je souffletterais mille fois mon visage.

(III, v, ll. 977–1001)[29]

ARNOLPHE

See how I have to mortify myself in front of him {Horace}!
What torment to hide my burning agony!
What? for an innocent to have such presence of mind!
She pretended to be so in my eyes, the traitress,
Or the devil has prompted her mind to this cleverness.
This deadly letter has struck the final blow.
I see, traitor, he has bewitched her,

By ousting me, the more he has attached her to him;
And this brings my despair, my deadly agony.
I suffer twice by him stealing her heart,
And love is on the rack as well as honour,
It maddens me to find my place usurped,
It maddens me that all my prudent thought has been deceived.
{...}
Heavens! have I philosophized so long to choose her,
And must I really lose my head over her charms!
{...}
Fool, have you no shame? Ah! I die, I am furious,
And I could a thousand times smack my own face.

Molière draws on the heavyweight vocabulary of the tragic stage: *peine, traître, funeste, désespoir*, but from the comic tradition he derives the forms in which it is experienced. The idealized conceptions of Arnolphe fall to the ground not only in the absurdity of his conclusions, that it is somehow appalling to love the woman he has chosen (philosophically) to be his wife, but also in the physical assault on himself. The realism of his procedure is vital to its intellectual impact. Molière as the miser in *L'Avare* would later demonstrate that as an actor, he was wholly capable of smacking his own face.

The role is built on an internal debate manifested in energy, tension, and a close attention to the forms of action. The effort made by Arnolphe to explain and then master his rage at the conclusion of Act III is followed by a veritable replaying of the imagined events of the entr'acte at the beginning of the next.

ARNOLPHE

J'ai peine, je l'avoue, à demeurer en place,
Et de mille soucis mon esprit s'embarrasse.

(IV, i, ll. 1008–1009)[30]

ARNOLPHE

I can scarcely, I confess, stand still,
And my mind is confused by a thousand troubles.

The lengthy speech which follows characterizes both the tranquillity of Agnès and the movements of passion which have overpowered Arnolphe, and which the actor now demonstrates to the audience. The comic discrepancy, so apparent in the farce, between the effrontery of the young wife and the rage of the husband, is played out within the single role, bringing the actor to consider the tensions of his actual performance, and the moral character of the objectives he examines. For Molière this meant venturing into a territory where comic extravagance became more intensely personal to the actor and more absorbing for the audience. The eccentricity of the farce character was transmuted into an internalized disorder which exploded a façade of gentility. This was the role without which his individual form of dramatic comedy could not develop.

Part 2

A CELEBRATORY THEATRE

6

THE COURT DRAMATIST

I chose to assume the form of the sun, because of the unique quality of the radiance that surrounds it; the light that it imparts to the
other stars, which compose a kind of court; the fair and equal share
of that light that it gives to all the various climates of the world;
the good it does in every place, ceaselessly producing joy and activity on every side; the untiring motion in which it yet seems always
tranquil; and that constant invariable course from which it never
deviates or diverges – assuredly the most vivid and beautiful image
of a young monarch.

Louis XIV, *Mémoires*

Magnificence was vital to royal propaganda in the *grand siècle* of Louis,
and at the outset, festival, with the figure of the monarch at the centre,
was a chief instrument of display. The King's liking for the *ballet de cour*
is well known, and he was a proficient, even a gifted dancer, participating in shows created by artists working in the inner circles of the
court, among whom Molière was prominent. Louis's involvement in
theatre is noteworthy, but hardly surprising given the society in which
he moved. He was young, with the tastes and the social skills of any
courtier of the day, and would have adopted the habitual entertainments of an earlier age: like his father, he would be expected to take to
the floor as the first personnage of the *ballet de cour*, or exhibit his skill
at any of the performances of martial or equestrian arts where the court
displayed itself and celebrated its accomplishments.

The contemplation of the monarch in the symbolic exercise of
power is indispensable to the functioning of even a modern monarchi-
cal state. Where power tended to the absolute its virtual manifestation
on an almost daily basis was a vital confirmation of the actual political
supremacy of the sovereign. The spectacle of the young Louis triumphant in the *carrousel*, or resplendent in the allegorical ballet, was

part of a narrative of success and glory, broadcast by telling and re-telling in word and in print. Charles Perrault was capable of publishing in 1670 a handsome volume of engravings, presenting in a new medium *Le Grand Carrousel* of 1662, in which the King represented the Emperor of the Romans. As with the 1664 *fêtes* at Versailles, the illustrations narrated the event so that the significant episodes of the actions, and, above all, the idealized characters could once more make their impact.

From his return to Paris in 1658, Molière was a court entertainer. By the happiest of coincidences the sovereign was entering a period of personal and political security where the monarchy was in the ascendant. The King, although only twenty years of age, had ruled since 1651 (when he declared the end of the Regency of his mother Anne of Austria), and with the aid of the gifted *premier ministre* Cardinal Mazarin, he had survived the potentially disastrous period of civil disturbance from 1648 to 1652 known as the Fronde. Elements in the nobility and the Parisian bourgeoisie had grouped in opposition to the Queen Regent, and were particularly hostile to the influence of the Italian cardinal who was believed to be effectively governing the realm. These years had also seen the precipitation of tensions between the crown and reforming elements in the Parlement de Paris, the prime judicial assembly of the capital.

Figure 6.1   *Les Plaisirs de l'Île enchantée.* The first day, Louis XIV leading the parade of knights. *Courtesy of the Bibliothèque nationale, Paris*

Figure 6.2   The second day of *Les Plaisirs*. The King watching *La Princesse d'Élide*, with Molière in the cast. *Courtesy of the Bibliothèque nationale, Paris*

Nevertheless, through this turbulent time, entertainment occupied the young Louis. In 1652 the Venetian Ambassador observed that the King (aged fourteen) had no taste for his council but that 'games, dances and comedies are the King's sole pursuits'[1] and Choisy contrasted the efforts of Mazarin with the indolence of his master who 'amused himself at the reviews, at the dances, at the ballets; [...] he lived as a private person without troubling himself with anything'.[2] Some suspected that the apparent frivolity of the monarchy was cultivated by Mazarin as a cloak for the severer aspects of his own ambitions. The cardinal 'invited gaiety to approach the throne ... to render his power less invidious'.[3] Whatever his enthusiasm for such amusements there was an element in the upbringing and personality of the King which integrated his pleasures closely with his sense of identity and mission. The shrewd memorialist Madame de Motteville noticed that despite the King's devotion to his *divertissement* there was a certain preoccupation: 'I often noticed with astonishment that in his games and amusements the King never laughed'.[4]

After the death of Mazarin in 1661, Louis would create a civil service of royal officers, but never again a Prime Minister. In his *Mémoires* he urges his son Louis to adopt a similar absolute rule:

I determined, above all, not to have a Prime Minister; and if you have faith in me, my son, the title will be abolished for ever in France. For nothing is more unworthy than to see all the power on one side and only the title of King on the other.[5]

Molière's theatres were part of a topography of places into which Louis translated his court, substituting the imagination of roles and performances for the reality of political struggle. Molière and his fellow artists and performers created a kaleidoscope of entertainments which paralleled and inspired the theatrical rituals of government and life at court. The aesthetic of these works is closely linked to the symbolism of absolute monarchy, with the person of the King characterized as semi-divine.

Spectacle needs to operate as a language if it is to be effective as a signifier. Thus the impression of wealth and generalized status that is evident in processional forms becomes refined with the growth of the court festival as the reign proceeds. Louis assumed a particular character through his inclusion in the Pantheon of classical deities, and from his earliest years was depicted in portraiture as Jupiter, Mars or Apollo.

In the elaborate *ballet de cour*, which had flourished in the decades after 1587, the date of the *Ballet Comique de la Reine*, the royal participant could assume a role, and, with it, the qualities of an idealized figure from myth, literature or history. Similarly he might appear before the court, and frequently the population, in a whole spectrum of essentially theatrical events, including jousting, tilting, carousels, nautical entertainments, royal triumphs and parades. In all of these, actual magnificence could supply the occasion for art to attribute virtual qualities to the participants. The theatrical vehicle which conveyed most effectively the icons of baroque neo-classicism was the court ballet, and it readily adapted to the needs of court propaganda. In 1651, at the age of thirteen, Louis had danced in the first of a series of ballets written by the court poet Benserade, in which appeared a character that would furnish the emblem of his reign. In 1653 in the *Ballet de la Nuit* the fifteen-year-old monarch took the role himself: it was Apollo, the Sun King.

The changing political situation of the kingdom is well reflected in the types of entertainment staged, their places, and their occasions. The truly public display rapidly declined after the establishment of the young King. The royal entry of 1660 was the last to assemble all the social orders. It was also the occasion of a protest at the precedence of the Comte de Soissons by the dukes and peers, who ultimately refused to participate. These forms were regarded as clear public signals: a theatrical gazette in which preference and rank were easily understood. Two major shifts in emphasis can be seen in court and political show: after 1662 and the *Grand Carrousel*, the movement from Paris to the residences at Fontainebleau, Saint Germain-en-Laye, Chambord and later Versailles; and the shift from garden to apartment after 1674. The movements implied a restriction, and doubtless a refining of the audience. They also altered the nature and focus of spectacle. As the 'stage' altered, the 'audience' became distilled into a smaller and an ever more élite fashion: the public of Paris in 1660 and 1662 witnessed the last of the great royal entrées and equestrian tournaments after the tradition of the Renaissance. While parade and equestrianism were practised elsewhere, the King's dislike and avoidance of Paris and its *canaille* were made clear in the great project which created Versailles and eventually made it the seat of government in 1682. After 1662 the monarchy effectively turned its back on the people, and played to the only significant audience: the court. The old public shows were subsumed into entertainments which, although even more lavish, were scaled to the needs of the court alone, and were increasingly produced at the royal residences outside the capital.

The theatricality of court entertainment is so comprehensive and elaborate that it cannot be ignored in any attempt to understand the art of Molière. His was an age which gloried in the magnificence of theatre as show, but in which there were many theatres differing very considerably in their stages of evolution, and in the aesthetic they employed. The very notion of 'theatre' must be detached from our present-day understanding of the buildings which house stages of different types.[6] The word in seventeenth-century France conserved its original Greek force, meaning 'viewing place' and was often synonymous with 'stage'. 'Sur nos théâtres' is the phraseology of a culture which concentrates on theatre as a medium for the organization of viewpoint, and sees it as being essentially malleable. Physically the term refers to a stage as it is set up to be viewed, implying thereafter the framing devices and the way the audience is grouped and organized within an auditorium. Wherever theatrical entertainment is created it is set up within given spaces: public, private or court.

During the months that followed Molière's eviction from the Petit-Bourbon in 1660, the actors were without a playhouse, but the court connection ensured that they played *en visite* at various aristo-cratic residences. They were generously remunerated for their performances of one or both of *Les Précieuses ridicules* and *Le Cocu imag-inaire*, receiving sums of from 150 *livres* for one play at the house of the duc de Mercoeur to 330 *livres* for a performance of both for a Treasury official, Monsieur de la Bazinière. But the most generous engagement came from the *surintendant des finances*, Nicolas Foucquet, who, for the same double bill, rewarded the troupe with the sum of 500 *livres*, as much as the receipts for an average perfor-mance at their former theatre. Foucquet again was quick to bring the actors to his château at Vaux-le-Vicomte on 11 July 1661 to play their newest success, *L'École des maris*, less than three weeks after its opening. He may well have brought this novelty to the King at Fontainebleau on 13 July since La Grange records that performance alongside one for Foucquet's wife at Vaux. A single, generous pay-ment of 1,500 *livres* is recorded from the Foucquet purse. The next day La Grange records the marquis de Richelieu paying 880 *livres* for *L'École des maris* to be played before the Queen's ladies.

The actors were fortunate to enjoy this currency in court circles, where entertainment was offered as evidence of duty towards the dedicatee, and gratified the self-esteem of the patron. Foucquet's offering was duly recorded by the journalist Loret:

> *Besides concerts and airs,*
> *He {Foucquet} offered them a play;*
> *To wit* L'École des maris,
> *The charm, at present, of all Paris,*
> *A new play and greatly admired,*
> *Which Monsieur Molière has composed.*
> *A subject so comical and fine,*
> *It was required that at Fontainebleau,*
> *This troupe, practised*
> *In serious and comic plays,*
> *For the contentment of the King and Queens,*
> *Should go and play it once again.*[7]

Foucquet was to be the source of Molière's first significant commis-sion, a new play to be offered as a tribute to the King. The entertainment reflected the lavish ambitions of the patron, and Molière was asked to write for new technical facilities and material resources, in a theatre which would be constructed as part of the cele-bration of the royal visit to Foucquet's astonishing new house and gardens at Vaux-le-Vicomte. Ironically Molière's first work for the fête was dedicated to the King's pleasure but not ordered by him. It was, however, the occasion for the creation of a style of theatre which was to be substantially that of Versailles and the other country residences.

The commission gave Molière all the resources he could reasonably desire, and more: an almost overpowering luxury of means, and the necessity of employing them with imagination. The result was the creation of *Les Fâcheux*, a collaboration with Torelli the stage engineer, Le Brun the painter, Pellison the poet and secretary to Foucquet, and most significantly Beauchamp the dancer. It would be a work that would prove enduringly successful in Molière's lifetime, after its dazzling success at Vaux, when the very wonder of the occasion created the royal envy or suspicion, whichever it was, that led to Foucquet's disgrace and imprisonment.

LES FÂCHEUX AT VAUX-LE VICOMTE

Les Fâcheux was something, Molière told his reader, out of the ordinary:

> ... c'est un mélange qui est nouveau pour nos théâtres, et dont on pourraient chercher quelques autorités dans l'antiquité; et, comme tout le monde l'a trouvé agréable, il peut servir d'idée à d'autres choses qui pourraient être méditées avec plus de loisir.[8]

> ... *this is a mixture which is new on our stages, and for which one could seek authority in antiquity; and, as everyone has found it pleasing, it can serve as an idea of other things which may be contemplated at greater leisure.*

Molière was prophetic and, in 1661, *Les Fâcheux* pointed towards forms he would indeed develop over the next decade. His curious anxiety to legitimize a mixed-media entertainment must have arisen easily in a man trained by the Jesuits as a dancer and a scholar. Equally, that training must have encouraged an interest in the acted performance integrated with the ornaments of music, dance and spectacle. Molière had certainly danced professionally, and it may be that the *Ballet des incompatibles*, created for the Prince de Conti and the 1655 States-General at Montpellier, had been in part devised by him. It is clear from the *livret*, that Molière and his company danced side by side with the courtiers.

Vaux afforded an environment already conceived as a pleasure ground. The theatre was to be placed, at will, among the waterways and fountains, the avenues and the foliage of a palace which was, in the words of La Fontaine, 'The Dream of Vaux'. The gardens of Vaux were its glory, and the greatest such enterprise that had been undertaken in France. The plans had been drawn up at least ten years previously, and their final form owed much to the great designer Le Nôtre who had supervized the work since 1657. Its scale had been staggering, involving the razing of three inconvenient villages, the building of a hostel for the accommodation of the workers, and the shifting of massive volumes of earth to create terraces and parterres. Le Nôtre organized the various levels of the garden within a perspective which stretched to the horizon, aided by the rising gradient of the hill opposite the château. The design brought enormous spaces within the compass of the human eye, placing the volumes and areas of the garden in a disciplined but graceful relationship with the noble promenade which moved through the garden and discovered its enchantments. As the series of engravings by Israel Sylvestre demonstrates, the garden ordained a certain human progress along its paths and avenues and moments of pause for the contemplation of set pieces. Chief among these were combinations of stone and water: the creation of a series of magnificent fountains and waterfalls, and a canal, three thousand feet long, all fed by the diversion of the river Angueil.

As Molière looked back some months after the performance and wrote his preface to the printed text, he must have dwelt upon the description he would give of the *fête*, so remarkable had been its impact on the court and so dreadful the consequences for the unfortunate Foucquet, thrown into prison by the King and accused of embezzlement. The brilliance of the house and of the entertainment must have seemed to the young monarch an inappropriate display in his minister: 'cette fête a fait un tel éclat qu'il n'est pas nécessaire d'en parler (*this festival caused such a sensation that it is not necessary to speak of it*)'.[9] It was probably wiser to speak of the practicalities of the theatre. The object had been to perform a ballet in addition to a comedy, presumably to be written for the occasion. However, the surprise desired by Foucquet meant that no court dancers could have been used for the usual *ballet de cour*, and dances would be performed only by the professional dancers and by Molière's actors. This accounts for the absence of any *livret*, the explanatory booklet giving the identities of amateur dancers from the court.

Le dessein était de donner un ballet aussi; et, comme il n'y avait qu'un petit nombre choisis de danseurs excellents, on fut contraint de séparer les entrées de ce ballet, et l'avis fut de les jeter dans les entr'actes de la comédie, afin que ces intervalles donassent temps aux mêmes baladins de revenir sous d'autres vêtements.[10]

The plan was to perform a ballet also; and, as there was but a small choice number of excellent dancers, we were obliged to separate the entrées of the ballet, and the decision was to interpolate them in the entractes of the play, so that these intervals might provide time for the same dancers to return in other costumes.

The dances had to be new in their invention and in their relationship to the action of the comedy. The juxtaposition of comedy and ballet was not an innovation, but the team that created *Les Fâcheux* adopted a principle which probably only the Jesuits had considered, namely that there should be a degree of integration of the different elements of acting, music and dance. The moral objectives of the Fathers justified dance as a mute explanation of the themes which were presented in the Latin play.

The interaction of performance media was to be carried further at Vaux-le-Vicomte with a similar close integration of the means of presentation. Still living in France, although supplanted by Vigarani at court, was the Italian *machiniste* Giacomo Torelli, creator of the decors for the Petit-Bourbon fifteen years before.[11] It was the imagination of Torelli which was behind the scenic marvels which entertained Louis XIV on a lovely summer's evening on 17 August 1661.

His Majesty travelled in full view in his *calèche*, as every account testifies, accompanied by Monsieur, his brother, and three ladies of the court. The Queen Mother came after in her carriage followed by Madame, in a litter and a suite which included most of the court. The King's choice of conveyance harmonized with the aesthetic of the evening in which the theatrical aspects of court social life were transmuted and formalized into an entertainment in which he and his court were part participants and part audience. The *calèche* (introduced only in 1646) was fashionable among young gentlemen, and was particularly suitable for personal display. An *équipage* of this sort was the equivalent of the modern open-topped sports car, attractive in itself, and a foil to set off the attractions of its occupants. Furetière's *Dictionnaire* gives a definition which *mutatis mutandis* explains the sovereign's liking for this mode of travel, and his choice of his companions:

A little cut-down coach down which has several ornaments. It is used by young men who wish to drive in parade.[12]

In *Les Fâcheux* there is an early mention of the fashion and the need to be seen in the Cours la Reine, the promenade beyond the Tuileries gardens which had been created by the expansion of the city some years earlier, and where it was fashionable to drive.

> Marquis, allons au Cours faire voir ma galèche;
> Elle est bien entendue, et plus d'un duc et pair
> En fait à mon faiseur faire une du même air.
>
> (I, i, ll. 76–78)[13]

> *Marquis, let us go and show off my calèche at the Cours;*
> *It is beautifully finished, and more than one duke and peer*
> *Has made my maker make one in the same style.*

Louis's arrival was the first act in a sequence which stressed movement and the quasi-scenic environment of Le Nôtre's gardens.

Torelli, as anxious as Fouquet to enjoy the good offices of the King, created the theatre and its transformations, together with a firework display to crown the evening. D'Olivet was charged with the some of the dance *entrées*, while the great Beauchamp was responsible for the ballet which framed and concluded Molière's comedy, and may also have supplied the evening's music. Torelli's collaborator in the painting of the scenes and set pieces was Le Brun, then at the beginning of his enormously successful career as painter and interior decorator. Whatever could be done to enchant the eye and ear was to be provided to impress the twenty-three-year-old monarch. The punishment of Fouquet is, ironically, as much an indicator of the sumptuousness of the entertainment as are the reports of the gossips and eyewitnesses of the day. For the collaborators this was a critical production: Fouquet's secretary Pelisson, who supplied verses for the prologue to the *comédie*, was arrested with his master; Torelli failed to expiate the sin of being associated with Mazarin and was expelled to Italy. The newcomers Molière and Le Brun went on to greater success, as did Le Nôtre, the creator of the garden.

La Fontaine's account of the evening evokes the enchantment of Vaux, from the moment the King alighted from his open carriage to the court's departure by the light of torches at two the next morning. Display was everywhere, and the occasion measured the glory of Fouquet and his royal guests:

Every sense was enchanted;
And the celebration had beauty
Worthy of the place, and of the master,
And worthy of their Majesties
If such a thing could ever be.

In the beginning was the drive. All of the Court beheld the waters
with great pleasure. Never again will Vaux be more beautiful than it
was that evening … {…} There was rivalry between the Cascade, the
Water Spray, the Fountain of the Crown, and the Animals, as to
which would please more; the ladies for their part did no less.[14]

La Fontaine links the beauty of the garden to that of the ladies: one
setting off the other. Vaux was a theatre to be admired and to lend
grace to those who paraded upon its stage.

After the promenade, La Fontaine's account notes the supper which
followed, but moves on rapidly to *la comédie*, the entertainment devised
by Molière and his collaborators. La Fontaine's characteristic wit tem-
pers the eulogistic tone that might be expected of the retainer writing
of the triumph of his master's house, and the result is a singularly rich
impression of the audience's experience. Thus the static elements of the
evening, in chief the supper, are glossed over, and the description concentrates on movement and change.

From the house the court moved again through the gardens to where
the theatre was placed at the end of one of the avenues. The theatre and
the stage design were conceived as an extension of the garden with its
own subtle illusionistic effects. In particular, the layout of the *allées* created the impression of perspective as in architectural painting or in
stage setting. La Fontaine's description suggests the fantasy in nature.

Au pied de ces sapins et sous la grille d'eau
Parmi la fraicheur agréable
Des fontaines, des bois, de l'ombre et des zephyrs
Furent préparés les plaisirs
Que l'on goûta cette soirée.
De feuillages touffus la scène etait parée,
Et de cent flambeaux éclairée;
Le Ciel en fut jaloux. Enfin figure-toi
Que lorsqu'on eut tiré les toiles,
Tout combattit à Vaux pour le plaisir du roi:
La musique, les eaux, les lustres, les étoiles.[15]

At the foot of the pines and beneath the waterfall
Amidst the sweet coolness
Of the fountains, the woods, the shade and the soft winds
Were made ready the pleasures
That were tasted that night.
The stage was decked with bursting foliage,
And lit by a hundred torches:
Heaven itself was envious. At last, imagine for yourself
That once the canvas was drawn back,
All Vaux vied for the pleasure of the king:
Music, waters, chandeliers, the stars.

The play of light on painted canvas as well as on foliage and water constituted part of an exchange between actuality and illusion, whereby, in La Fontaine's impression, the natural world was drawn into a fantasy as one more element in the satisfying of the King. La Fontaine evokes the spaces which are occupied by the spectators, and the way in which illusion and imagination combine in a series of moments and places which dissolve one into another. Either the audience moves, or the theatre set changes, or the drama passes like a parade through a moment of pause. Molière's invention must be seen as part of this passing show.

Curiously La Fontaine's relation does not mention the best joke of the evening, where Molière momentarily disrupts the effortless progress of the fantasy. The stage and its remarkable set were erected, as La Fontaine relates, at the end of an avenue of pines, and when the curtain, a canvas drop, was raised (La Fontaine says 'les toiles' but may be searching for a rhyme), the set continues the walk in the perspective painted by Le Brun. Le Brun's design is plainly intended for the drop or *ferme* which completes the perspective effect. Other accounts clarify La Fontaine's reference to the use of *feuillages touffus* in the set, for these could have been painted. De Choisy's *Mémoires* tersely observe the integration of the set with the actual perspective on the fountains of the garden, *fontaines véritables*, and the incorporation of trees, *véritables orangers*. Le Brun and Torelli's theatre melted into the actual elements of the garden, and into this illusion, according to Molière's *Préface*, walked the dramatist himself.

D'abord que la toile fut levée, un des acteurs, comme vous pourriez dire moi, parut sur le théâtre en habit de ville, et, s'addressant au Roi avec le visage d'un homme surpris, fit des excuses du désordre sur ce qu'il se trouvait là seul, et manquait de temps et d'acteurs pour donner à Sa Majesté le divertissement qu'elle semblait attendre.[16]

As soon as the curtain was raised, one of the actors, you might say myself, appeared on the stage dressed for the town, and addressing the King with the look of a man who was caught off guard, made excuses for the confusion of his being there alone, and without the time and the actors to give to His Majesty the entertainment which it seemed to expect.

The intrusion of street costume and the comic disclaimers of the dramatist are then overtaken by theatrical fantasy with fountains, lights, and stage machinery.

[...] au milieu de vingt jets d'eau naturels, s'ouvrit cette coquille que tout le monde a vue, et l'agréable Naiade qui parut s'avança au bord du théâtre, et, d'un air héroique, prononça les vers que Monsieur Pellison avait faits ....'[17]

{...} amid a thousand natural water-jets, there opened the cockle-shell that all had seen, and the fair Naiad who appeared came to the front of the stage and, in an heroical manner, recited the verses Monsieur Pellison had composed ...

One change replaces another: a rock changes to a cockleshell and that in turn opens to reveal the actress. Madeleine Béjart's prologue then extols the power of fantasy: the nymph will produce 'un spectacle nouveau' at the service of the greatest of kings. The prologue thus ends with the painted set dissolving into live figures of dancers who appear from the statuary of Le Brun's design. La Fontaine plays upon the exchange between the theatrical invention and the fantasy of the garden itself. Béjart represents the nymph of the fountain 'where the action takes place' and which is part of the water gardens in which the audience has walked before the show. Her assertion that the spirits of the garden will appear at Louis's command reflects its most notable forms, in particular the terms, the statuary half-figures, present in Le Brun's design.

Ces Termes marcheront, et si Louis l'ordonne,
Ces arbres parleront mieux que ceux de Dodone.
Hôtesses de leurs troncs, moindres divinités,
C'est Louis qui le veut sortez, Nymphes, sortez.[18]

These Terms will walk, and if Louis should command,
These trees will speak, better yet than those of Dodona.
Guardians of their trunks, lesser divinities,
Louis wills it: come forth, Nymphs, come forth.

At this point Torelli's scene dissolved and dancers appeared as dryads, fauns and satyrs for the first *entrée* of Beauchamp's ballet. Molière and Beauchamps were particularly concerned to exploit the limited number of performers so that the flow of invention was not interrupted. Thus at the conclusion of the prologue it is made plain that part of the cast exits with La Naïade, Madeleine Béjart, 'for the play', while the remainder entertained the audience with the dancing of the *entrée*. As La Fontaine remarked: 'It is a most pleasing matter to see a term give birth, and to see the child dance on coming into the world'.[19] It was indeed a delightful invention to produce, almost out of the garden itself, the forms and figures of the dance.

The play continued the scenic invention which drew the audience into the spectacle as dwellers, albeit temporary, among its carefully ordered spaces. The device on which the *comédie* was based was slight: as Molière explained it was the first *noeud*, knot or intrigue, which came to mind and which would sustain a play. A lover, Éraste, is given an assignation to meet, in the *allée*, his beloved, Orphise, who must circumvent by these means the objections of her tutor, Damis. Damis is thus the most infuriating person, *fâcheux*, of the action, intent as he is on preventing the marriage of the lovers. Molière puts the accent on the meeting rather than on the consent that Éraste desires, which is delivered at the conclusion of the play by the perfunctory means of the tutor's deliverance from ruffians at the hands of the disregarded suitor. So there is effectively no intrigue, and the knot is speedily loosened with the gratitude of the victim spared and the recognition of Éraste's valour. All this is the work of a few moments, no hesitation and a little, presumably virtuosic, swordsmanship on the part of La Grange who took the part.

The amusement was supplied by the parade of court bores who button-hole the luckless Éraste and keep him from his rendezvous. The advantage of this form was that the interruptions and disturbances were supplied at will by actors or by dancers, suitably double-cast. There was no structural reason to recall a character or a group once they had exited, beyond the quartet of the two lovers, and the two enraging *fâcheux* with whom they are paired, Éraste's servant and Orphise's tutor.

Perhaps Molière's boldest stroke was to introduce the idea of his play through a five-minute stand-up performance for La Grange: over a hundred lines of text which have remained extremely well known in theatre history but which can also seem to a modern reader an overpowering irrelevance. Eraste describes how, wherever he goes, the world is full of *fâcheux* who persecute him. Today he has been interrupted, almost, one might add, on his way to the theatre, by a theatre bore who has battened on to him, at the playhouse, where he has been quietly seated, acccording to the recent fashion, on the stage.

Il faut que je te fasse un récit de l'affaire,
Car je me sens encor tout ému de colère.
J'étais sur le théâtre, en humeur d'écouter
La pièce, qu'à plusieurs j'avais ouï vanter;
Les acteurs commençaient, chacun prêtait silence,
Lors que d'un air bruyant et plein d'extravagance
Un homme à grands canons est entré brusquement
En criant: 'Holà ho! un siège promptement!'
Et de son grand fracas surprenant l'assemblée,
Dans le plus bel endroit a la pièce troublée.[20]

I really must relate to you the tale of this business,
For I can feel myself still smarting with anger.
I was on the stage prepared to listen to
The play, which I had heard many persons praise;
The actors were beginning, everyone grew silent,
When, with a raucous manner, and extravagant display,
A man with long canons abruptly entered
Shouting: 'You there! A seat and smartly too!'
And with his great commotion surprised the house
And disrupted the play in its finest passage.

In the context of its original audience this was a daring tour-de-force. Given the rich initial scenic illusion, the expectation might have been of a series of transformations, instead of which the locus of the audience's imagination was returned to the garden theatre with a performance which initially describes an audience participating in another performance. No actor can undertake the account that Molière writes without investing the actual stage space with the imaginative coordinates of the recounted stage on which his *fâcheux* disturbs the play. At the very point where the actor might be expected to transport the imagination of the audience to another place, the actor reaffirms the actuality of the stage and the fragility of its illusions. Were one to expect a psychologically persuasive characterization one would be sadly disappointed: this lover spares few thoughts for his lady until he has concluded the first vignette in the play. Molière is far more intent on celebrating the theatre than the delights of love.

The length of Éraste's account is well calculated both in terms of the imaginative shift from the optical spaces of garden and stage, to the more expansive mental spaces of acting, and also in terms of the practical rhythm of entrances and exits of a cast which was doubling to produce an illusion of almost giddying profusion in the social types displayed. Molière thus gained additional time for the costume changes which were necessary for the entrance of the performers in Scenes ii and iii, who must have been part of the initial company for the opening ballet.

The parade of grotesques which follows is sustained by writing for varying styles and different characterizations in both acting and dance. The dramatist ensures a spicy and sometimes highly topical reflection of the life and interests of the court, while his use of the medium stresses the power of fancy in performance. The valet is importunate in his solicitude and clumsiness, and even Orphise is a teasing sketch of the tantalizing coquette that Molière was later to create in the role of Célimène. A parade of curious *extravagants* blocks Éraste's path to the accomplishment of his rendezvous. The focus of the first act is Lysandre, the amateur choreographer and composer who detains Éraste while he demonstrates the *courante* he has composed, obliging his victim to dance the steps of the lady, and probably played by Molière himself. One can feel how freely Molière's imagination uses the opportunities of the dramatic form he has discovered, easily basing a character on the demonstration of steps and music in the fashionable dance, and creating dramatic interest out of the physical encounter between the two characters. To an audience trained to enjoy the attitudes of dancing, the pursuit of dramatic objectives through a familiar set of physical forms must have been absorbing. The pleasure of the scene would have seemed doubly appropriate given the evening's dedication to the most distinguished connoisseur, Louis himself. Appropriately enough there is a direct tribute to the declared objectives and emerging authority of the young King early in the play with the outrageous interruption caused by a bellicose would-be duellist, who is rebuked by the martial Éraste for his contempt of royal interdictions.

The second act involves Eraste in a lengthy and, for a reader, truly tedious description of a card game, which is then followed by a debate between two *précieuses* which Éraste must adjudicate, and so the play proceeds. In the final act the focus is upon the chief spectator of the action: Louis himself, and Molière reappears as the insufferable Monsieur Caritidès, intent upon having a petition presented to the king by his chosen intermediary, Éraste. The scene allows a suitable tribute to the paternalism of a sovereign who has declared that he is to be accessible to the least of his subjects. Caritidès, who is the true heir of the farce pedant, is a new and topical clown. Molière seizes on the snobbery of the Hellenist and the ingenuity of those who sought advancement through the purchase of offices of different sorts. Caritidès proposes to put his linguistic gifts at the service of the Crown in seeking a *charge* of inspector of spelling irregularities on the house and trade signs of the Paris streets. This combination of the virtuosity of the farce actor and the newest forms of social extravagance reaches a peak in the final *fâcheux*, Ormin, the *donneur d'avis*, the highly marginal breed which sought advancement through schemes which were proposed to the crown as means of revenue.

Les Fâcheux cannot rival the structural achievement of the five-act masterpiece Molière created the following year, but he can be seen taking the measure of his audience and weaving together a resplendent and celebratory display of theatrical art. Performance rises to the challenge of the new stage and its scenery, and does so by engaging the social and intellectual concerns of the court. It contains material probably as topical as any Molière treated at any other time, and could conceivably have come too close to matters of government and finance in the shape of Caritidès and Ormin, had the touch not been light and the dramatic distortions so clear. As it was, the King favoured Molière with the suggestion of an additional character. Menage recounts the genesis of what became Dorante the fanatical huntsman, which Molière gratefully acknowledges in his preface to be the result of the King's inspiration:

> *In the play* Les Fâcheux, *which is one of the finest of Molière, the huntsman bore whom he introduces in one scene is M. de Soyecourt. It was the King himself who gave him this subject and here is how. On leaving the first performance of this play which took place at the house of M. Foucquet, the king said to Molière showing him M. de Soyecourt: There is a great model that you have not copied. No more needed to be said, and the scene in which Molière introduces him in the guise of a huntsman, was composed and learned by the actors in*

*less than twenty-four hours, and the King had the pleasure of seeing
it in its place, at the following performance of the play.*[21]

The play was given again, with the new scene included, at
Fontainebleau on 25 and 27 August. Almost symbolically
Foucquet's offering was taken and moved bodily to the King's residence where it was almost certainly reinforced with the addition of
new dancers. Loret relays the belief that the play was even finer, and
there was additional dancing. Whether this meant the inclusion of
courtiers in the ballets we cannot tell, but a certain Mademoiselle
Giraut scored a success, such was the attractiveness of 'her person and
her steps'. The suggestion that the performances were yet more
splendid is strengthened by the costs at Fontainebleau. For *L'École des
maris* and *Les Fâcheux* 'scenery, tumblers, dancers, food and wages of
the actors', the treasury paid out 15,428 *livres*.

Not only did the play move to Fontainebleau but Le Nôtre, the
designer of the garden setting, was appointed to create the gardens at
Versailles, where Molière would collaborate in a series of royal divertissements growing directly out of *Les Fâcheux*. Foucquet could
hardly have realized he was drawing up a model for a royal 'divertissement' and the fact reflected badly on the wealth of a mere
servant of the crown. When *Les Fâcheux* was played for an expectant
Parisian public in November 1661 Foucquet had been in prison for
two months. He would remain there until his death in 1680.

Les Fâcheux must have amazed its first audience, however well
used to court entertainment. Even in the troubled aftermath of the
Fronde in 1653, the *Ballet de la Nuit* had allied the traditions of the
native *ballet de cour* with an Italian stage setting, and such settings
were already employed before the Fronde in 1639 and 1641 at the
Palais Cardinal of Richelieu. Molière now brought a new concern for
integrity into the multi-media entertainments which had prolifer-
ated through the century. Although to the modern reader *Les Fâcheux*
might appear to be a somewhat elastic series of turns and little more,
considered in the context of its original performance, it is more significant and its success is clearly understandable. In particular
Molière's essential gift was to discern the potential which could
allow the *ballet de cour* to evolve as drama. Hitherto invention was
applied to an increasing elaboration of either scenic effect or the fantasy of costume, always presented with an abundance of theatrical
magnificence whatever the glory or misery of the represented scene
or character. Now Molière took the essential step of applying a dramatic principle to potentially overpowering theatrical means.

Nothing could so attract Molière's audience at Vaux-le-Vicomte or Versailles as this element of realism in a highly artificial proceeding. If life was lived and understood in terms of the ethics of class, then there was no better way of exploring this experience than in the restricted *'theatrum mundi'* which Molière offered them.

The episodic structure of a play like *Les Fâcheux* hides Molière's achievement when it is judged beside the intellectual plan of his great works. The contrast between the parade of bores in *Les Fâcheux* or (differently presented) in *L'Impromptu de Versailles* and the organization of the intrigue of *L'École des femmes* is indeed considerable. Nevertheless Molière was aware of what he was undertaking and in his remarks on *Les Fâcheux* he makes this plain. In particular he understands that some, misconstruing his purpose, will find the parade unrepresentative of the rich variety of importunate eccentrics at the court. Given the need to 'distract the august persons', he conceived a species of royal *entrée* for folly and extravagance. This relaxed attitude to the question of form shows a signal freedom from constraints and an ability to risk all on acting, dance and song. In these years of the early 1660s it is the pragmatism of performance that prevails over the dignity of literature.

7

STAGES

Molière's entrance in *Les Fâcheux* at Vaux-le-Vicomte set a tone which he would echo from time to time: that of the 'innocent' actor finding himself in a place whose dignity he cannot maintain. Between 1661 and 1663 the company played twenty-nine engagements for the court or its principal members *en visites*, where no permanent stage could be expected. Some engagements were brief, a performance played in the evening at one of the great *hôtels* of the nobility in Paris itself after a regular afternoon performance, often of the same play. Others were lengthy, predominantly ordered by the King for one of the palaces outside the town. The company was at Fontainebleau in August 1661; at Saint-Germain-en-Laye in May 1662 playing the best of their repertoire over a seven-day period; and again at Saint-Germain between 24 July and 11 August, when thirteen performances were given. Winter performances were given in the Louvre in December that year and the following January. The King attended Molière's playhouse twice in 1663 to see *L'École des femmes*, and then, in September and October, the company played before him at Vincennes and Versailles.

This last engagement was a novelty. Versailles was witnessing the beginnings of the transformation of Louis XIII's modest hunting lodge which would ultimately create the greatest palace in Europe. In 1663 much work had been done on the gardens by Le Nôtre, but the enveloping of the original château had not yet begun. This was adequate to the needs of a small court of intimates, and was a place where the King might pursue in privacy his love affairs. Around 1661 he had made the acquaintance of Louise de la Vallière, but, by the time of Molière's summons to Versailles in October 1663, she was his mistress. For this *visite* Molière wrote the third panel to the triptych of *L'École des femmes*, *La Critique de L'École des femmes* and now *L'Impromptu de Versailles*. The invention of *L'Impromptu de Versailles* rests upon the 'failure' of the actors to transform their efforts into the show that the King has commanded. The stage remains a rehearsal space in which performances are tried out, are criticized, and break down. The very appropriateness of the play being rehearsed is questioned, and Molière's idea for an alternative is recalled by one of the company. The printed text specifies the location of the scene as *à Versailles, dans la salle de la comédie*,[1] and the play opens with the distracted Molière trying to get his cast on stage, calling the reluctant actors by name. It is impossible to know how the stage space was organized: that is, whether or not there was a painted scene which would be appropriate to the nameless new play. It seems at least possible that Molière played on a stage with no setting save the architectural surround of the *grand salon* itself, for his initial instructions on place teasingly stress that the actors should imagine the scene: the very hall in which the stage has been erected:

MOLIÈRE

Figurez-vous que la scène est dans l'antichambre du Roi; car c'est un lieu où il se passe tous les jours des choses assez plaisants.[2]

MOLIÈRE

Imagine that the scene is set in the antechamber of the King; for that's a place where amusing things happen every day.

When they are interrupted by a *marquis fâcheux*, a connoisseur, especially of the actresses, played by La Thorillière, the latter enquires about the fashion of their costumes, only to be told they will play as they are dressed. It appears that the company is unready, with the properties and technicalities of the stage laid bare. As the 'performance' approaches, the rehearsal is thrown into confusion by court busybodies coming to enquire about the start, depriving the actors of the final moments in which to ready themselves. The *impromptu* is ultimately 'postponed by the King' until such time as the actors have learned their parts. Molière conceives an entire performance which addresses the problems which actually attend the difficult practice of theatre, which must be brought to a point of perfection at a determined time and place.

The effect of this little play should be considered against the background of a series of performances of already familiar works being played as part of a short residency: *L'École des maris*, *Le Dépit amoureux* and the still popular *Les Fâcheux*. The company was living within the château or in its dependencies and clearly for these few days Molière and his comrades were familiar figures to a court of the King's intimates who shared his taste for theatrical performance and enjoyed a close acquaintance with Molière's practice. By shifting the accent from painted scenes to the bare stage on which the actor must finally exercise his art, Molière inverted the pleasure of scenic illusion, to exploit an informed appreciation of theatrical wit and topicality in a play stripped of ornaments. The King himself may have had some involvement in matters of presentation and technique. The inclusion of Louis as an off-stage character is both part of the obligation felt by the courtier to the sovereign, but also an acknowledgement of a theatrical environment where he can be credited with the creation of the very stage on which the play is given. The description of a later performance of *Les Fâcheux* refers to the stages which Louis had caused to be erected in the grand salon leading to his royal apartments.

> And in the evening, His Majesty caused to be played, on one of the double stages which his universal genius had invented, the play called *Les Fâcheux*, created by Monsieur de Molière, combined with ballet *entrées*, and most ingeniously fashioned.[3]

When Molière refers in *L'Impromptu de Versailles* to the *antichambre* as being the setting of a play, he almost certainly refers to the space in which the theatre had actually been constructed.[4] For those days of residency, Louis lived in the closest proximity to the preparations for the entertainments being prepared.

The form of the stage can only be conjectured. Couton believes that it was a removeable platform set up in one of the pairs of alcoves at either end of the room. This does not account for the use of the term *théâtre double* implying a double stage, and not two stages. The professional town playhouse required a *théâtre supérieur* which was available for both simple balcony or window scenes, but which, with the aid of stage machinery, could be used for celestial apparitions. The fact that *Les Fâcheux* was played on this stage at Versailles means it must have been moderately well equipped, and capable of reproducing the scene changes of Vaux-le-Vicomte. Although the credit given to the King for the design of the stage may be loyally exaggerated, his involvement in the creation of the entertainment cannot be doubted. If only by the exercise of the royal *fiat* Louis became almost the equivalent of the modern impresario, providing the physical facilities and determining the occasion and the repertoire to be played. Thus the staging of *L'Impromptu de Versailles* within the rooms that the court habitually occupied was part of its charm, and the stressing of stage and preparation was part of shared amusement between actors and audience.[5]

Molière's next piece for the court was *Le Mariage forcé*, and this was again a late commission requiring haste. Nevertheless a *comédie-ballet* was prepared where the promise of *Les Fâcheux* could be exploited: a small cast of actors and dancers was assembled with provision made for an *entrée* to include the King. Madeleine Béjart and Cathérine de Brie were to dance and sing a scene, while French and Italian singers would contribute airs and a chorus. The music was composed by Lully, who was also to participate as a dancer. Such a tightly knit company was able to work quickly and flexibly in a simple staging, and there is no mention of sets and costumes. The play was given in mid-winter as part of the carnival celebrations in the Louvre, and its form strongly suggests the adaptation of farce to supply a framework for the ballet expected as part of the celebrations. The stage was created in the *appartement bas* of the Queen Mother, and was probably modest.

In the new *comédie-ballet*, actors and dancers were closely integrated, performing in the same space, and distinctions of degree were minimal: the King and a chosen few nobles danced alongside a small group of professional dancers. The intimacy of the composition could arise only from the authority of the King and the sense that the stage could unite professionals and amateurs in a shared fantasy. In the first act of the *comédie-ballet* (as opposed to the later, cut version in one act), performers interact and media of performance overlap. Sganarelle, played by Molière, sleeps at the side of the stage, exhausted by his pursuit of an answer to the question whether he should marry as an old man, whereupon 'in a dream' a singer appears praising beauty, followed by an *entrée* depicting jealousy, cares and suspicions. The *intermède* concludes with a scene of mockery danced by the Comte d'Armagnac and three professional dancers. The King himself appeared in the second act in an *entrée* of *deux Égyptiens et quatre Égyptiennes* (fortune-tellers), and was suitably accompanied as an *Égyptien* by the Marquis de Villeroy; but of the other dancers, three were professionals. Again, the action of the play kept Molière on stage pondering the ability of the dancing characters to see into the future. Sganarelle then asks two *Bohémiennes* for help. (In the version adapted for the town it is two *Égyptiennes* who dance and sing their mocking replies.) The *livret* explains the action:

> Il prend fantaisie à Sganarelle de se faire dire sa bonne aventure, et rencontrant deux Bohémiennes, il leur demand s'il sera heureux dans son mariage. Pour réponse, elles se mettent à danser en se moquant de lui, ce qui l'oblige à trouver un magicien.[6]

Sganarelle takes it into his head to have his fortune told, and meeting two gypsy-girls, he asks if he will be happy in his marriage. In reply, they begin to dance, making fun of him, which obliges him to go and find a magician.

The magician duly appears, played by Destival, who answers Sganarelle in song, conjuring up four demons, the fourth *entrée* of the ballet. Once Sganarelle has been persuaded, with the aid of a beating, that he cannot escape marriage, the concluding sequence of the play engages him in celebratory dance and song. D'Olivet the dancer, who worked alongside Molière in creating *Les Fâcheux*, enters to teach Sganarelle a *courante*, before a final *mascarade* is announced to honour the wedding. This takes the form of a *concert espagnol* with a sextet of mixed voices leading into the final three *entrées*, which assemble, indifferently, courtiers and professional dancers, among them Lully the composer.

In these two experimental pieces, conceived for an intimate performance within the *élite* circles of the court, Molière casts himself, Prospero-like, at the centre of the action and in a position where he can exploit the possibilities of the unencumbered stage. The two plays afford him the full range of available performance, from the virtuoso effects of his topical acting satires in *L'Impromptu de Versailles,* through the traditional physical farce of *Le Mariage forcé* to the integration of song, music and dance into a comic action. But in contrast to entertainment where the theatre itself must be richly treated, these are plays for a stage set up at the briefest notice. The fundamentals differ little from Tabarin's stage in the Place Dauphine.

In 1664 Louis created astonishing *fêtes* at Versailles lasting for a period of days, to which Molière would contribute new works. The entertainments which commenced on the 7 May 1664 set the tone for what Versailles was to become: the King's pleasure palace and the symbol of his glory and the devotion of his subjects. *Les Plaisirs de l'Île enchantée* would incorporate every sort of activity that could ravish or divert the spectators, and the whole would be framed by a fantasy.[7] The official account announces a theme: the pleasures were to be those of the magical island of the enchantress Alcina, which the Duc de Saint-Aignan had selected from the pages of Ariosto's *Orlando furioso* to provide a design whereby a group of knights led by the King as Roger would be held in thrall by beauty and art. There would have been little difficulty in associating the charms of Louise de la Vallière with the spells of the fictional enchantress.

A *livret* was produced with a *relation* to convey to distant subjects the magnificence that would be seen by only an *élite*. The account is detailed and the handsome engravings which illustrated the three principal days record a multi-media performance encompassing the whole assembly. The basis of the *fêtes* was the organization and the decoration of the different spaces of the palace and its grounds. The *relation* sets the scene:

> Le Roi voulant donner aux Reines et à toute sa cour le plaisir de quelques fêtes peu communes, dans un lieu orné de tous les agréments qui peuvent faire admirer une maison de campagne, choisit Versailles, à quatre lieues de Paris. C'est un château qu'on peut nommer un palais enchanté, tant les ajustements de l'art ont bien secondé les soins que la nature a pris pour le rendre parfait. Il charme en toutes manières; tout y rit dehors et dedans, l'or et le marbre y disputent de beauté et d'éclat; et quoiqu'il n'ait pas cette grande étendue qui se remarque en quelques autres palais de Sa Majesté, toutes choses y sont si polies, si bien entendues et si achevées, que rien ne le peut égaler. Sa symétrie, la richesse de ses meubles, la beauté de ses promenades et le nombre infini de ses fleurs, comme de ses orangers, rendent les environs de ce lieu dignes de sa rareté singulière.[8]

> *The King, desiring to give to the queens and to all his court the pleasure of some uncommon festivities, in a place decorated with all the delights which mark out a country house for praise, chose Versailles, four leagues from Paris. This is a house which may be termed a palace of enchantment, so well have the touches of art assisted the care taken by nature to ensure its perfection. It is charming in every way; there everything smiles both inside and out, there gold and marble vie with one another in beauty and splendour; and although it may not have that great scale which characterizes other palaces of His Majesty, everything is so finished, so well conceived and so well carried out, that nothing is its equal. Its symmetry, the richness of its furnishings, the beauty of its walks and the infinite number of its flowers, as of its orange-trees, make the surroundings of this place worthy of its rare singularity.*

Within the rooms of the house and amid the fountains and walks of the garden were created the stages for *Tartuffe* and *La Princesse d'Élide*. While it is the former play which has survived in the canon, it was the latter which had pride of place in the entertainment. The chief amusements were enjoyed over the first three days from 7 to 9 May, and these were linked by the Alcina theme. *La Princesse d'Élide* was the *comédie* given the second evening in the *Allée Royale*, between the carousel and banquet of the first evening and the *Ballet d'Alcine* of the third which culminated in a spectacular firework display as part of the destruction of the palace of the enchantress. The progress through these events showed a particular regard for location. The residence itself was relatively small, a fact acknowledged by the official account in crediting its beauties, and rued by many attending the *fête* who had no proper lodging. Louis had overlooked the difficulty of billeting his *petite armée* of followers. The gardens, on the other hand, were developing in magnificence and novelty under the masterly supervision of Le Nôtre to say nothing of the King himself, to whom Colbert (Foucquet's successor) made periodic reports. House and garden were being developed with particular regard to perspective. The geometrical arrangements yielded particular delights to the spectator occupying different positions and moving between one and the other. Louis's liking of fountains and waterways was evident both in their number and in his involvement in their design and regulation.

In this setting theatre spaces took shape as part of the overall aesthetic. Vigarani was charged with the engineering of the *Plaisirs* and must have had a hand with Le Nôtre in designing the spaces and elaborating the effects they could sustain. Three stages were employed: the first owing much to the continuing fashion for carrousel as a theatre occasion. The first great *bassin* in the main *allée* was covered over and a circus constructed (see Figure 6.1). The illustration shows three arches, although there may well have been, symmetrically, four with both groups of spectators similarly framed. The circular space accommodated first a series of *entrées* incorporating Vigarani's machines, with then a barrier being erected for the tourney, and finally a semi-circle of tables was introduced and set with baskets and dishes brought in by servants forming part of a ballet. The semi-circle defers to the position of the King, who must be placed on the axis of a performance which, in the celebratory engraving, is symmetrically arranged for an observer to admire a perspective with the distant chateau in the background.

For the second day, a stage had been erected lower in the *allée*. The account makes clear that its position was determined by the progress of the knights towards the island of Alcina further off, and the King himself, presumably still identifiable in his role as Roger, presided over the place where the Queen would be offered the pleasures of the *comédie*, Molière's *La Princesse d'Élide*. The account reports a circular auditorium bounded by palisades, within which the audience sat on tiered seating arranged around a rectangle reminiscent of *ballet de cour*. The playing area and the perspective beyond was framed by an arch which despite its classical regularity continued the verdant themes of the garden. The auditorium was roofed (the weather was actually good but windy) by a *velum* which also created a satisfactory acoustic out-of-doors for strings and voices, and bordered by foliage, some of which at least was painted scenery, and which afforded concealed positions for musicians. The auditorium grew out of the garden and the stage itself took its place within a perspective of the garden walk and the château beyond, with a painted scene replacing the view down the *allée*, at the time of performance in darkness (see Figure 6.2). The natural continuity of auditorium and stage is evident in the placing of pairs of musketeers on stage and in the auditorium. Finally, Molière himself is to be seen in the role of Moron offset to stage left, controlling the balance of the space. For the third day the castle of the enchantress had been erected on an island created in the *bassin d'Apollon* at the further end of the *allée*. The narrative which embraced the celebrations was taken up again in a ballet of sea monsters devised by Vigarani, and culminated in the destruction of the palace amid splendid fireworks. The staging of the ballet (like the opening ballets and banquet) was timed to extend from daylight into dusk, and finally to end (as had been the case at Vaux-le-Vicomte) with a brilliant effect over water and against the night sky.

At the conclusion of *Plaisirs*, as if unwilling to abandon Versailles, Louis continued for four more days to amuse his guests, each event and each assembly providing a stage upon which could be played a more or less self-conscious role, sometimes preserving the identities of the earlier fantasy. On the evening of the sixth day the play given was 'a comedy named Tartuffe that Monsieur Molière had made against the hypocrites',[9] and, after more jousting on the following day, the play was a reprise of *Le Mariage forcé* played earlier in the year at the Louvre. So ended a full week of festival: a sustained performance for which Versailles provided continuously varied stages upon which the King played alongside the more obviously sustaining talents of his actors, dancers and musicians.

The imagination behind these displays made every entertainment fit its location and offer a spectacle, sometimes to the assembly, but sometimes so that the participants beheld each other as if on a stage, caught up in the singular theatricality of the occasion.

TARTUFFE AT VERSAILLES

The first performance of *Tartuffe* must be imagined among the different pleasures of Louis's enchanted isle to recognize the dramatic
vigour of a new subject, using the methods of the old farce stage, and
to understand the repercussions of the performance in the worlds of
theatre and politics beyond the gardens of Versailles. *Tartuffe* concentrated the hostility of the pious faction towards the hedonism and
licence of the occasion. Although *La Princesse d'Elide* justified the
conduct of the King by linking love to nobility and valour, and flattered 'un jeune prince' mirrored in the action, Louis could not be
criticized. However, the three-act *Tartuffe* represented attempts at
seduction in a town play, where the King could be respectfully
reproached with tolerating a dangerous work which, as the *Relation*
maintains, might mislead those of lesser discrimination. The laughter of the King and his court could be allowed given their superior
gifts of understanding, but other audiences might be corrupted by
such a show. Despite its success with the court, Louis banned the
play from public performance, and it took five years and two reworkings before the order was rescinded and a licence was granted for the
performance of *Tartuffe ou L'Imposteur*, a play in five acts.

Quite apart from the struggle to influence the King, Molière gave
grounds enough for hostility. Like *L'École des femmes*, *Tartuffe* renewed
the farce with a daring and topical conception of the defeat of a
cramped and jealous husband by a younger and more attractive lover,
but his characterization as a *faux dévot* established far too specific a
reference for safety, and the religious mania of the husband brought
true zeal uncomfortably close to ridicule.

In one of a later series of *Placets* requesting the licensing of the
play, Molière speaks of changes of costume in his expanded version,
re-titled *L'Imposteur*,[10] in which his imposter was renamed Panulphe,
and was clearly more worldly in appearance:

> En vain, je l'ai produite sous le titre de *L'Imposteur* et déguisé
> le personnage sous l'ajustement d'un homme du monde; j'ai
> beau lui donner un petit chapeau, de grands cheveux, un
> grand collet, une épée, et des dentelles sur tout l'habit, met-
> tre en plusieurs endroits des adoucissements, et retrancher
> avec soin tout ce que j'ai jugé capable de fournir l'ombre
> d'un prétexte aux célèbres originaux du portrait que je
> voulais faire: tout cela n'a de rien servi.[11]

In vain I have brought the play out under the title of The
Imposter *and disguised the character in the apparel of a man of
the world. To what good have I given him a small hat, long hair, a
wide collar, a sword, and lace over all his dress, put in many places
softer terms, and cut out carefully everything that I judged capable
of furnishing the shadow of a pretext for the celebrated originals of
the portrait that I wished to paint: all has served for nothing.*

The *Placet* reveals how closely he must have come to portraying his
first Tartuffe as a priest, or at least as one of the urbane and worldly
abbés who took minor orders as the route to a living. Molière's satire
on religious hypocrisy turned his comic genius upon the very group
that was mounting an increasingly energetic campaign against the
theatre. He could scarcely have had this as an end, but the attraction
of the new subject was too great: it promised a novel role and
employed the language of devotion to promote shocking behaviour.
Molière must have seen in some of the darker currents of religious
life a sort of preciosity which could animate a sinister *docteur*. In his
role as master of ceremonies, Louis knew what he was offering his
companions. *Tartuffe* was the farce.

The precise form of the three-act work cannot be known, but the
indications are that it is substantially present, reworked, in the present five-act text.[12] One may presume that the play would conclude
with the triumph of the amorous rogue over his rival, and might
well contain the two episodes of seduction that are witnessed by
Damis and then Orgon, with the truth being overturned or sup-
pressed in both. What we may imagine is a play moving more
rapidly, almost certainly without the Act II *dépit amoureux*, and
clearly without the events of the fifth act. The love interest of Valère
and Mariane is hard to place in such a play, and Cléante or Damis
might be sacrificed in imagining a three-act version. However,
Madame Pernelle is known to have been cast, and also her *gagiste*
servant Flipote with her one line. It seems likely that some coercive
ending such as in *Le Mariage forcé* or *George Dandin* must have been
employed, leaving at the conclusion *Tartuffe* and a compliant Elmire
undisturbed in their affair.

This more condensed version might explain the response of a
young pleasure-seeking court and of distant critics hearing of its
distilled bawdy and irreligion. Molière having introduced his
'softer touches', one can only speculate on the daring of the original
entertainment. What remains clear in the five-act version is the
appeal to an audience to engage in the joyful world of the farce. For

five years Molière had been the *farceur* to the court, and from the opening moments of his play we see how well he could supply such an audience.

Madame Pernelle is the traditional figure who opens and closes the play. An inheritance of the Alison of the old farce, she serves as the blinkered relative to whom the husband has to defer, as when she refuses to accept the guilt of Tartuffe. *Discours* and *choses* confront one another in a riddle that can be understood only by those who listen, which she will not. If one does not believe the old saying that the art of the actor lies in part in an ability to listen, then the example of the comic inattention of Molière's characters can be instructive. While the audience listens and understands, Molière's actor plays as if hearing and recognition were gone:

ORGON
Mais que fait ce discours aux choses d'aujourd'hui?

MADAME PERNELLE
On vous aura forgé cent sots contes de lui.

ORGON
Je vous ai dit déjà que j'ai vu tout moi-même.

MADAME PERNELLE
Des esprits médisants la malice est extrême […]

ORGON
C'est tenir un propos de sens bien dépourvu.
Je l'ai vu, dis-je, vu, de mes propres yeux vu,
Ce qu'on appelle vu: faut-il vous le rebattre
Aux oreilles cent fois, et crier comme quatre?

MADAME PERNELLE
Mon Dieu, le plus souvent l'apparence déçoit:
Il ne faut pas juger sur ce qu'on voit.

ORGON
J'enrage.

(V, iii, ll. 1667–1681)[13]

ORGON
But what's all this to do with today's events?

MADAME PERNELLE
They will have made up a hundred wild stories against him.

ORGON

But I have told you already I saw it all myself.

MADAME PERNELLE

Malice in spiteful minds knows no bounds {...}

ORGON

This is an argument deprived of any sense.
I saw it, I tell you, saw, with my own eyes, saw,
The word is 'saw': do I have to hammer it in your ear
A hundred times, and shout like four?

MADAME PERNELLE

Heavens above, most often appearances deceive:
One should not judge on what one sees.

ORGON

She drives me mad.

This is consummate writing for performance. The dramatic action
lives in the encounter between mind and space: Tartuffe's attempted
seduction of Elmire has been seen twice by characters in the play,
and obviously seen by the audience for whom it has an absolute
value as empirical knowledge. The events are richly planted in their
experience, imbued with the performance life of bodies in space.
The tension between the moralising *discours* of Madame Pernelle (a
reflection of Orgon's own similar earlier dismissal of accusations),
and Orgon's concrete witnessing of betrayal is brilliantly drawn out.
Molière invites the audience to share the rhythm of frustration in
the actor. The nervous overload of dramatic information leads to a
mental construction of possible events which pass the bounds of
decent utterance. The audience 'sees' the completion of the infamous event in the description which Orgon begins and abandons as
a 'sottise', gross foolishness. The table is there and so, too, is the
lady who was lately, one may reasonably suggest, all but
spread-eagled across it.

MADAME PERNELLE
                                        Il est besoin,
Pour accuser les gens, d'avoir de justes causes;
Et vous deviez attendre à vous voir sûr des choses.

ORGON
Hé, diantre! le moyen de m'en assurer mieux?

Je devais donc, ma mère, attendre qu'à mes yeux
Il eût ... Vous me feriez dire quelque sottise.

MADAME PERNELLE
Enfin d'un trop pur zèle on voit son âme éprise;
Et je ne puis du tout me mettre dans l'esprit
Qu'il ait voulu tenter les choses que l'on dit.

(V, iii, ll. 1684–1692)[14]

MADAME PERNELLE
It is necessary,
Before you accuse people, to have good reasons;
And you should have waited to see and be sure.

ORGON
What the devil! how could I be more sure?
Should I then, mother, wait until before my eyes
He had ... You are going to make me say something very stupid.

MADAME PERNELLE
After all, anyone can see that his soul is possessed by too pure a zeal;
And I can't get it into my head
That he would attempt the things that you say.

The drama stresses the importance of the mental construct: for this character to refuse the image '[le] mettre dans l'esprit' is to raise pleasantly a question of epistemology. The audience knows the event referred to, has seen it delineated in the space of the theatre, and conserves the form of the event in memory. The style moves the cruder explorations of the farce stage to philosophically challenging lengths. Empiricism is the governing mode of the drama, and in the theatres of Molière it is constantly testing the abstractions and idealistic systems which impose ideas on the world.

Whereas Molière had failed to solve the problem of a new staging in his *L'École des femmes*, his three-act *Tartuffe* enjoyed the advantage, typical of the old farce, of the lover entering the victim's house in disguise. This serviceable procedure is never abandoned in Molière's work and reappears in, say, *l'Avare*, or *Le Malade imaginaire*, and *mutatis mutandis* it is to be found all along the way. The simplicity of the principle should not obscure the rich consequences for the stage setting and the quality of dramatic action which flows, essentially, from a given space containing at one and the same time two representations: in *Tartuffe*, a superimposition of lechery upon religion, obsession upon piety, dangerous violence upon paternal duty.

The methods of the old farce make meanings clear in space, and often they are consequently crude and morally shallow. Now Molière had welded some steel into the old structures. No longer did the action proceed in a happily amoral fashion, but embraced and questioned codes and practices the audience knew to govern serious moral affairs. The rambling improvisations of the generalized pedant gave way to the nuanced theology of the contemporary cleric. The shift from generalized to specific codes of both conduct and conversation offered the actor–writer an opportunity to refine his schemes of performance. The crude oppositions of *discours* and *choses* which inspire the comedy of Madame Pernelle are part of an old method, but they fit happily into a play which examines the opposition with a new finesse.

The opening of the play depends upon one of Molière's more celebrated stage effects: he brings on almost the whole cast as they pursue the vengeful Madame Pernelle on stage to prevent her leaving. They meet in the *chambre basse* of which Elmire will later speak to Tartuffe, the room which will lead from below the parlour out onto the street. The comedy comes directly from the opposition of things and words: persons, and the withering descriptions the grandmother applies to them. The playing of the role by a man (Louis Béjart) burlesques the sentiments expressed, and allows Molière to have his cast grotesquely reviewed by a puritanical critic. That they are never allowed to reply makes apparent the contrast of concrete realities and intolerant upbraiding. This is taken forward in the debates which follow Madame Pernelle's departure.

ORGON

Qui suit bien ses leçons goûte une paix profonde,
Et comme du fumier regarde tout le monde.
Oui, je deviens tout autre avec son entretien;
Il m'enseigne à n'avoir affection pour rien,
De toutes amitiés il détache mon âme;
Et je verrais mourir frère, enfants, mère et femme,
Que je m'en soucierais autant que de cela.

CLEANTE

Les sentiments humains, mon frère, que voilà!

(I, v, ll. 276–280)[15]

ORGON

Whosoever follows his teaching tastes the deepest peace,
And regards everyone else as so much dung.
Oh yes, I'm quite different when I speak with him;

He teaches me to entertain affection for nothing,
From all friendships he separates my soul;
And though I saw the death of brother, child, mother and wife,
It would not bother me as much as that.

CLEANTE
What human feelings you show, my brother!

Such is the power of doctrine that the pleasures of social life are repudi-
ated. At every turn (as Madame Pernelle has made clear) daily life, its
amusements and assemblies run counter to religious prejudice. The
traffic of the stage is blocked by the words of a false and dangerous
piety. Absent or present, the space is haunted by the figure of Tartuffe
himself. Orgon fancies Tartuffe incorporated into the family as his son-
in-law, but the ironic reality is his partnering Elmire about the house.

The perspectives of subtle deception and irrational gullibility are
revealed by language which embraces both moral fastidiousness and
violent physicality:

TARTUFFE
Si vous pouviez savoir avec quel déplaisir
Je vois qu'envers mon frère on tâche à me noircir ...

ORGON
Hélas!

TARTUFFE
Le seul penser de cette ingratitude
Fait souffrir à mon âme un supplice si rude ...
L'horreur que j'en conçois ... J'ai le coeur si serré,
Que je ne puis parler, et crois que j'en mourrai.

ORGON (*Il court tout en larmes à la porte par où il a chassé son fils*)

ORGON
Coquin! Je me repens que ma main t'a fait grâce
Et ne t'ait pas d'abord assomé sur la place.
Remettez-vous, mon frère, et ne vous fâchez pas.

(III, vii, ll. 1143–1151)[16]

TARTUFFE
If you but knew my vexation when I see
Them try to blacken me in my brother's sight.

ORGON
Alas!

114

TARTUFFE
The merest thought of such ingratitude
Inflicts upon my soul such torture that …
The horror I see when … My heart is overwrought,
I can speak of it no longer, and it will be my end.

ORGON (Runs in tears to the door through which he drove out his son)

ORGON
Wretch! I repent that I stayed my hand,
And I did not strike you down on the spot.
There, be calm my brother, and don't get angry.

Moments such as this continue to exhilarate, and perturb, theatre audiences, as language is brought to the very limit of its capacity to control action, and spite erupts into physical activity on the stage. The clash of fine mental discrimination and gross bodily energy is evident, as in farce, but now identified with contemporary life, morals and thought.

Entrances are powerful: energetic, or abrupt, or dislocated in some way. Almost invariably Molière seeks a fine spatial effect. Orgon enters in Act I anxious to fix his mind elsewhere in the house on the image of his beloved *Tartuffe*, and inattentive to the words of Dorine, or to the greeting of Cléante, his brother-in-law. The split focus is adopted in scene after scene, played out strongly, with bold use of moves and bodily attitudes. This physical life is more than mere 'stage business' with the implication of an amusement accessory to the play proper. The incarnation of the incongruities of thought and action is the stuff of comedy, and is so discussed in the penetrating *Lettre sur L'Imposteur*. The part Molière writes for himself illustrates well how the movement of the body is integrated into the texture and rhythm of thought which is fundamental to dramatic play. Thus Orgon's second entrance opening Act II is an absurd display of thinking within a spatial environment: he summons his daughter, and promptly disappears into a *petit cabinet* to check within:

ORGON
Mariane.

MARIANE
Mon père.

ORGON
Approchez, j'ai de quoi
Vous parler en secret.

MARIANE
Que cherchez-vous?

ORGON *(Il regarde dans un petit cabinet.)*
Je vois
Si quelqu'un n'est point là qui pourroit nous entendre;
Car ce petit endroit est propre pour surprendre.
Or sus, nous voilà bien.

(II, i, ll. 427–431)[17]

ORGON
Mariane.

MARIANE
Father.

ORGON
Come here, I need
To speak to you in secret.

MARIANE
What are you looking for?

ORGON (He looks into a side room.)
I am looking
To see there is no one there to overhear us;
For this little room is just the place for spies.
Ah, good, we're quite alone.

This sequence involves an almost balletic movement about the stage, with the actress summoned to the actor who announces a close conference and then sweeps away at the point of salutation. The movement to the wings beautifully disorients her performance: 'Que cherchez-vous?', leaving her centre-stage to receive the incomprehensible reply that the domestic accommodation has some furtive use, to see her father disappear once more, and reappear contented.

The scene extroverts into negotiable stage space Orgon's mental world as he plans Mariane's marriage to Tartuffe. The actor looks to a positive outcome, which he then urges. The shape of this is adopted by the actress, but with no clear focus for the mind. Language flows or is broken as the issue is examined in the spatial tensions of the scene. Molière's stage directions confirm the vectors of the playing: Orgon moving in on Mariane, Mariane pulling away:

ORGON

[...] Que dites-vous de *Tartuffe* notre hôte?

MARIANE

Qui, moi?

ORGON

Vous. Voyez bien comme vous répondrez.

MARIANE

Hélas! j'en dirai, moi, tout ce que vous voudrez.

ORGON

C'est parler sagement. Dites-donc ma fille,
Qu'en toute sa personne un haut mérite brille,
Qu'il touche votre coeur, et qu'il vous serait doux
De le voir par mon choix devenir votre époux.
Eh?
(*Mariane se recule avec surprise.*)

MARIANE

Eh?

ORGON

Qu'est-ce?

MARIANE

Plaît-il?

ORGON

Quoi?

MARIANE

Me suis-je méprise?

ORGON

Comment?

MARIANE

Qui, voulez-vous, mon père, que je dise
Qui me touche le coeur, et qu'il serait doux
De voir par votre choix devenir mon époux?

ORGON

Tartuffe.

MARIANE

Il n'en est rien, mon père, je vous jure.

Pourquoi me faire dire une telle imposture?

(II, i, ll. 438–450)[18]

ORGON

{…} What do you say of our guest, Tartuffe?

MARIANE

Who, I?

ORGON

You. Look well how you reply.

MARIANE

Alas! I'll say, well, anything you'll have me say.

ORGON

Well said. Say then, my child,
That his person shines with merit to the highest degree,
That he moves your heart, and nothing would be as sweet
As to see him, by my choice, become your husband.
Eh?
(Mariane starts back in surprise.)

MARIANE

Eh?

ORGON

What's the matter?

MARIANE

I beg your pardon.

ORGON

What?

MARIANE

Did I hear right?

ORGON

How?

MARIANE

Who, do you want me to say, father,
Moves my heart, and nothing would be as sweet,
As to see him, by your choice, become my husband?

ORGON

Tartuffe.

MARIANE
Father, I want nothing of the sort, I swear.
Why would you make me speak such a falsehood?

As with Agnès in *L'École des femmes,* the actress playing Mariane repeats the lesson she has been given. She adopts the physical forms of the actor she partners, up to the point where she breaks out of the exchange to affirm that the marriage cannot be. Orgon's tyranny is imposed finally as a sort of theorem to be accepted without a proof:

ORGON
Mais je veux que cela soit une vérité;
Et c'est assez pour vous que je l'aie arrêté.

(II, i, ll. 449–450)[19]

ORGON
But it is my wish it be the truth;
And it's enough for you that I have decided so.

If one attends to the rhythms and tensions of the encounter one can discern the classic comic double-take played on either side. The method stresses the sensual values of space, where actors urge one another in real time and space to invest on- and off-stage areas with a particular significance and to place there particular images. The meanings in the roles are constructed out of the crudest energies, powerfully directed: 'Eh?', 'Eh?', 'Qu'est-ce?', 'Plaît-il', 'Quoi?'. The lack of cohesion in the exchange is the condition for the audience to enjoy its wonderful geometry.

The attempt to gain mastery by words over things is interrupted by the sly intrusion of Dorine into the space of this private encounter. The geometry is pleasantly complicated as Orgon has to play on two fronts, commanding Mariane to embrace the marriage and trying to dismiss Dorine's refusals to accept the seriousness of his intentions. This culminates in the absurd physicalization of the comedy as Orgon simultaneously lectures his daughter and threatens Dorine with a beating if she does not hold her tongue. The scene cannot even be read without the sense of bodies balanced on the stage; in performance the significance of acting is felt powerfully in the complex play of energy, attitude, expectation and space.

With the appearance of Tartuffe, played by the chubby and certainly appealing Du Croisy, space becomes yet more eloquent, and instantly a detail is picked up on-stage:

TARTUFFE

(Il tire un mouchoir de sa poche.)
Ah! mon Dieu, je vous prie,
Avant que de parler prenez-moi ce mouchoir.

DORINE

Comment?

TARTUFFE

Couvrez ce sein que je ne saurais voir.

(III, ii, ll. 858–860)[20]

TARTUFFE

(He takes a handkerchief from his pocket.)
Ah! heavens, I beg you,
Before you say a word, take this handkerchief.

DORINE

What?

TARTUFFE

Cover your breast, which I cannot bear to look upon.

The switch from what Dorine characterizes as 'affectation et forfan-terie' to the on-stage reality of her handsome breasts, with the distancing gesture of the extended handkerchief, shows how carefully Molière plots the focus of the audience's attention. The space has been one of surveillance, supervision and inhuman control. It now becomes more tightly focused on a detail of the physical body and the expressive power of distance. On this stage the detail of relationships in social space emerges potently: matters of costume and bodily presentation, gesture and customary attitudes, and, notably, the positioning which is governed by the social etiquette attaching to domestic space and furni-ture. It offers little in the way of furniture and properties. Stage painting supplies the function of localizing the action within appro-priate limits, and, where required, a stool or armchair could be brought on. In *Les Précieuses ridicules* the servants struggle to please their fashionable mistresses in bringing appropriate seating for the fine visitors they have received. In *Dom Juan* a servant brings Monsieur Dimanche a stool as the proper seat for a merchant, only to be chased away by the Don and told to return with the preposterously flattering armchair; and in the same play Dom Luis is forced to stand for lack of his son's order to bring him a chair at all. The very poverty of this pro-vision on Molière's stage makes his effects the clearer.

In *Tartuffe* furniture and its position on stage becomes a crucial ele-ment in the meaning of the playing. The frontispiece illustrations for *Tartuffe* naturally choose as the high point of the play the moment of comic *anagnorisis* where Orgon emerges from beneath the table where he has ignominiously agreed to hide himself and from which he has incomprehensibly failed to emerge on his proper cue.[21] The table cre-ates a now-familiar comic effect. It is also a master stroke in the definition of acting space. Orgon is placed on the stage so that Elmire can play in his presence a scene almost of the utmost indecency. The space is invested with differing significance by the two performers: for Elmire it includes Orgon, witness of his friend's crime; for *Tartuffe* it is the place of his satisfaction, which can only be 'réalités':

ELMIRE
Cependant ce n'est pas encore assez pour vous,
Et l'on ne peut aller jusqu'à vous satisfaire,
Qu'aux dernières faveurs on ne pousse l'affaire?

TARTUFFE
Moins on mérite un bien, moins on l'ose espérer.
Nos voeux sur des discours ont peine à s'assurer
[...]
Et je ne croirai rien, que vous n'ayez, Madame,
Par des réalités su convaincre ma flamme.
                                        (IV, v, ll. 1457–1467)[22]

ELMIRE
Yet still it's not enough for you,
And you are not to be satisfied,
Without pressing the affair to the ultimate favours?

TARTUFFE
The less deserving we are of happiness, the less we dare to hope for it.
Our vows of love can scarce be reassured by speeches
{...}
And nothing can be credited, until you, dear Madam,
Are able to convince my passion with realities.

When Orgon fails to appear, Elmire's performance becomes increas-ingly focused on her hidden accomplice, and progressively more frenzied as she indicates transparently the progress of events. The cli-max is engineered with enormous skill: as Elmire ostensibly prepares to 'yield' and grant *les dernières faveurs*, she demands that Tartuffe go out into the gallery to ensure that Orgon is not there. Tartuffe rejects the need to examine the space of the stage, since he can do as he pleases in the house of the gullible Orgon:

C'est un homme, entre nous, à mener par le nez.

(IV, v, l. 1524)[23]

He's a man, between ourselves, you lead by the nose.

Similarly in the earlier scene between Tartuffe and Elmire, the space between the two is controlled by the use of furniture, with again a hidden listener, whom neither suspects. The audience has seen Damis withdraw only as far as a 'petit cabinet', the adjoining room which Orgon so presciently searched before speaking to Mariane. Whatever language is employed to refine the 'realities' of Tartuffe's approach, the scene is as carefully staged to allow its physical forms to develop with the tumescent enthusiasm of Tartuffe and the adept manoeuvrings of Elmire. The performers must take chairs at the outset as is appropriate for conversation, given the invitation to Tartuffe to wait on the lady. Tartuffe must lean from his to take Elmire's hand as he develops the theme of his now clearly priapic zeal:

TARTUFFE
(Il lui serre le bout des doigts.)
Oui, Madame, sans doute, et ma ferveur est telle ...

ELMIRE
Ouf! vous me serrez trop.

TARTUFFE
C'est par excès de zèle.
De vous faire aucun mal je n'eus jamais dessein,
Et j'aurai bien plutôt ...
(Il lui met la main sur le genou.)

ELMIRE
Que fait là votre main?

TARTUFFE
Je tâte votre habit: l'étoffe en est moelleuse.

ELMIRE
Ah! de grâce, laissez, je suis fort châtouilleuse.

(Elle recule sa chaise, et Tartuffe approche la sienne.)
(II, ii, ll. 913–918)[24]

TARTUFFE
(He squeezes the tips of her fingers.)
Yes, Madam, without a doubt, my fervour is such …

ELMIRE
Ouch! you're hurting me.

TARTUFFE
It's just excess of zeal.
I could never mean to do you any hurt,
And rather I would like to …
(He places his hand on her knee.)

ELMIRE
What is your hand doing there?

TARTUFFE
I am feeling your dress, the material is soft.

ELMIRE
Ah! please, stop, I am very ticklish.
(She moves her chair away, and Tartuffe brings his nearer.)

From the material of the skirt Tartuffe moves to lace elsewhere on her person. One may suppose that this is not merely another opportunity to take the lady's hand. The stage directions, let us say again, are not the indication of some useful but inessential 'stage business'. They define physical forms: the inclination of the bodies, the focus of the eyes, the position of the hands. The movement of chairs is accompanied by an ebb and flow of energy, and best of all by the readjustment of bodily attitude and the redefinition of attention which act so powerfully upon an audience.

8

SCENES AND COSTUMES

Scenes

The more public entertainment became at the court of Louis XIV, the more important it was that the King's guests and the official accounts should report the splendour which attended *le plus grand Roi du monde*. Presentation elevated the occasion beyond the everyday, into a world of myth, contingent on the presence of the mythologized Louis XIV. Such a relocation of the imagination required that the scenic stage, and its presiding stage engineers, present the visual aspect of the almost divine omnipotence which attached to the figure of the King himself.

The intellect could only marvel at the *scena ductilis*, the painted wings and shutters of the changeable scene. The Italian theatre, with its false depth produced by perspective painting and its defeat of gravity by engineering, appeared to conjure a reality out of the counterfeiting of nature.[1] The mounting of virtual perspectives within the actual space of the stage baffled the willing mind with artifice. When technical capacity was seconded by extravagance, as in the court of *le Roi soleil*, then the victory of the eye over judgement was a particularly blatant one. Prodigality distorted performance and risked overwhelming acting in its generalized display.

It is no surprise that the accepted canon of Molière's works are those plays written with the plain means of the town stage in mind, or those *comédie-ballets*, particularly *Le Bourgeois gentilhomme* and *Le Malade imaginaire*,[2] conceived for the intimate conditions of winter performance at Chambord or Saint-Germain-en-Laye, where the dramatist exercised greater control over the entertainment,[3] and its smaller scenic variation. The mixed media of court performance remained, but the aesthetic was human in scale.

The appeal of scenery and its dangers were well illustrated in the French *pièce à machines* of which Corneille's *Andromède*[4] was the first and most celebrated example. Corneille recognised the threat to drama inherent in the new technology and the allied fashion for extended musical elements. On the other hand he evinced a certain professional pride in his ability to incorporate the changing face of the stage. Molière followed suit, but, of all the elements he absorbed into his performances, the Italian manner of staging most threatened to de-stabilize his theatre. For the actor the decoration of the stage was not problematic until it turned to elaborate and mobile pictorialism, when the strain was manifestly great.

In 1668, when *fêtes* were announced for Versailles, no longer was the King to be a participant, but rather the spectator of what were to be seen as the effects of his universal genius. Where before he had been recognized in his own performances, here he commanded a show unrelated to the all-too-human proportions of his actual person. The emphasis shifts from the living presence of the King in his private life and pleasures to the puissant symbols of his political role. The *fête* lasted hours rather than days, with a larger assembly brought together for a public purpose, namely the celebration of Condé's successful *Blitzkrieg* in the Franche-Comté, for which Louis naturally assumed credit. The military power and brilliance of the King was reflected in the similar qualities of all his peaceful endeavours, even in the entertainments and amusements he procured for a grateful court at Versailles.

The *fête* would comprise an initial light collation followed by a play, then a banquet, a ball, and finally a fireworks display. For each save this last the guests would move to a separate locality. This meant the creation of four 'salles' within the grounds for amusements which would last a matter of hours. Each location differed with the fancy of its decoration. Lighting and fountain engineering were remarkable, and the gardeners had laboured to procure architectural effects, particularly for the initial collation. Vigarani's theatre was built at the intersection of two walks in the park, and based on a square of 80 feet. The stage was 36 feet in width and extended in depth some 80 feet east into the *allée du Roi*, to add depth to the scenes, and left an auditorium of approximately 80 feet wide and 50 feet deep. Twelve hundred persons were seated in an amphitheatre on three sides of a central rectangular *parterre*, in the centre of which stood the dais for Louis and the royal party, surrounded by still more spectators, making a house of approximately 3,000.

When the curtain was raised the painted scene beguiled the eyes so that 'one thought one saw indeed a garden of extraordinary beauty'.[5] The description indicates an *allée* of great trees, each separated from the other by a series of 'houses in rustic architecture'; in the distance, a 'superb building in the form of a dome, pierced by three gateways', and beyond, a landscape. The first ten sets of wings were terms, half-statues on a base, supporting baskets of flowers beside terraces on each side of the stage with a canal into which fountains played from gilded masks, presumably in conformity with Louis's desire to see Versailles's fountain works used as part of the spectacle. The formal, brilliant setting framed a *pastorale* depicting in action and song the misfortunes of a quartet of lovers, whose ultimate happiness was celebrated in dance by a chorus of votaries of Love. The rejoicing was accompanied by a change of scene, admiringly described by the *Relation*:

> Here the decoration of the theatre changes in an instant, and one cannot understand how so many actual fountains are no longer visible, nor by what means, in the place of the buildings and allées, only great rocks appear, interspersed with trees, where a number of shepherds are seen singing and playing all manner of instruments.[6]

Into this pastoral Molière inserted the play he had rapidly conceived for the occasion, *George Dandin*. Rather as the sets of wings replaced one another in Vigarani's setting, the shepherds and shepherdesses of the pastoral came and went upon the stage in alternance with the play of George Dandin and his wayward wife.

Vigarani's designs flattered Louis's taste and imagination. The account repeatedly suggests actual water effects, and elsewhere in the halls constructed for dining and dancing, water and light constituted a theme. It appears that yet again the park, as the expression of the King's almost miraculous power, was the source of the evening's invention. If we imagine the bourgeois interiors of *Tartuffe* or *Le Misanthrope* as appropriate to Molière, then the setting for *George Dandin* may be judged preposterous.[7] The responsibility of designer, costumier and dramatist was to make a play, and invention was not to be hidden. Setting and effect were the object of the *fête* and art and nature were related in the contemporary mind. The function of art is perhaps demonstrated by the account of Louis's instructions to his designers.

> He pointed out to them himself the places where the disposition of the site could through its natural beauty contribute more to its decoration; and because one of the finest ornaments of this house is the quantity of water which art has

brought there, despite the fact that nature has refused it,
His Majesty ordered them to make use of it, as much as possible, to embellish the place, and even provided the means
for them to use it and to extract its proper effect.[8]

Molière writes the framing dialogue and lyrics of the pastoral as the
means of transposing to Vigarani's scene a piece which, we have seen,
requires only the simplest staging to realise its dramatic effect.[9] One
sees the light touch with which Molière was accustomed to play at
the interface between the illusions of acting and those of the formalized court entertainment. In presenting the *comédie en musique*, he
amusingly invites our recognition of the artificiality of the pastoral
which frames the play.

TIRCIS ET PHILENE

Puisqu'il nous faut languir en de tels déplaisirs,
Mettons fin en mourant à nos tristes soupirs.
*(Ces deux Bergers s'en vont désespérés, suivant la coutume des
anciens amants, qui se désespéraient de peu de chose. Ensuite de cette
musique vient* LE PREMIER ACTE DE LA COMÉDIE *qui se récite.)*[10]

TIRCIS ET PHILENE

*Since we must now languish in such pain
Let death end our sorrowful complaint.*
(These two shepherds go off in despair, according to the custom of lovers in ancient times, who would despair for little
cause. After this music comes THE FIRST ACT OF THE PLAY
which is spoken.*)*

Molière did not expect his sophisticated audience to find in his lyrics
more than a conventional expression of the lovers' pain. This would
hinder in no way Lully's music. Similarly Vigarani set the stage to
grace the players and please the eye with the play of light on gilding,
water and painted canvas.[11] Scenery and stage effects did not impede
the acting of the play.

The aesthetic of the ballet with its varied *entrées* was such as to
hold back the changeable scene and the rival delights of stage
machinery. This is not so with the nascent opera, for which the scenic
stage was more suitable. The Italian manner naturally embellished
lyric performance but threatened the clarity of the drama, as had
been recognized by Corneille when he felt the need to confine music
to choruses accompanying the movement and noise of stage

machines.[12] Nor indeed was Lully convinced that the form was suited to the French stage and language.[13]

Molière's own opinion is possibly rendered in the remarks on *comédie en musique* at the head of the livret for *George Dandin*: despite the achievement of Lully, singers may fail to please. Exposed in long musical episodes, the person of the singing actor is open to criticism by the connoisseur:

> Notre nation n'est guère faite à la comédie en musique, et je ne puis pas répondre comme cette nouveauté-ci réussira. Il ne faut rien souvent pour effaroucher l'esprit des Français: un petit mot tourné en ridicule, une syllabe qui, avec un air un peu rude, s'approchera d'une oreille délicate, un geste d'un musicien qui n'aura pas peut-être encore au théâtre la liberté qu'il faudrait, une perruque tant soit peu de côté, un ruban qui pendra, la moindre chose est capable de gâter tout une affaire; mais enfin il est assuré, au sentiment des connoisseurs qui ont vu la répétition, que Lully n'a jamais rien fait de plus beau, soit pour la musique, soit pour les danses, et que tout y brille d'invention.[14]

> *Our nation is hardly made for musical plays, and I cannot say how this novelty will succeed. It often requires nothing to discomfit the mind of the French: the slightest word which can be mocked, a syllable which, with a jarring air, comes near a delicate ear, a gesture from a singer who has not yet acquired the necessary composure on stage, a wig worn slightly awry, a ribbon hanging down, the least thing is capable of spoiling the entire business; but in fact it is sure, in the opinion of connoisseurs who have seen the rehearsals, that Lully has never made anything as fine, both as regards the music and the dances, and that invention shines through everywhere.*

Molière does not comment on the scenes directly, but addresses an audience which is alert to nuances of performance and enjoys the direct relationship with the actor. At Versailles, time, money and the summer weather favoured movement to different places of assembly, each with its appropriate pleasures. The freedom of these occasions also licensed the imagination of the actor–dramatist whose instinct was always to invite the audience to challenge the rigidity of a seemingly autonomous scenic staging.

The *fêtes* at Versailles differed in many respects from the scenic fantasy which procures the illusion of space and movement in one building, for a fixed audience, and in a limited compass of time. Molière encountered these conditions finally at the *Salle des Machines*, the theatre Vigarani had designed for the Tuileries in 1659 and which he had opened in 1662 with Buti and Cavalli's opera, *Ercole amante*. An anecdote records what may have been the origin of *Psyché*: the use of a scene from Vigarani's 1662 production. The commission required the dramatist to write for a painted scene, and to stage the choruses and dance *entrées* of a nascent opera. This was to be Molière's *tragédie-ballet*. *Psyché* was driven by the requirements of the stage picture and was no vehicle for the acting of the author. The printed playtext warned the original readership of the play that *Psyché* could not be expected to observe the academic rules of composition since the dramatist 'was more concerned with the beauty and the grandeur of the show than with exact regularity'.[15] There were to be eight separate scenes, allowing a variation of garden and architectural effects, and also evoking isolation and horror, particularly in the re-used scene of hell in the fourth act.

The commission has every mark of the *raison d'état*. The account of the event was broadcast across Europe, as with this report, sent to the court of Savoy.

> I am sending to my Royal mistress, at the behest of the Comte de Saint-Aignan, one of the *livrets* of the ballet which is being danced here [...] we were at it for five hours [...] I have not yet seen anything better done nor more magnificent and these are things that cannot be done elsewhere because of the quantity of dancing-masters, there being seventy who dance together in the last *entrée*. Equally marvellous is the quantity of violinists, of instrumentalists and singers who are more than three hundred in number, all magnificently dressed. The hall is superb, built for the purpose, the stage commodious, marvellously well decorated; machines and scene changes are magnificent and function well, Vigarani acquitting himself honourably in this respect; but for the last scene, it is indeed the most astonishing thing that may be seen, for one sees appear in an instant more than three hundred persons suspended either in clouds or in a glory, and this makes the most beautiful symphony in the world with violins, theorbos, lutes, harpsichords, oboes, flutes, trumpets and cymbals. It can well be seen that in this manner of things that they must have been brought to follow the ideas of the Italians.[16]

The one name which he records is that of Vigarani. If *Psyché* was the harbinger of opera's victory over spoken drama,[17] the triumph was assured, above all, by changeable scenery.

Far from the garden festivities which show Louis in the comparative relaxation of his private palace, the Tuileries theatre could accommodate 7,000 spectators in the most formal setting.[18] Vigarani devoted 140 ft of the building's 240 ft to the depth of stage required by an unusually large number of pairs of wings leading up-stage to a *ferme* or paired shutters which in turn opened on to the depth of a further vista stage with back scenes. Distance was important if a convincing perspective effect was to be achieved with considerable numbers of dancers and singers occupying positions within the medium ground of the stage. Space permitted also large aerial machines in which performers, including royalty, could descend to the stage and thereafter into the dancing space of the theatre.

Despite the expectation in the town that Molière's presence promised comedy, he wrote himself an uninteresting role as Zéphire, the servant who waits, Ariel-like, on L'Amour, a role he swiftly relinquished when the play was taken into the repertoire at the Palais-Royal. The massive scale of the *Salle des Machines* scarcely favoured the performance of the singers in the new opera (its acoustics as well as its size were unfavourable), let alone the intelligent exchanges of actors and audience possible in the town playhouse or the theatre in the King's apartments. One sees that Molière responds to the scenic stage as to an unseen hand that threatens to engineer the performances of the human society of the theatre, and as such it is to be exploited, gently mocked but never allowed to dominate.

The presentation of the entertainment in scene and costume was an integral part of Molière's aesthetic, and even the simplest stages on which he might have played admitted the back scene and the theatrical costume. Both announced the pleasures of play and imagination, and both could be made part of the shared imagination of actor and audience. In the impromptu plays for the court, or in its *divertissements*, we see acting foregrounding the illusions of staging, as when Molière appears 'taken unawares' by the opening scenes of *Les Fâcheux*. In the second *intermède* of *La Princesse d'Élide*, the *agréable Moron* who climbs 'a tree', actually a painted wing, to escape a bear, plays mischievously with the illusions of scenic stage, as does Sganarelle in *Dom Juan*, standing gazing as the pairs of wings slide in and out around him to reveal the tomb of the *Commandeur*.

(Le tombeau s'ouvre, où l'on voit un superbe mausolée et la statue du Commandeur.)

SGANARELLE

Ah! que cela est beau! les belles statues! le beau marbre! les beaux piliers! Ah! que cela est beau! qu'en dites-vous, Monsieur?

(III, v)[19]

(The tomb opens, where there can be seen a superb Mausoleum and the statue of the Commander.)

SGANARELLE

Oh! Isn't it lovely! The lovely statues! The lovely marble! The lovely pillars! Oh! Isn't it lovely! What do you think, sir?

This is the characteristic image of Molière, the performer, controlling the stage with his actor's imagination appealing to the judgement of the audience. It is at work also in the other key element of theatrical presentation, the interaction of performer and costume.

Costume

Donnez-moi ma robe pour mieux entendre ... Attendez, je crois que je serai mieux sans robe ... Non; redonnez-la-moi, cela ira mieux.

Le Bourgeois gentilhomme (I, ii)[20]

Give me my gown so I can hear properly ... Wait, I think I would be better without the gown ... No, give it back to me, that will be better.

For Monsieur Jourdain dress affects actions in the society to which he aspires. Just as much as dancing, music or elegant speech, dress is a means of playing a role. The question is not, however, merely how fine he will appear, but is this what he should do? The functional aspect of stage or social dress in Molière's age concerns us, not because the significance of dressing has greatly altered, but the experience of representation in drama is different. The audience sought understanding in the images of the stage before it sought likeness to everyday reality. In our present-day reading and staging of plays, the question is one of resemblance: what does costume look like? We are grounded in ideas of description: the modern designer and director locate plays in worlds which are strongly determined by imagined or researched historical and cultural prototypes.

All ages know how dress and scenic design can call into play exotic or bygone environments which will colour the illusions of the drama, and this was the case when Molière played in Corneille's *Mort de Pompée*. The costume had historical connotations, but mediated by an unashamedly contemporary taste. The breastplate and *tonnelet*, a kilt, were worn with the wig and ribbons of the modern gentleman to create the costume *à l'antique* which in sculpture and painting had become as recognisable as contemporary dress. The King would be portrayed in this dress as often as in any other, and naturally it would dignify the statue of the *Commandeur* in the mausoleum of *Dom Juan*.

The extent to which costume moves along a scale from the functional to the descriptive is determined as much by organization and practice in the theatre as it is by aesthetics. The costume designer was active only in the court entertainment, working alongside the scene painter and the stage engineer in the *ballet de cour*, to show to advantage the persons of the performers, but pursuing the themes and emblems of the show through ensembles of costume. When it is the responsibility of the actor to dress for the role then the result will inevitably lack, or indeed simply neglect, this visual unity. Molière's company knew three ways of dressing: on their own stage the Mascarilles and Sganarelles, costumed for farce, cohabited with the Valères and the Horaces, dressed for the street and salon, while at court they were costumed by the designer in a mythic or pastoral scenic fantasy.

We have seen how part of the appeal of the 1664 *fête* lay in the enjoyment of different locations pleasingly embellished with a variety of architectural and scenic elements. These went hand in hand with costume highlighting of the *dramatis personae*, from Roger's knights in the lists to attendants serving food in ballet *entrées*. Whatever the ingenuity of the designer, stage space preserved a prime position for the costumed performer. These effects conserved a practice of the pageants and *tableaux vivants* of the royal *entrée*, or the carousel. Vigarani may have impressed with the design of his temporary theatre-building, but for *La Princesse d'Élide* he created only a single scene integrating the play with the spaces of the garden. Only at the conclusion did there appear 'from beneath the stage a machine in the form of a great tree bearing sixteen fauns'.[21] The ingenuity of the designer–machinist was largely employed in assisting the movement of the ballet and in varying its spectacle. The actors were not to be challenged by the dissolving picture within the proscenium arch.

The composition of the *ballet de cour* included all the available languages for the description of a sequence of events. The sequence itself was abstracted in an *argument* conveyed to the onlookers by the indispensable *livret* which was distributed at the opening of the ballet. In *Le Bourgeois gentilhomme* the concluding ballet incorporates the audience scrambling for their copy:

PREMIERE ENTRÉE
Un homme vient donner les livres du ballet, qui d'abord est fatigué par une multitude de gens de provinces différentes, qui crient en musique pour en avoir, et par trois Importuns, qu'il trouve toujours sur ses pas.[22]

FIRST ENTRÉE
A man comes to give out the book of the ballet, who is firstly bothered by a multitude of people from different provinces, who cry out in music for their copy, and by three Importunates, whom he finds everywhere under his feet.

The dance was not expected to convey the narrative, which the *livret* could make clear. Similarly the dressing of the dancers identified them within a performance which self-consciously argued its meaning. The aesthetic was theatrical rather than dramatic, with the audience bringing together a wealth of impressions and experiences in a conscious interpretation. In performance the dancer knew the representative position which he occupied: how he was to be seen by others, and what meaning they attached to his presence. Thus music, dance, scene and costume were linked as species of display.

The requirement of ballet costume across the century was twofold: that it accommodate the style of dance and movement which prevailed, and that it obey the demands of richness and ingenuity in theatrical display. The costumes of gardeners or locksmiths or birdcatchers or peasants alike needed to share in the splendour of the occasion. There was no thought of naturalism in representing these trades, indeed quite the reverse, for these tradesmen were the creation of fancy and the costumier. Dress was brilliant and expensive, and its form functional only within a ballet where the identification of the part played was the first priority, and the admiration of the artifice of its display was the second. Early in the century the accent was very much upon the grotesque and fanciful possibilities of costuming: the drunkard wears an extraordinary headdress which makes clear to an audience the 'character' they should attach to him.

Similarly the invention of the ballets of the first half-century includes all manner of stage effects, with pieces of dress walking without any visible human occupant, in a fashion worthy of twentieth-century Dadaist theatre, and with strange beasts and birds being brought into the dance. The ballets of Louis XIV's court were no less theatrical, but their argument favoured a greater dignity in the characters, and their object was a more stately delight, given the direct participation of the King himself.

For *Le Bourgeois gentilhomme* almost two decades later one would hardly expect an equivalent grotesque in the dressing of the *Quatre Garçons tailleurs*, and some designs from the workshop of Henry de Gissey (or conceivably his pupil Jean Bérain) may indicate the style of musicians and Turks appearing in the play (see Figures 8.1 and 8.2). For the concluding *Ballet des Nations* the costuming brought together dancers representing spectators together with Italian *commedia* costumes long familiar in dramatic and dance theatre. All this was costumed to be admired, not because of strict resemblance to anything the audience knew, but for the invention and the splendour with which it presented performers to its privileged audience (see Figure 8.3).

Figure 8.1 Ballet performers: musicians. *Courtesy of the Nationalmuseum, Stockholm*

Figure 8.2 Turkish costume for the ballet. *Courtesy of the Nationalmuseum, Stockholm*

Figure 8.3 Working drawing for a ballet costume: a gypsy-girl. *Courtesy of the Nationalmuseum, Stockholm*

The actor in the town company provided his own costume, and the inventory of Molière's wardrobe shows the relative expense to which the actor would go in presenting the performance. Thus we see that the value of a set of ordinary town clothes is made at 15 *livres* and much finer suit is estimated at 25 *livres*:

> Item, a jerkin and rheingrave of musk-rose Dutch cloth with a coat of white China satin, the garters and hose of silk, trimmed with satin, valued at twenty-five *livres*, that is ... 25 1.[23]

For the stage, the dress for Harpagon in *L'Avare* with its black satin and black silk lace seems ill chosen for a miser and is valued at 20 *livres*. Orgon in *Tartuffe* might be expected to express some religious sobriety, but Molière's costume for this role is estimated at fully 60 *livres*. It is, however, suitably sober in colour and presumably, style.

> Item, another chest where is the costume for playing *Tartuffe*, consisting of a doublet, breeches and a coat in black Venetian cloth, the coat lined with *tabis* and garnished with English lace, the garters and the slippers similarly garnished, valued at sixty *livres*, that is ... 60 1.[24]

The costumes which remain from the early roles in Molière's repertoire, that is Sganarelle in *Le Médecin malgré lui*, Sganarelle in *L'École des maris*, and Mascarille in *L'Étourdi*, and Sganarelle in *Le Cocu imaginaire*, taken together reach a valuation of 25 *livres*. These costumes were presumably both older in material and archaic in style and were serviceable only in Molière's own roles. The most costly items are for the ballets: Clitidas in *Les Amants magnifiques* at 60 *livres* and Jourdain in *Le Bourgeois gentilhomme* at 70.

L'ajustement is a matter of class and position. Impossible for one who is unaware to cut the figure of a gentleman. Thus the provincial Monsieur de Pourceaugnac is described by Sbrigani alighting from the Limousin coach on his way to the marriage arranged with the despairing Julie:

> Pour sa figure, je ne veux pas vous en parler: vous verrez de quel air la nature l'a desseiné, et si l'ajustement qui l'accompagne y répond comme il faut. Mais pour son esprit, je vous avertis par avance qu'il est des plus épais qui se fassent.
>
> (I, ii)[25]

As for his features, I will say nothing of them: you will see in what spirit Nature drew them, and see if the apparel which accompanies them is not entirely suitable. But as for his wit, I must warn you in advance it is one of the dullest you could find.

A man's features, his clothes and his wit are linked as if one were the natural manifestation of the other. (Molière, playing Sbrigani, refers to the cut of his own unusual Neapolitan costume, clearly that of the comedy player.) When the disordered mind of a Harpagon is horrified by his son's fashionable clothes, he raises the ignoble and obsessive question of cash. Nor does Molière merely follow fashion and the possible prejudices of his audience. The balance between *ajustement*, pleasing physical appearance and good sense can be lost by those who believe themselves to be possessed of all three in good measure. From the pranks of the servants in *Les Précieuses ridicules* to the *petits marquis* in *Le Misanthrope*, Molière stages characters whose mental processes are as exaggerated as their physical appearance or their costumes. The length of the petits marquis's *canons* corresponds to the inflation of their pride; and when Molière rehearses the marquis, *le plaisant de la comédie*, in *L'Impromptu de Versailles*, space is required for an entry, and he advises Brécourt the actor to enter combing his wig with his fingers.

For the actor the chief criterion is the view of the audience, and his own feeling that he is appropriately dressed for the physical performance he must give. This is an extension of social dressing, and exploits his own society's language of dressing in the composition of the character. Costume is contemporary, what Hollander speaks of as 'that most subtle kind of costume, modern dress', and conveys to wearer and watcher a pointed impression of social and moral identity.[26] Present-day conceptions of the individuality of persons would not be understood. The individual was identifiable in terms of a distinction earned by the effortless avoidance of excess, and the happy blending of qualities which could only be appreciated in their unforced integration. This was seen in the gentleman, the *honnête homme*, a rational conception of man in society, which will be discussed in the third part of this book.

Costume, manners and social accomplishment all played their part in the appreciation of the individual, who was thus more a social creation than a natural phenomenon. The actor's art similarly involved the recognition of the relationship of performance and dress, and the matter of conformity or deviation from accepted standards is frequently an element which Molière introduces into the actor's performance.

There is no example more extravagantly entertaining than *Le Bourgeois gentilhomme*, where the role of appearances in Molière's society is brilliantly exploited, and the actor gains control within the role of the elements which present him to his audience.

9

ACTING

Through the fifteen years of Molière's mature Parisian career he was subject to serious personal and professional attack, all the more intensely focused since his success was enjoyed through the plays in which he himself was the chief performer.

His plays were made to serve the curiosity and imagination of the audience he knew well from his position as their principal actor, addressing them from the stage. No other dramatist of the age could be held as personally responsible for the tastes and pleasures of his theatre, nor for what might be its alleged failures or excesses. The success of his plays was so comprehensive that, as with *L'École des femmes*, both play and performance were decried as vulgar and overdone: the play was carelessly made, and ignorant of the rational principles of dramaturgy, *les règles*, and offended propriety, *les bienséances*, in the vulgar material that suited the ill-judged and excessive methods of the playing.

More dangerous for the dramatist was the affair of *Tartuffe* beginning in 1664, which carried over the next year to include *Dom Juan ou le Festin de Pierre*, an even more scurrilous play in the opinion of Molière's enemies, and one whose theatrical power they well understood. The author of an anonymous attack, the *Observations sur le Festin de Pierre*, deplores the effect of persuasive acting, which he succeeds in evoking with some vigour. Heresy, having been driven out of the kingdom by the piety and dreadful power of the King, is taking to the stage to preach its blasphemy.[1] In condemning scandal, the critic reveals the delight produced in the (misguided and misled) audience by Molière at work.

> ... an eccentric who reasons grotesquely on God, and who by a contrived fall, wrecks his arguments; a damnable valet, fit for the repartee of his master, whose whole belief comes

139

down to the bogeyman, for provided one believes in the bogeyman, all is well, and the rest is a trifle; a devil who meddles in every scene, and who spreads over the stage the blackest smoke of Hell; and finally a Molière, worse than all this, dressed as Sganarelle, who makes fun of God and the Devil, who plays the fool with Heaven and Hell, who breathes hot and cold, who confuses virtue and vice, who believes and who does not believe, who cries and laughs, who reproaches and approves, who is critic and atheist, who is hypocrite and free-thinker, who is man and demon together: a devil incarnate, as he defines himself.[2]

The style of the acting with its physical strength and violent contrasts is recorded together with the grossly inappropriate presentation of morals and theology by a 'damnable valet'. The valet is moreover Sganarelle, recognisable by his costume from half-a-dozen other plays. The writer identifies the key element in Molière's reckless playing with 'the most holy matters',[3] as incongruity of matter and manner, the mismatch between a physical style of acting and the orderly thought appropriate to such matters. The account shows an awareness of the function of acting in creating an intellectual rhythm, and in engaging the mind of even the most hostile spectator in the pleasure of ideas. If Molière was to be dismissed as a buffoon, he was dangerously focused in his buffoonery, and caused his audience to entertain criminal and, even worse, impious ideas. Molière's enemies were excellent dramatic critics, and far more alert to Molière's comedy than the pedants and envious poets of the salons.

The author of the *Observations* both accuses Molière of urging irreligion, and also of being a particularly low type of actor. Repeatedly he speaks of farce as the form adopted by Molière, and how this in itself reveals the malicious intent of the dramatist. At the same time Molière is damned as being a less gifted *farceur* than the well known precursors at the Bourgogne.

It is true that there is something *galant* in the works of Molière, and I would be loathe to steal the esteem that he has got himself. We must agree that, if he comes off badly in the play, he has a certain talent for the farce; and although he has neither the quips of Gaultier-Garguille, nor the *impromptus* of Turlupin, nor the bravado of the Capitan, nor the naïveté of Jodelet, nor the paunch of Gros-Guillaume, nor the science of the Docteur, he does not fail to please sometimes, and to amuse after his own fashion. He speaks French passably; he translates Italian quite well, and copies not at all badly the classics; for he does not pride himself on having the gift of invention nor the fine genius of poetry, and his friends confess freely that his plays are theatre business, where the actor counts for more than the poet, and where the beauty consists almost entirely in the action. What makes us laugh in his mouth often provokes pity on the page [...] I leave out those critics who would have much to say against his voice and his gestures, and who say that there is nothing natural in him, that his postures are forced, and that by dint of studying grimaces, he does always the same thing ...[4]

Dom Juan was dropped from the repertoire and was never revived by Molière. In early 1665 Molière's thinking about his art was conditioned by two great successes which he could not play again, and by the quarrels of the previous three years. His opponents were animated by more than a simple puritanism: they linked the currents in the plays to the great issues of the day, to the suppression of Protestantism and the defeat of *libertin* attacks on piety. Acting and comedy were feared because of a danger which was well understood: this was a medium in which ideas were not only contemplated, but where they were manifest.

Among the replies to Molière's critics came the anonymous *Lettre sur L'Imposteur*[5] describing the altered version of the play in 1668, and which might be by Donneau de Visé, now allied to the Molière camp, or, at least in part, Molière's own work. The *Lettre* discusses the revised play, and then goes on to discuss the effect of comedy, and consider how it improves manners by attacking impropriety. This leads to a theory of comedy, and the identification of an experience of 'the comic', termed *le ridicule*, based on the idea of the rational deficit which is felt in any object, or, in this case, dramatic encounter, which is incongruous or improper. The sense of *le ridicule* is planted in us by a benevolent nature to guide us towards the good and make us sensitive to error as a sort of deformity. Thus the behaviour of Tartuffe in the play is *ridicule* or comic, and would be seen so by any lady exposed subsequently to advances such as his.[6] Whereas *le ridicule* is ultimately a moral question, it is known as a matter of sense and sensation. The spectator knows the comic as a feeling, and as the experience of physical form, apprehended directly through the processes of empathy.

Given our weakness or our laziness, providential Nature has attached a mark to reason which makes knowledge of it easier: 'an external form and recognisable outside appearance'.[7] This form is the occasion of a pleasurable recognition of a moral object, either in the delight we experience in virtue or in the pleasure of *ridicule* when we encounter ignorance and error. The strength of the theory lies in the equation of pleasure in moral objects with the sensations provoked by the experience of form. Comic pleasure is defined in terms of knowledge and sensation, the key words in the argument being *connaissance* deriving from a *forme extérieure et sensible*, attached to any object which is acutely lacking in reason. For a contemporary of Descartes and his philosophy of reason as the only guarantor of truth, this is a bold theory: that knowledge lies in bodily forms, and that the moral world can be apprehended through the physical forms of action.[8] Most importantly for the actor, the theory unifies what in English we could term 'integrity' and 'integration'. It is the business of acting to assume the physical forms of the drama and to realize their moral character.

What was outwardly irrational, eccentric or socially threatening, presented, as the *Lettre* shows, a physical form capable of exercising the moral sense of the spectator. Thus acting was a matter of specific physical presentation of generally relevant moral positions (rather than the opposite in much modern playing where there is a generalised presentation of desired specific and often idiosyncratic states of feeling). The acting of Molière's day was by no means unemotional, and feeling, or passion, had an important role in tragedy and comedy alike. The essential question in the acting style of both genres is the degree to which passion is licensed by the events of the drama, and the extent to which the forms of passionate expression are in keeping with the moral quality of the action. It will be clear that this was a juxtaposition that Molière exploited in his own acting, while reproaching excess in the tragic actors who were his rivals.

As we have seen above, the word *caractère* is applied to the nature and configuration of a moral being, before it begins to be applied to the *dramatis personae* of the play or to persons living in the world. 'Character' was used in the Theophrastian sense of a set of moral attributes (not unlike the English usage in a phrase such as 'a person of good character');[9] in French the person of the play was, and still is, the *personnage*. Both terms are used in French to discuss play-acting, but neither should suggest to us a pursuit of an individualized psychology. In this sense the 'characters' of the drama are an opportunity for playing. What then was the nature of this playing? How might it have been conceived in the mind and, most importantly, the technique of the individual actor? The rehearsals of *L'Impromptu de Versailles* describe a practice which is not that of today.

As the actors appear, their irritation and anxiety are directed at Molière for undertaking a performance at such short notice. The parts have been distributed, each containing only the character's own words. Molière alone knows 'la pièce', the play as a whole. As they complain about the difficulty of the preparation there is a coincidence of ideas of *'personnage'*, *'rôle'* and *'mots'*; that is, character, part and words.

MOLIÈRE

... employons ce temps à répéter notre affaire et voir la manière dont il faut jouer les choses.

LA GRANGE

Le moyen de jouer ce qu'on ne sait pas?

MADEMOISELLE DU PARC

Pour moi, je vous déclare que je ne me souviens pas d'un mot de mon personnage.

MADEMOISELLE DE BRIE

Je sais bien qu'il me faudra souffler le mien d'un bout à l'autre.

MADEMOISELLE BÉJART

Et moi, je me prépare fort à tenir mon rôle à la main.

MADEMOISELLE MOLIÈRE

Et moi aussi.

MADEMOISELLE HERVÉ

Pour moi, je n'ai pas grand-chose à dire.[10]

MOLIÈRE

... let us use the time we have to rehearse our business and see how the thing should be played.

LA GRANGE

How can we play something we do not know?

MADEMOISELLE DU PARC

For my part, I tell you that I do not recall a word of my character.

MADEMOISELLE DE BRIE
I am sure that I shall have to be prompted from one end to the other.

MADEMOISELLE BÉJART
And as for me, I am resigned to keeping my part in my hand.

MADEMOISELLE MOLIÈRE
And so am I.

MADEMOISELLE HERVÉ
As for me, I haven't much to say.

The rehearsal method depends upon parts being known before the whole play (*la pièce*) is tackled. Since the part is precisely that, a part with only the *réplique* or cue to speeches being supplied, the actor knows *le personnage* initially in terms of the actions implied by the forms of the text. From a modern point of view there is a limited idea of what many actors would term 'motivation', since the actions are not linked in a prior conceptualization of the action of the play over-all. On the other hand, rehearsal practice must have involved careful attention to the 'parts' of other players,[11] for without this neither the cue could be picked up nor the sense with which each part engages.[12]

The way in which these parts are to be played emerges from the actual 'rehearsal' of the unnamed play being prepared for the court, and the discussion of another project which Madeleine Béjart calls to mind. In this, Molière imagines a young company being in effect auditioned and criticized by an established Bourgogne dramatist, with two styles of playing contrasted, in their physical representation of an observed ethical character. Molière's own playing may reasonably be identified with the young actor whom he describes playing 'in the most natural fashion in the world', much to the dissatisfaction of the Bourgogne dramatist. Everything about the young actor is unsatisfactory, starting with his size and bearing. There is a subtle joke in the description of an appropriate royal figure, given the presence in the audience of the undoubtedly *galant* and slender Louis:

> – Et qui fait les rois parmi vous? – Voilà un acteur qui s'en démêle parfois. – Qui? Ce jeune homme bien fait? Vous moquez-vous? Il faut un roi qui soit gros et gras comme quatre, un roi, morbleu! qui soit entripaillé comme il faut, un roi d'une vaste circonférence, et qui puisse remplir un trône de la belle manière. La belle chose qu'un roi d'une taille galante.[13]

And who among you plays the kings? – Here is an actor who tries his hand at that sometimes. – Who? That well made young fellow? Are you joking? You need a king who is big and fat as four men, a king, dammit! with the right sort of stuffing, a king with a vast circumference, and who can fill a throne in fine fashion. Just imagine a king with an elegant figure.

When the actor has recited a few lines of *Nicomède*, the verdict is yet more unfavourable.

Comment? Vous appelez cela réciter? C'est se railler! Il faut dire les choses avec emphase. Écoutez-moi.
(Imitant Montfleury, excellent acteur de l'Hôtel de Bourgogne.)
Te le dirai-je, Araspe? ... etc.
Voyez-vous cette posture? Remarquez-bien cela. Là, appuyer comme il faut le dernier vers. Voilà ce qui attire l'approbation et fait faire le brouhaha. – Mais, Monsieur, aurait répondu le comédien, il me semble qu'un roi qui s'entretient tout seul avec son capitaine des gardes parle un peu plus humainement et ne prend guère ce ton démoniaque. – Vous ne savez ce que c'est. Allez-vous-en réciter comme vous faites, vous verrez si vous ferez faire aucun ah!14

What? You call that declamation? You are joking! You must speak these things with emphasis. Listen to me.
(Imitating Montfleury, an excellent actor at the Hôtel de Bourgogne.)
Shall I tell you, Araspes ... etc.
Do you see this posture? Look at it carefully. There, put the right stress on the last line. That is what brings approval and creates a stir. – But, sir, the actor would have replied, it seems to me that a king who converses alone with his captain of the guard speaks in a more human fashion and does not adopt that devilish tone. – You do not know what you are about. Go and recite as you do, and you will see if you produce a single 'ah!'.

Clearly Molière mocked rivals who were demonstrably successful in a genre where he himself never succeeded. The implication is that Molière's style was unsuited to tragedy because of his leanings towards the natural, possibly towards something we would describe as naturalistic. This is to misinterpret the evidence. Molière's style reflected a necessary closeness of comedy to everyday reality as opposed to the grandiloquence of tragedy with its elevated subject matter. There is no suggestion here that the comic performance was any the less physical, but only that its forms were more judicious.

The forms of comic acting certainly struck others as highly calculated, albeit in another style. As we have already seen, when Molière is attacked, it was for a supposedly grotesque performance, pratfalls and all. These attacks were important enough for him to wish refute them in the *Critique*, and professionally interesting enough for him to repeat them for the delight of his well informed theatre audience, who remember the alleged excesses.

> Et ce Monsieur de la Souche enfin, qu'on nous fait un homme d'esprit, et qui paraît si sérieux en tant d'endroits, ne descend-il point en quelque chose de trop comique et de trop outré au cinquième acte, lorsqu'il explique à Agnès la violence de son amour, avec ces roulements d'yeux extravagants, ces soupirs ridicules, et ces larmes niaises qui font rire tout le monde?[15]

> *And this Monsieur de la Souche, after all, who is presented to us as a man of wit, and who seems so serious in so many places, does he not gravitate to something too comical and too exaggerated in the fifth act, when he explains to Agnès the violence of his love, rolling his eyes in that overdone fashion, sighing in that ridiculous way, and with those simpleton's tears which make everyone laugh?*

While stressing the audience's laughter, Molière foregrounded the criticisms made of his playing. The later satire *Élomire hypocondre* contains an extensive picture of Molière 'in training' with Fiorilli, his colleague at the Palais-Royal:

> *For example, Élomire*
> *Wishes to perfect himself in the art of making others laugh:*
> *What does he do, the rogue, in this bold endeavour?*
> *Night and morning he visits the great Scaramouche.*
> *There, glass in hand, and opposite the great man,*
> *There is not a contortion, a posture nor a grimace,*
> *That this great pupil of the greatest of clowns,*
> *Does not practise and practise again in a hundred ways and again*
> *a hundred:*
> *Now to express his household cares,*
> *His frowning face is lined a thousand times;*
> *Then adding pallor to the lines he has created,*

He becomes the very portrait of a wretched husband.
After this, pressing further this sad visage,
He draws the portrait of a cuckold, or jealousy;
Sometimes with measured step, you will see him seeking out,
Something which before his eyes he is afraid to find;
Then stopping short, foaming at the mouth with anger
You would say that he catches out an unfaithful wife,
And believe, so well his eyes portray the outrage,
That he has rage in his heart and horns upon his head.[16]

The accounts make two things clear: the extreme calculation of physical effects in the body and face of the performer, and the illusion of a moral and passionate state in the character. The language of painting is yet again applied to explain the likeness of the performance to life, and yet the actual descriptions of performance make clear means of playing which are abstract and elaborated within the terms of the stage and the progress of the human body in theatrical space. The evolution of this style has its roots in a tradition of simple, accurate, popular playing, in which meaning must be conveyed cleanly and clearly.[17] The sharing of understanding between the player and the audience cannot be blurred if the pleasure of comedy is to be enjoyed. The measured, balanced step of the comic actor, the bodily posture and the controlled facial expression embody both attention and attitude and 'show' the audience the dramatic action, but more importantly still they are the means of engaging the actor in the clear execution of the action itself.[18] An important definition must be made at this point, for it is at the heart of the process of acting itself, and in particular it explains difficulties which arise in the modern performance of classical roles.

There is a distinction to be made between information and knowledge in any epistemological system. The first is data-based, and its status is dependent upon the circumstances of its transmission and reception. The second is dependent on the processes of life whereby the data which are encountered are incorporated into individual experience. Information cannot be said to be 'known' until it is recalled or in some way represented mentally. The question of recognition which is so crucial in all art embraces the means whereby the mind discovers its knowledge as a connected process in which experiences involve the tiering of knowledge layer upon layer. Not only does one 'know' the state of affairs one encounters, but this is known as part of a pattern of interconnectedness in mental experience. So one knows the object, but also knows that it stands in a relationship to a general field of experience by which the understanding is informed. Every performance manifests a performer (and an audience) coming to know certain states of affairs, and the fact that conditions for this knowledge are plotted in advance in the rehearsal does not undermine the fact of the performance being known only at the point where it is given and shared.

The habit of referring to Molière's acting as 'painting' reflects a convenient comparison and a ready terminology, but also raises a crucial question. Could his acting have been 'indicative'; that is, aimed at the creation of an impression in the audience that the character expresses a view or experiences a reaction. A certain interpretation of the 'passionate' description of his performance might lean in this direction, given also the accounts of his contortions and grimaces. This would be to interpret a primitive critical language in favour of a particularly modern error. The language of painting goes only so far in expressing the liveliness of the impressions of acting, and it does not convey anything of its methods. On the other hand, the practices of contemporary painting make clear that the concerns of painters themselves set a premium on knowing rather than showing in the experience of the work of art. The moral dimension of painting is evident in Poussin, where physical form was a means of 'knowing' moral qualities, and in the physiognomical investigations of the painter Le Brun, which would have been known to Molière, since the latter was effectively Molière's colleague at court.

Le Brun's *Conférence sur l'expression générale et particulière*, published in 1698,[19] outlines a way of classifying the human passions, largely in conformity with Descartes *Des Passions de l'âme* (1649), and goes on to assist the artist in the representation of these states by the depiction of different physical forms.[20] The treatise takes up a long tradition which seeks to analyse the passions in terms of the relationship of the individual to the world. The discussion identifies physical and moral objects through the agency of a contemporary physiology. Here, in discussing the drawing of physical form, Le Brun is drawn into a dramatic evocation of human response:

> The soul, as hath been already observed, is so united to all the parts of the body, that she easily expresses all the different Passions: for Fear may be expressed by a man flying away, Anger, or Wrath, by a man clinching his fists, and seeming to strike.[21]

The system is built up symmetrically about the central relationship of the subject to the object, which is termed admiration. This relationship is experienced before the object excites the nervous system, or as contemporary medicine would have it, the spirits flow from the brain, to stimulate the body to clear movement, visible in muscle and bodily form. This movement and form arise as a response by the integrated body to the moral quality of the object. Then, as the operation of the spirits engages the subject further, attraction or aversion follows, and a movement towards possession or avoidance of the object will be experienced, and different passions may be suffered or enjoyed, dependent on the movements of the soul. A reading of this short treatise makes an excellent accompaniment to the *Lettre sur L'Imposteur* with its description of the power of moral objects to produce a sensible movement of the soul, dependent on esteem or contempt.

> Admiration is a surprise, which inclines the Soul attentively to consider the objects that seem rare and extraordinary to her; and this surprise has such a power as sometimes to force the spirits towards the Part which receives an impression from the Object, and she is so taken up with considering such an impression, that few spirits are left to supply the Muscles: hence the body becomes as a statue, without motion; and this excess of Admiration causes Astonishment; and Astonishment may happen before we know whether such an object be agreeable to us or not.
> Thus it is plain that Admiration may be joined with Esteem or with Contempt, according to the grandeur or meanness of the object. From Esteem proceeds Veneration; as from Contempt, Disdain.[22]

Thus the meaning of the object to the viewer is morally founded, and that meaning is ultimately experienced in muscle. It is indeed a dramatic scheme. Molière would have seen Le Brun's frontispieces for the 1647 edition of Corneille's works, and it is scarcely imaginable that he would not have discerned the physical forms of passions aroused in plays, some of which he played.

There is a danger that these studies in fine art may be seen under their worst aspect as a sort of codification of the passions, whereby painting may be simply 'read'. There would be a link to modern semiology where the work is seen as a conscious signing system referring back to an encoding of meanings which are variously understood by the given response to signs. There is something more in the matter which relates directly to acting and spectator response. As has been observed above, the face-pulling of the actor, or the face-making of the painter, can be seen as a means of coming to know human experience as opposed to a way of conveying the known. The schematic drawings which accompany Le Brun's discussions present a language of physical form, corresponding, it is true, to observation, but also to a programme for understanding, and primarily offered as an aid to composition.

This interest in physiognomy is naturally paralleled in the identification of gesture in the body as the embodiment of an ethical character. This is visible in the 'staging' of the scenes of painting, and in the illustrations of plays which accompany the printed text. The language of gesture in Le Brun's portrayal of Louis XIV is the same as that employed in the depiction of Corneille's heroes in the frontispieces by the same artist. Whereas Le Brun's setting cannot be expected to represent the reality of the performance in the seventeenth-century playhouse, one may well suppose that acting style is indicated by these strongly physical depictions of heroic attitude. Neither in painting nor in illustration should one seek naturalism: characters are rendered in accordance with a decent and credible representation of a given ethics and a given ideology. One may remember, for all his denunciation of the tragic actors of the Bourgogne, that Molière chose to be painted by his friend Mignard in the costume of Caesar in Corneille's *Mort de Pompée*,[23] holding the general's baton, while his detractors showed him opposite his 'master' Fiorilli as a second Scaramouche. In each case 'character' emerged from physical control in the body.

The understanding of such a physical language could be expected in a culture where every day the body was controlled in the presentation of a social persona. The placing of the limbs in the classicizing portrait could be replicated in the bearing of the courtier, and was surely based in either case on the custom and exercise of dance. One would expect the subjects of portraits to be flattered in the composition of the picture, and the natural way to do this is to show them adopting the elegant forms which were taught in the dance and adopted in the salon. Louis XIV dancing as Apollo shows the same elegant bearing, the same studied carriage of the arms and turn-out of the foot in second position as is displayed in van der Meulen's depiction of the King in the trenches at the seige of Douai and amid the carnage of the conquest of the Franche-Comté in Simmoneau's allegorical battle scene.

Molière's plays reflect this awareness of physical form, and it is at the heart of the rational structures of comedy he created. The *petits marquis* naturally expressed the fashions and social refinements of the court, and in the *Impromptu de Versailles* Molière makes clear that such manners give free play to the extravagance of comedy:

MOLIÈRE

Souvenez-vous bien, vous, de venir, comme je vous ai dit, là,
avec cet air qu'on nomme le bel air, peignant votre perruque
et grondant une petite chanson entre vos dents. La, la, la, la,
la, la. Rangez-vous donc, vous autres, car il faut du terrain à
deux marquis; et ils ne sont pas gens à tenir leur personne
dans une petite espace. Allons, parlez.

LA GRANGE

'Bonjour, Marquis.'

MOLIÈRE

Mon Dieu ce n'est point là le ton d'un marquis; il faut le
prendre un peu plus haut.

(Sc. iii)[24]

MOLIÈRE

*Now, you, remember well to enter, as I told you, with that bearing
which they call the air of breeding, combing through your wig and
growling out a little tune between your teeth. La, la, la, la, la, la.
Stand back the rest of you, for two marquises you need lots of room;
and they are not the sort to confine their persons in a small space.
Go on, speak.*

LA GRANGE

'Good-day, marquis.'

MOLIÈRE

*Great heavens, that is hardly the tone of a marquis; you must pitch
it higher.*

As the rehearsal proceeds, the accent is placed upon the form of the
playing: Molière demonstrates to Brécourt the virtuoso display of
false civilities and mannered greetings which can be exploited in his
role, and, as la Du Parc and Mademoiselle Molière enter, the civilities
continue, with the play of bodies predominating. Trunks serve as
armchairs, and the actresses take their places with exaggerated deference for one another.

MADEMOISELLE DU PARC

'Allons, Madame, prenez place, s'il vous plait.'

MADEMOISELLE MOLIÈRE

'Après vous, Madame.'

MOLIÈRE

Bon. Après ces petites cérémonies muettes, chacun prendra place et parlera assis, hors les marquis, qui tantôt se leveront et tantôt s'assoiront, suivant leur inquiétude naturelle.

(Sc. iv)[25]

MADEMOISELLE DU PARC

'Come, madam, be seated, if you please.'

MADEMOISELLE MOLIÈRE

'After you, madam.'

MOLIÈRE

Good. After these little mute ceremonies, everyone is to sit down and speak seated, except for the marquises, who from time to time will stand and sit in accordance with their natural restlessness.

These roles had been among the first in which Molière's style had won approval, as in *Les Précieuses ridicules*, where, before a discriminating court he played a virtuoso mockery of the parade and the dance of the nobleman.

MASCARILLE

Ce n'est ici qu'un bal à la hâte; mais l'un de ces jours nous vous en donnerons un dans les formes. Les violons, sont-ils venus?

ALMANZOR

Oui, Monsieur; ils sont ici.

CATHOS

Allons donc, mes chères, prenez place.

MASCARILLE

(Dansant lui seul comme par prélude)
La, la, la, la, la, la, la, la.

MAGDELON

Il a tout à fait la taille élégante.

CATHOS

Et a la mine de danser proprement.[26]

MASCARILLE

This is nothing more than an improvised ball; but one of these days we shall give one for you that is correct in every respect. Have the violins come?

ALMANZOR

Yes sir; they are here.

CATHOS

Come on then, dear fellows, take your places.

MASCARILLE

(Dancing alone, as if in a prelude)
La, la, la, la, la, la, la, la.

MAGDELON

His figure is elegance itself.

CATHOS

And he has the air of a perfect dancer.

As Mascarille takes Magdelon on his arm to dance the courante, and
Jodelet breathlessly dances in turn (he was actually recovering from
an illness), the masters burst in to reveal the deception: two servants
aping the manners of their betters. In dancing, their crime is the
more manifest: 'to wish to play men of consequence'.

Just as dance is the physical training which underpins the successful social performance, so too Molière's own acting, to say nothing of
his new dramatic forms, shows everywhere the imprint of dancing.
Not only is dance the source of the social forms which need to be
adopted by even the ill-humoured Alceste, but from time to time
dance will be the basis of a scene, or the dramatist transforms the play
and the ballet takes the place of the drama.

So it is that in *Les Fâcheux* the boor Lysandre brings the *courante* he
has composed and sings it to Éraste, together with words which have
been composed by one of twenty admirers of the air who immediately took up their pens, so great was the appreciation at court.
Lysandre's satisfaction links this achievement to the fine position he
holds in the life of the state, and judges it to be an equal mark of his
dignity.

ÉRASTE

J'ai le bien, la naissance, et quelque emploi passable,
Et fais figure en France assez considérable;
Mais je ne voudrais pas, pour tout ce que je suis,
N'avoir point fait cet air qu'ici je te produis.
La, la, hem, écoute avec soin, je te prie.
(Il chante sa courante.)
N'est-elle pas belle?

ÉRASTE

Ah!

LYSANDRE

Cette fin est jolie.
(Il rechante la fin quatre ou cinq fois de suite.)
Comment la trouves-tu?

ÉRASTE

Fort belle assurément.

LYSANDRE

Les pas que j'en ai faits n'ont pas moins d'agrément.
(Il chante, parle et danse tout ensemble, et fait faire à Éraste les figures de la femme.)

(I, iii, ll. 183–191)[27]

ÉRASTE

I have wealth, birth, and a worthy commission,
And in France I pass for a man worthy of consideration;
But I would not forgo, for all that I am,
The making of this air which I shall do for you.
La, la, ahem, listen with care, I beg you.
(He sings his courante.)
Is it not lovely?

ÉRASTE

Ah!

LYSANDRE

The ending is pretty
(He sings the end again four or five times.)
How do you find it?

ÉRASTE

Very beautiful indeed.

LYSANDRE

The steps that I made for it are no less pleasing.
(He sings, speaks and dances together, and obliges Éraste to execute the woman's part.)

The superimposition of a physical and moral exercise is clear: Éraste is forced against his better or more impulsive judgement into the moves of a social exercise: both praise and dancing.

Instruction of all sorts abounds in Molière's writing, from Agnès being rehearsed in the duties of a wife, to Sganarelle being taught his function as a doctor on pain of a good beating. In *Le Mariage forcé* he is similarly taught behaviour by his future son-in-law, before being instructed in the steps of a *courante* by the dancer Dolivet. When one examines the phenomenon closely it reveals itself for what it is: the anatomy of acting. Acting requires the adoption of the forms of action within which the actor comes to know the significance of what he does, and as such it is intimately related to the routines which engage the mind in new understandings of the self and the world. Molière's lessons allow the partial dismantling of the process of acting so that the eventual integration which is the source of its power is the more intensely felt by the audience.

Thus scenes of remarkable power can occasionally lack apparent 'matter' viewed from any particular social or political standpoint. They are too abstract, too concerned with the way meanings are made rather than with their effect. *Le Bourgeois gentilhomme* is Molière's eternal schoolroom and the pupil graduates as gloriously stupid as when he enrolled.

LE BOURGEOIS GENTILHOMME AT CHAMBORD

This was in some senses Molière's *Tempest*: a monument to his theatrical art. It was the work in which he exploited most happily the resources of the court, and his collaboration with Lully the composer and the dancing-master Dolivet. While it has been seen as a work of social criticism, with the 'original' of Jourdain identified, we should recall Molière's own caution that in comedy the resemblances to the social world are not an end, but a means to recognition. If *Le Bourgeois gentilhomme* is inspired by anything it is by performance: the accent is on the acquisition and the integration of the skills which make the nobleman, and they are similar when the performance is given by the nobility at court, or by an actor, Molière, for the court. Music, dance, fencing and the practice of speech and elegant address; the selection of appropriate costume and the furnishing of appropriate decorations and properties; these are both the business of Monsieur Jourdain the besotted social climber, and Molière the actor.

Viewed as performance, the play is a remarkable study in the processes of active learning. A character deprived of the power of performance is accordingly ignorant of the world and blind to the preposterous ambitions he entertains in it. The delight is in the topsy-turvy enjoyment of a consummate performer, Molière, playing the buffoon who cannot understand, appreciate or follow the instructions of an accomplished gallery of venal, but professional, instructors. The effect is to foreground the medium of performance itself in the wreckage of Jourdain's best endeavours. The consummation of the play in the fantasy of a Turkish ennoblement, where language, manners and culture are remote, is the master stroke in the composition of a theatrical extravaganza, where the means of representation are intimately linked to the matter treated.

Played before the court at Chambord, *Le Bourgeois gentilhomme* concentrated attention on a small élite cast of performers and made few demands on the stage engineer: a single set-change was required for the finale in which Jourdain is made a *mamamouchi* (by Lully, playing the Mufti), and conceivably again for the ballet which followed the play.[28] This initially staged the preliminaries for a ballet: the distribution, to an audience of singers, of the *livret* in which the assembly can follow the different *entrées*. Molière's theatrical imagination is manifest in the mirroring of the audience in the first *entrée* of an entertainment which, despite its habitual fantasy, is essentially a bridge between stage and auditorium, and where the assembly of spectators admires the display of its own representatives. Thus the *Ballet des Nations*, which ultimately concludes the entertainment, is postponed in favour of two *entrées*, one between Dolivet the dancer, distributing the livret and a chorus of singers demanding a copy so that they may enjoy the show, and another, danced by an ensemble of *importuns*, particularly difficult spectators. When the four *entrées* of the ballet proper follow, they mingle song and dance in a display of theatrical forms: Spanish, Italian and French performances. The whole concludes with a chorus of praise, not addressed, as customarily, to the King, but to the occasion and the sharing of a ravishing theatrical show: *Quels spectacles charmants, quels plaisirs ....*[29]

While the *Lettre sur L'Imposteur* stresses the relationship between moral judgement and physical form, it also asserts that the direct experience of playing will invest the spectator with the imprint of a dangerous event, affording states of knowledge which the physical memory recalls when similar events are encountered. Acting operates at the level of muscular effort integrated with nervous and intellectual experience, and Molière's practice frankly exposes the elements as they are assembled into a sophisticated social and moral exemplum. In *La Critique de L'École des femmes* one encounters a mischievous Élise protesting how she learns from the affected prude Climène.

ÉLISE

Je vous étudie des yeux et des oreilles; et je suis si remplie de vous, que je tâche d'être votre singe, et de vous contrefaire en tout.

(Sc. iv) [30]

ÉLISE

I study you with eye and ear; I am filled with your example, I am your ape, and I imitate you in everything.

When Jourdain sets out to ape his betters, the fatuity of his convictions must not obscure the sublime composition of the role, revealing the building blocks of a technique, assembled in the creation of a pitiful edifice, but where paradoxically the beauty and power of acting is abundantly felt. The role is a process of inversion, *contre-sens*, worse and more delightful than nonsense because it has its topsy-turvy composition. The task imagined in Jourdain is the learning of a part. If the fictitious circumstances are for a moment ignored, then Jourdain/Molière appears as a singularly inept actor painfully preparing a role which will never be mastered.

Le Bourgeois gentilhomme brings Molière back to the beginnings of his own training in the absorption of good manners and the practice of the exercises appropriate to a gentleman. The inspiration of the play is in the display of acting as a process of learning, magisterially revealed in the clumsiness and naïvety of the pupil. Jourdain is trained first in the recognisable media of performance, and then in the fantasy of the device which animates the play: the Turkish nonsense of the conclusion. Jourdain, the *mamamouchi*, convinces in the way that Bottom does as the ass.

The training is based in physical exercise: not only dance, music and fencing, but a singular approach to language in the hands of the Master of Philosophy. Here speech itself is reduced to the articulation of sound in possibly the most primitive scene of comedy Molière ever conceived. The forms of the acting are *de facto* fixed by the instructions of the master, and the lessons learned are daringly infantile. The moral constructions of the role are nonetheless important, and sometimes appalling, as with the malediction of the parents who never taught Jourdain the obvious:

MAÎTRE DE PHILOSOPHIE

Vos deux lèvres s'allongent comme si vous faisiez la moue: d'où vient que si vous la voulez faire à quelqu'un, et vous moquer de lui, vous ne sauriez lui faire que: U.

MONSIEUR JOURDAIN

U, U. Cela est vrai. Ah! que n'ai-je étudié plus tôt, pour savoir tout cela?

MAÎTRE DE PHILOSOPHIE

Demain, nous verrons les autres lettres, qui sont les consonnes.

MONSIEUR JOURDAIN

Est-ce qu'il y a des choses aussi curieuses qu'à celles-ci?

MAÎTRE DE PHILOSOPHIE

Sans doute. La consonne D, par exemple, se prononce en donnant du bout de la langue au-dessus des dents d'en haut: Da.

MONSIEUR JOURDAIN

Da, Da. Oui. Ah! Les belles choses! Les belles choses!

MAÎTRE DE PHILOSOPHIE

L'F en appuyant les dents d'en haut sur la lèvre de dessous: Fa.

MONSIEUR JOURDAIN

Fa, Fa. C'est la vérité. Ah! mon père et ma mère, que je vous veux de mal![31]

MASTER OF PHILOSOPHY

You push forward your two lips as if you were pouting: therefore it is the case that if you wished to do so to anyone, to make fun of him, you could do no other to him than to say: U.

MONSIEUR JOURDAIN

U, U. It is true. Ah! Why did I not study before, to know all this?

MASTER OF PHILOSOPHY

Tomorrow, we shall look to the other letters, which are the consonants.

MONSIEUR JOURDAIN

Are there things about them as strange as with these?

MASTER OF PHILOSOPHY

Without question. The consonant D, for example, is pronounced by placing the tip of the tongue above the upper teeth: Da.

MONSIEUR JOURDAIN

Da, Da. Yes. Ah! What wonders! What wonders!

MASTER OF PHILOSOPHY

The F by applying the upper teeth to the lower lip: Fa.

MONSIEUR JOURDAIN

Fa, Fa. It is true. Ah! father and mother, how I wish you could suffer for this!

This rehearsal is followed by another equally concerned with the forms of language:

MONSIEUR JOURDAIN

Marababa sahem veut dire 'Ah! que je suis amoureux d'elle'?

COVIELLE

Oui.

MONSIEUR JOURDAIN

Par ma foi! vous faites bien de me le dire, car pour moi je n'aurais jamais cru que *marababa sahem* eût voulu dire: 'Ah! que je suis amoureux d'elle! [...] Voilà une langue admirable que ce turc!

(IV, iii)[32]

MONSIEUR JOURDAIN

Marababa sahem *means 'Ah! How I love her'?*

COVIELLE

Yes.

MONSIEUR JOURDAIN

Heavens! you were right to tell me that, for I would never have believed myself that Marababa sahem *meant 'Ah! How I love her!' {...} What an admirable language is this Turkish!*

Molière sometimes expressed reservations about the publication and reading of his plays, observing that the printed record betrayed the stage reality. This is nowhere more evident than in a masterpiece such as this, where the roles are dismantled before our eyes and reassembled from the simple maladroit movements, barely articulated sounds, and a gobbledegook language which signifies nothing. Molière's anti-hero, Jourdain, is the comic celebration of a refined society, which needed all its finesse to follow the intricate clumsiness of the actor. With *Le Bourgeois gentilhomme* Molière combined the celebration of the art of the theatre with the creation of the most fantastical of his comic characters, happily enshrined in the theatrical form best fitted for the play of fantasy, the *comédie-ballet*.

Part 3

A POLITE AUDIENCE

10

THE TOWN PLAYHOUSE AT THE PALAIS-ROYAL

On 11 October 1660, Molière and his Italian colleagues faced eviction from the Petit-Bourbon theatre when Ratabon, the superintendent of the King's buildings, summarily ordered its demolition. The King seems to have been sympathetic to the plight of his actors, for he granted them Richelieu's old theatre in what was now the Palais-Royal, and moreover, he ordered his superintendent to undertake repairs in the *Grande Salle* where they would perform, for, as La Grange records, three beams were rotten and half of the hall was 'uncovered'. It was for the actors to fit out the space themselves.

Unusually in the *Grande Salle* (there was a smaller theatre) there was a permanent rake: twenty-seven stone steps, each twenty-three inches deep, ran across the body of the rectangular hall, with a gradient of almost 1:4 providing improved sight-lines for spectators in a central tier of seats, the *'amphithéâtre'*.[1] The arrangement suited Richelieu's court audience which was accustomed to the construction of raked seating positioned around the monarch, particularly to give a view of the scenic stage and its changes. Such an audience is aware of precedence, but enjoys a relative freedom of association, all the more necessary on the narrow benches of the narrow rake, and in the upper and lower galleries which ran the length of the side walls, and which were not subdivided into *loges* as in the public theatre. An illustration of Richelieu entertaining Louis XIII and his family at a performance of the *Ballet de la prosperité des armes de France* in 1641, the year the large theatre opened, shows the fine ceiling painted in *trompe l'oeil*, and the proscenium arch, identical with that in the della Bella engravings for *Mirame* which opened the theatre the same year. The artist does not include a platform on which the King and Queen might have been seated, but sets their chairs on the flat floor of the usual court dancing space, giving no indication of the steps.[2]

However other evidence makes clear that at this event spectators sat in an *amphithéâtre* and, for the ballet, a bridge flanked by peacocks came forward to allow the Queen to cross directly from a scaffold, which bore the throne, to the stage itself. Whatever modifications had been made to the rake, a level dancing floor was not among them, and a special effect was required to create a space for the ball. Without a clear dancing area, the *Grande Salle* was designed, not for the forms of the old *ballet de cour*, but for the staging of *comédies*, plays, the writing of which the Cardinal did so much to encourage.

What then did Molière's company do with this dilapidated court theatre? If it was tempted to experiment with the scenic potential of the new hall, which had been the theatre of Torelli, the stage engineer for *Les Fâcheux*,[3] its immediate objective was to re-open, and to recreate its usual auditorium (see Figure 10.1). This followed the familiar model of the *jeu-de-paume* or tennis-court theatre, which they had exploited at two locations during the abortive 1643–1645 period in Paris, and which they would have encountered in the towns and cities of France during the years of provincial touring. The form of these courts was conveniently similar to that of a hall in a great house, being rectangular and measuring 17 *toises* by 6 *toises* (a *toise* being equivalent to 6 ft). Staging and playing were adapted to the demands of this narrow house and the end-on stage which was easily erected. The space favoured the actor, playing at some 50 ft from the

Figure 10.1   Abraham Bosse: A theatre interior around 1630. *Courtesy of the Bibliothèque nationale, Paris*

most distant spectators. In the public theatre the area immediately before the stage was devoted to a *parterre*, or pit, housing a large number of standing spectators, around which elevated positions allowed a wealthier section of the public to enjoy both a view of the performance and a degree of social segregation.

Such was their haste that the actors were obliged to improvise, even after the repairs ordered by the King. The dilapidation had presumably affected the ceiling and its supporting timbers, and it was presumably in this sense that the hall was 'uncovered', rather than being actually exposed to the elements. At all events, when the timbers were restored, a canvas was rigged in place of a ceiling, which was finally installed only when a further alteration of the auditorium was carried out by the troupe in 1671. The prime concern of the company in 1660 was to create a space which was suitable for its audience.

Its town audience required a degree of social separation, and the wealthier members would not wish to enter the level *parterre*, the pit where, for 15 *sous*, patrons stood facing the stage to watch the performance. For those who could pay more, the town playhouse offered one or two tiers of boxes, *loges*, around the three sides of the long rectangular building, with the transverse *loges de fond*, facing the stage, reconciling the demand for privacy and a direct view. Above the *loges* on a second or third level there would be a *galérie*, an undivided tier, which came to be known as *le paradis*, and at this level, built above the *loges de fond*, would be a steeply raked bank of bench seating facing the stage. This was the *amphithéâtre* of the town playhouse.

There is little reason to suppose any ambitious re-thinking of the auditorium at the Palais-Royal. Two contracts were signed by Du Croisy[4] on behalf of the troupe which laid out pressing terms for the *charpentier*, the general builder, who dealt with timber framing, and the *menuisier*, the joiner who was responsible for other woodwork. The contract with the carpenter, Paul Charpentier, dated 18 November 1660, set a deadline of twenty working days for the completion of the new auditorium, to include the dismantling and transportation of the theatre timbers from the Petit-Bourbon. Even so, the new theatre opened only on 20 January 1661.

The size and layout of Molière's Parisian playhouse can be considered with the aid of the November contracts. They indicate an intimate auditorium constructed within a larger hall. (The available width of the Palais-Royal is established by the length of its celebrated cross-beams which were 10 *toises* in length, giving an internal dimension of 9 *toises*, or 54 ft.) The carpenter was to re-construct the Petit-Bourbon interior giving the familiar rows of boxes:

... deux rangs de loges, l'un sur l'autre et un appui au-dessus d'environ trois pieds de haut dont il y aura dix-sept loges à chaque rang, lesquels auront six pieds de mitan en mitan des poteaux du devant desdites loges ...[5]

... two rows of boxes, one above the other and a support above of about 3 ft high, in which there will be seventeen boxes in each tier, which will measure 6 ft from centre to centre of the supporting posts of the front of aforesaid boxes ...

The dimensions of the auditorium are indicated by the boxes, the *loges*, in two tiers of seventeen each. These would be symmetrically distributed around three sides of a rectangle, the fourth of which was the stage opening. The contract helpfully records that the facings for the stage are 30 ft wide, that is 5 *toises*, which establishes the width of the auditorium as equivalent to five *loges de fond* opposite the stage. We then have a rectangular space with 6 *loges* to either side and 5 across, a rectangle measuring 36 ft by 30. This would be a theatre of considerable intimacy. There are, however, two questions which need to be answered, and both relate to the twenty-seven steps, which posed problems to Du Croisy that would not be encountered in adapting a tennis-court with its flat floor.

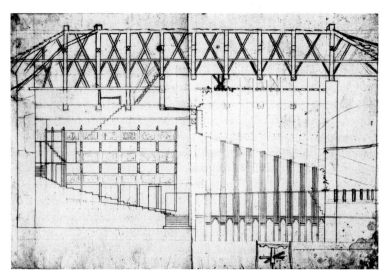

Figure 10.2   Elevation of the Palais Royal theatre in 1673. *Courtesy of the Nationalmuseum, Stockholm*

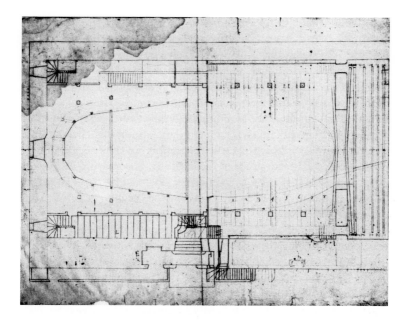

Figure 10.3 Plan of the Palais Royal theatre in 1673. *Courtesy of the Nationalmuseum, Stockholm*

We know from the dimensions of the steps that the depth of Richelieu's auditorium was at least 52½ ft. There was some level area between the bottom of the rake and the steps to the stage shown in the engravings of *Mirame*. With this depth available, would the company not seek to exploit its potential? On the other hand, how would the necessary *parterre* be constructed, given the raked floor? The contracts suggest that the company was not clear, technically, what needed to be done.

Initially, while not specifying the reason, they required the area of the *parterre* to be prepared with hard-core and lime, and provided for retaining walls to be built to support infilling. The contract notes that this new floor rises towards the back. This is then amended by Du Croisy as being '*inutile*'. The reason is clear later from the contract given to Buret. The anxiety to level the steps with hard core is misplaced, since wooden flooring will be sufficient. The rake must then have been boarded over to create a pit, reducing the slope and carrying it forward across the level area in front of the stage. The contract with Buret specifies flooring 'to serve as *parterre*' over the first four *toises*, 24 ft, and to be 6 *toises*, 36 ft, in width. Further up the rake, he was asked to construct a second floor, 5 *toises* deep and 8½ *toises* wide 'or thereabouts'. For this flooring (and for the stage) Buret must provide 'supports'. The stage presumably needed strengthening, or possibly needed to be raised given the presence of spectators standing in a pit. The extra flooring required supports to lift it above the gradient of the rake, and this leads to the conclusion that a wooden construction provided seated positions for spectators in a novel position in a public theatre. The vagueness of the contract as to the width, 'eight and a half *toises* or thereabouts', suggests unfamiliarity with this construction, where flooring would at some point, possibly for the needs of access, reach almost to the side-walls of the building, 9 *toises* apart. An area of raked seating bounded by *loges* on either side, and by the *loges de fond* behind and the *parterre* in front, could only be the new *amphithéâtre* for the remodelled interior.

Some discussions of the auditorium ignore the Buret floor and conclude that the transverse *loges de fond* were constructed no more than 7 *toises* from the stage opening, if not at the 6 *toises* established by the six-side boxes. Were this the case, after the 4 *toises* of the Buret's parterre, 2 (or 3) *toises* would remain for the further 5 *toises* of flooring contracted. This can hardly be correct, especially if we take into account the capacity of the *amphithéâtre*, on exceptional occasions, of 124 spectators.[6] With a maximum width of 30 ft the benches could hardly seat more than fifteen spectators each, and a depth of 12 or even 18 ft would be insufficient for the eight or nine benches required.

Although Du Croisy could have taken his datum-line as the front of the stage and had the boxes constructed backwards from that point, this would have resulted in an under-use of space which was already short. On one estimate of the stage depth, 6½ *toises*, there would remain a total of 60 ft in the hall for the 36 ft of the boxes. The evidence, not least the positioning of the boxes later in the century, suggests on the contrary that they were set back from the stage, and that the datum was the back wall of the house.

How then did Du Croisy ask Charpentier to install the boxes? Richelieu's old house terminated in an arcade possibly giving access to the upper part of the rake. Molière's company had to install the *loges de fond*, which cannot have been very much less than 6 ft in depth, and provide a suitable front-of-house area for access. (These were the boxes where noble and even royal patrons would sit.) It seems reasonable then to assume that Du Croisy would have set the transverse boxes no more than one *toise* on to the rake, using whatever space was available from the old portico for access. The side boxes would then terminate (taking the horizontal measurement of the rake at 52½ ft) ten feet short of the last step of the rake. One should assume at least one *toise* between the foot of the rake and the stage front which then gives a distance of 16 ft between the actor at the edge of the stage and the spectators in the first side boxes. We then have a total disposable depth for *parterre* and *amphithéâtre* of 52 ft horizontally, or 54 ft on the rake, or near to 8½ and 9 *toises* respectively. If four are clearly indicated for the pit, this leaves five for the *amphithéâtre* (the depth required by Buret's contract).

This leads to the conclusion that Du Croisy mistook only the width of the *amphithéâtre* flooring, unused as he was to the fitting out of the interior of a building with an existing sloping floor. This then establishes an *amphithéâtre* of some 30 ft in depth, capable of providing at least ten rows of benches and roomier places, particularly for ladies, for ten to twelve persons, consistent with a maximum recorded attendance of 124. The depth of the auditorium is not, then, 36 but 54 ft.

The existence of this *amphithéâtre* is the clearest innovation in Molière's theatre. At the *Illustre Théâtre*, in common with the Bourgogne and the Marais, the *amphithéâtre* was high above the transverse *loges*. It appears that there was no attempt to develop such seating when the Palais Royal was taken over, and the records of the troupe do not indicate the existence of any second *amphithéâtre*.[7] It is of course possible that the Petit-Bourbon possessed one, but there is no specific mention of any timbers being removed beyond those of the *loges*. Had there been any sort of timber rake for seating, it might have been worthy of mention in La Grange's account of their eviction, and included in the arrangements for the removal of the fittings, to say nothing of the contract for their dismantling, which is careful to establish that the contractor has no right to the planks of the *loges* which belong to Du Croisy. It appears that the division of what had been the *parterre* in the older forms of theatre into two new areas was a combination of the practice of the court theatre with its arrangements for the viewing of spectacle, and the town theatre where the largest number of patrons stood in the *parterre*.

The *amphithéâtre* brought new possibilities of accommodating the audience. The *parterre* spectators, for all their importance to the composition of the house, paid least, 15 *sols*, and custom, modesty and probably the discomfort of standing, let alone the difficulty for persons of small stature to get a good view of the stage, meant that ladies were not seen there.[8] The new *amphithéâtre*, however, increased the number of seats for patrons who were able to pay well (3 *livres*) for a good view of the stage allied to a degree of social separation, essential for women. Persons of both sexes could decently occupy an excellent position, close enough to the acting and well placed for the perspective scenes of the more spectacular shows. Thus in 1672, after the re-equipping of the theatre permitted the staging of *Psyché*, the King's brother and sister-in-law attended a public performance, and chose to sit in the *amphithéâtre*:

> Monsieur et Madame sont venus aujourd'hui à Psyché et ont eu deux bancs de l'amphithéâtre et, pour cette fois et deux autres, ils ont donné 440 livres qui ont été mise dans les mains de Monsieur de Molière.[9]

> *Monsieur and Madame came today to Psyché and took two benches in the amphitheatre and, for this occasion and two others, they gave 440 livres which were placed in the hands of Monsieur de Molière.*

The position of the *amphithéâtre* could scarcely be bettered, but the audience would pay more for the *premières loges*, 5 *livres* 10 *sols* and even more, a *demi-louis*, or 10 *livres*, for one of the thirty-two[10] seats upon Molière's stage. (On the other hand the higher *loges* were markedly cheaper, at 1 *livre* 10 *sols*, or 1 *livre*, when a third tier of loges were added in 1671.) At a later stage, after Molière's death, the price of the *premières loges* was reduced to 3 *livres* also, perhaps indicating a shift in taste with proximity to the actors being balanced against the pleasure of the symmetrical view of the scene. The stage seats, on the other hand, remained popular and were reduced only by ten *sols*. It was still better to be seen than to see.[11]

It is notable that the royal visitors to *Psyché* in 1671 sat in the *amphithéâtre* for a machine-play.[12] The scene itself was all-important and the formations of the dancing were best enjoyed if viewed symmetrically from the front.[13] For comedies and tragedies, the boxes nearer the stage and the stage seats permitted even closer contact with the actors and a desirable exposure to other members of the audience.

To theatre-goers of the present age the idea of the on-stage spectator is difficult to accept, particularly inasmuch as he[14] sat against the scenery which set the imagined location of the play. The effect has to be considered in terms of the original theatre, whose limitations were familiar to its audience. There were protests about the encumbrance to the stage, but it was a practice that continued well into the next century. Tallemant des Réaux complained in the 1640s about what he seemed to regard as a comparatively recent fashion.

There is at the moment an appalling nuisance at the play; it is that the two sides of the stage are full of young men seated on straw chairs; this comes from their unwillingness to go into the *parterre*, although there are often soldiers at the door, and no longer pages nor lackeys carry swords. The boxes are very expensive, and one must think to have one early: for an *écu*, or for a *demi-louis*, one may be upon the stage; but this spoils everything, and sometimes it requires only one insolent fellow to spoil everything.[15]

Molière recognised the comic potential of the nuisance when he sketched the portrait of the theatre bore among his *Fâcheux*, with some delightful exaggeration for comic effect. Éraste describes his late arrival upon the stage, interrupting the actors, and how he calls for a chair, and then sets it, not reasonably to the side, but in the middle of the stage blocking the view of three-quarters of the *parterre*. He then plays out unwittingly, and to the great embarrassment of Éraste, what is a comedy to the audience. A similar figure is created in *La Critique de l'École des femmes*, where the debate turns on social status, and the judgement of different classes of theatre-goer. Here the *extravagant* distinguishes himself by refusing to enjoy the play which amuses the *parterre*. Dorante and the Marquis discuss the success of *L'École des femmes*:

LE MARQUIS
Il ne faut que voir les continuels éclats de rire que le parterre y fait. Je ne veux point d'autre chose pour témoigner que la pièce ne vaut rien.

DORANTE
Tu es donc, Marquis, de ces messieurs du bel air qui ne veulent point que le parterre ait du sens commun, et seraient fâchés d'avoir ri avec lui, fût-ce de la meilleure chose du monde? Je vis l'autre jour sur le théâtre un de nos amis, qui se rendit ridicule par-là. Il écouta toute la pièce avec un sérieux le plus sombre du monde; et ce qui égayait les autres ridait son front. À tous les éclats de rire, il haussait les épaules, et regardait le parterre avec pitié; et quelquefois aussi le regardant avec dépit, il lui disait tout haut: Ris donc, parterre, ris donc. Ce fut une seconde comédie que le chagrin de notre ami. Il la donna en galant homme à toute l'assemblée, et chacun demeura d'accord qu'on ne pouvait pas mieux jouer qu'il ne fit.[16]

THE MARQUIS

*You need only see how the parterre continually bursts out laughing.
I desire nothing other to demonstrate that the play is worthless.*

DORANTE

You are then, Marquis, one of those fashionable gentlemen who cannot accept that the parterre has common sense, and who would be angry had they joined in its laughter, were it at the best thing in the world? I saw on the stage the other day one of our friends who made himself ridiculous in exactly this way. He listened to the play in the most sombre and serious manner imaginable; and everything that delighted the others brought a frown to his forehead. At every laugh he shrugged his shoulders, and looked down on the parterre with pity; and sometimes also, looking at them with scorn, he would say out loud: 'Go on, laugh, wretched parterre, go on, laugh!'. This was a second comedy, our friend's distemper. He acted it generously for the whole assembly, and everyone agreed that nobody could act better than he did.

In creating a comic portrait Molière touched on an unavoidable aspect of the stage spectator: he was representative of the audience, and his presence showed the artificiality of the performance. Self-important behaviour, particularly in the privileged spectator, breaks the unwritten contract which binds together the disparate social groups which constitute the audience. It is notable that Molière, who can hardly be regarded as pursuing any sort of populist agenda, is sensitive to the comedy of the man who destroys the cohesion of an audience. Dorante reproves the marquis for thinking that common sense is indicated by the price of the ticket, fifteen *sols* or a *demi-louis*. While there are ridiculous characters at court, there are far more among the self-declared connoisseurs: the courtier is as good a judge, and better than the pedants and the authors who disapprove of plays they are incapable of writing. Moreover, Molière was fortified by the knowledge that the King himself had attended a performance of *L'École des femmes* in the Palais-Royal.[17]

Molière's theatre had a form which, for all its disadvantages, assembled an audience which was socially diverse, and where the distinctions of class were displayed. The house was lit, so that actors could see spectators, and spectators could see one another. The accounts of the day remark on the pleasure given at various entertainments by artificial light and the agreeable effect it had on costume and complexion. The shimmering illumination of torches outdoors and the different qualities of candles indoors graced any assembly, and especially those for whom their costume and appearance were a matter of almost professional occupation and pride. Mademoiselle de Montpensier notes drily that on the occasion of the performance of Molière's *La Comtesse d'Escarbagnas*, Madame, the King's sister-in-law, looked better by the lights of the *ballet* than she did by daylight.[18]

The lighting of the room and the positioning of the spectators joined stage and auditorium in the creation of a shared illusion. Molière's audience was keenly aware of the collective reception of the play, and of its own function in sustaining the drama. It had, in the opinion of Molière himself, the most considerable effect on the nature and the quality of the work which he made for it.

11

THE POLITE AUDIENCE

The audience for Molière's plays was not large but it was influential, dominated by those able to afford an expensive entertainment, and who publicly demonstrated, by their presence at the play, enjoyment and approval of a pastime which elsewhere was criticized. The actors, being exposed to public censure, needed all the more the approval of this knowledgeable, committed audience. Playing before the court in the *Impromptu de Versailles*, Molière recognizes that such patronage imposes the heaviest responsibility on the playwright.

> Et pensez-vous que ce soit une petite affaire que d'exposer quelque chose de comique devant une assemblée comme celle-ci, que d'entreprendre de faire rire des personnes qui nous impriment le respect, et qui ne rient que quand ils veulent?
>
> (Sc. i)[1]

> *And do you think that it is a small matter to present something comical before an assembly like this one, to undertake to make persons laugh who demand our respect, and who laugh only when they wish?*

It is curious to imagine these persons of quality being inclined to govern their amusement, or even being capable of so doing. Yet in this society Molière could suggest that decorum was more precious than laughter. When Meredith explained 'the comic spirit' in Molière, a quality we might equate with the seventeenth-century concept of *le ridicule*, he distinguished the mental pleasure of comedy from the mere fact of laughter.[2] The 'agelast', the excessive laugher, was to Meredith a poor creature with no special sense of the comic. On the other hand, he saw the fine laughter of the connoisseur as being founded on judgement, and sensitivity to the moral and formal properties of human action, an argument we find also in the *Lettre sur l'Imposteur*. In both cases aesthetics are linked to the refinement of a given society in explaining the social function of comedy. Meredith, with hindsight, saw Molière's society as all-important in allowing comedy to flourish: men and women living together brilliantly, neither puritanical nor licentious, yet highly aware of the moral character of their lives.

Molière's audience was drawn from an educated urban class isolated from the hardships borne in the country at large, and enjoying the security of a degree of civil peace and military victory abroad. It embraced its good fortune and celebrated its prosperity under a young and attractive monarch, the living symbol of the civilizing pleasures to which it felt entitled.

The rising bourgeois and the urbanized noble enjoyed a society whose rituals and practices grew in sophistication. Increasingly the aristocracy was separated morally and politically from its material base in the provincial estate, much as the bourgeoisie gradually detached itself from the source of its wealth in actual trade, and from the commodities and skills of its professions. The more that men and women moved away from the concrete realities of daily life, the more they moved in an abstracted world, at liberty to reflect upon the business of living together, and to idealize their achievements. It was a society which valued personal quality and distinction, and pursued them in both theory and practice. They were the natural attributes of birth and position, but required exercise in society to manifest the conduct which engendered esteem.

A study of social accomplishment, almost a science of living, emerged in the concept of the *honnête homme*, characterized by *savoir-faire* as much as by virtue, in whom ethics were manifest in conduct, bearing and action. *Honnête* was the epithet which signalled social accomplishment in dress, manners or conversation, and explained the individual's ability to please. It guided social consciousness and a thoughtful engagement with the roles and relationships of gender, class, religion and politics, affording an ethical centre to the practices which make up complex social interactions. The principle does not solve specific problems of practice but underlines the systemic functioning of the social being and the necessary relationship of behaviour and circumstances.

It was an ideal whose manifestations need careful distillation to convey the spirit rather than a sometimes contradictory reality. The Chevalier de Méré, born in 1607 but reflecting in his chief writings of the 1680s the attitudes of Molière's day, was prominent among them. His declaration is typical of many contemporary theorists: *honnêteté* escapes all definition, being 'quelque chose d'inexplicable qui se connaît mieux à le voir pratiquer qu'à le dire (*something beyond explanation which can be known better when it is seen practised than when we speak of it*)'.[3] Identifying behaviour with ethics, the power of the term in contemporary ideology was formidable, most of all in formulating criticism of exaggeration or ignorance.

For the enemies of the stage, with its unseemly and depraved farces, an *honnête homme* could never be an actor. After Molière's death an apologist disavowed the actor's desire to maintain his profession at all, and contrasted his daily life and true inclinations as being *honnête*.

> Molière declaimed as an actor in the theatre and elsewhere, but he conversed as a gentleman [*honnête homme*]; in a word, there was nothing to be held against him but his profession, which he continued more for the profit of his fellows than for his own.[4]

However, there is a deeper problem when the role is the simulacrum or perhaps the epitome of *honnêteté*. We have seen how Molière conceived the tragic actor embodying elevated sentiments in presentation and delivery, without affectation or excess, much as would be expected of the *honnête homme* in society. This easy integration of the performance was paralleled by a greater achievement in the comedy, where *honnête* behaviour was adopted and as artfully relinquished in the comic role. The kinship of the actor and the *honnête homme* is paradoxically a key to Molière's understanding of the function of acting, and helps to explain the importance of contemporary ideas and behaviour for the creation of his comedy.

We see in the rehearsal and execution of the role a process of study and assembly. The actor derives from the bare text the elements of human interaction: mental and physical rhythms, objectives and actions, persuasive speech, and considered interaction, and these are to be brought together under the watchful eye of the socially aware spectator. This symbolic enactment reconstitutes personality as it would be experienced by the society of the time. Sensitive to the performative aspects of social reality, Molière's spectators were likely to be effective collaborators in the difficult art of comedy, and receptive to the symbolic reintegration of personality in the art of the actor.

Molière accommodated a genre characterized by its realism, to a society guided by an ideal. *Honnêteté* procured the greatest of social benefits: self-esteem, and the charge that a play was unfit for *les hon-nêtes gens* was seriously damaging. This was no puritanical clique but, by definition, the whole of good society, and in defending his comedy, Molière appealed to his audience as his natural collaborators. His stage was to be the mirror in which they recognized their age. This was tactically what he accentuated in *La Critique de L'École des femmes* by putting fair-minded and modest advocates, *honnêtes gens*, as characters (and of course actors) upon the stage of the Palais-Royal, addressing directly questions of taste and decency: *honnêteté* in the theatre. Dorante speaks for Molière when he links this moral quality in his audience with an equivalent aesthetic finesse in the play, and returns to the difficulty of an art which can please *les honnêtes gens*, the polite audience.

> Lorsque vous peignez les héros, vous faites ce que vous voulez. Ce sont des portraits à plaisir, où l'on ne cherche point de ressemblance; et vous n'avez qu'à suivre les traits d'une imagination qui se donne l'essor, et qui souvent laisse le vrai pour attraper le merveilleux. Mais lorsque vous peignez les hommes, il faut peindre d'après nature. On veut que ces portraits ressemblent; et vous n'avez rien fait, si vous n'y faites reconnaître les gens de votre siècle. En un mot, dans les pièces sérieuses, il suffit pour n'être point blâmé, de dire des choses qui soient de bon sens et bien écrites; mais ce n'est pas assez dans les autres, il y faut plaisanter; et c'est une étrange entreprise que celle de faire rire les honnêtes gens.
>
> (Sc. vi)[5]

> *When you depict heroes, you do as you please. These are portraits from invention, where we do not look for likenesses; and you have only to follow the strokes of a lofty imagination which often abandons the truth to seize the marvellous. But when you depict men, you must follow nature. We want likeness in these portraits; and you have done nothing if you do not make us recognize in them people of the day. In a word, in serious plays all you need to do to escape criticism is to say things which are good sense and well written, but it is not enough in others; there you must amuse and set laughing a polite company.*

When his plays were attacked, *honnêteté* animated the discussion. Boursault, the author of the malicious, but informative, satire *Le Portrait du peintre*, suggests in one of his *Lettres nouvelles* that in *Le*

Malade imaginaire Béralde's witty rebuke to Monsieur Fleuron the apothecary[6] was originally an evident *obscenité* (a new term, but enthusiastically adopted in the condemnation of Molière's plays). As Monsieur Fleuron approaches with his clyster to purge the bowels of his patient, Béralde intervenes:

> ... l'honnête homme répondit à l'apothicaire. Allez, Monsieur, allez, on voit bien que vous avez coutume de ne parler qu'à des culs. (Pardon, Monseigneur, si ce mot m'échappe; je ne le dis que pour le faire mieux condamner.) Tous les auditeurs qui étaient à la première représentation s'en indignèrent, au lieu qu'on fut ravi à la seconde d'entendre: Allez, Monsieur, allez, on voit bien que vous n'avez pas coutume de parler à des visages. C'est dire la même chose et la dire bien plus finement.[7]

> ... *the gentleman replied to the apothecary. Come, Sir, come, we can well see that you are accustomed to speak only to arses. (I beg pardon, my lord, if I allow the word to escape my lips; I say this only the better to have it condemned.) All those listening at the first performance were indignant, whereas they were delighted at the second to hear: Come, Sir, come, we can well see that you are not accustomed to speak to faces. This is to say the same thing and to say it with greater finesse.*

The implication is that Molière lacked the necessary propriety of the *honnête homme*, and was somehow forced into it by the greater refinement and, not without relevance, the wit, of his audience. In all the polemics which surrounded Molière's career, the charge is never distant, even when his genius is recognized, that he is the author of vulgar works such as *Les Fourberies de Scapin*, made expressly for 'the people' in his first biographer's view. The play occasioned the much-quoted rebuke from his friend Boileau who could not recognize in Scapin's sack the author of *Le Misanthrope*.

> Etudiez la cour, et connoissez la ville.
> L'une et l'autre est toujours en modèles fertile.
> C'est par là que Molière illustrant ses écrits
> Peut-être de son art eût remporté le prix;
> Si moins ami du peuple en ses doctes peintures,
> Il n'eût point fait souvent grimacer ses figures,
> Quitté pour le bouffon, l'agréable et le fin,
> Et sans honte à Terence allié Tabarin.

Dans ce sac ridicule où Scapin s'envelope,
Je ne reconnais plus l'auteur du Misanthrope.[8]

Study the court and learn to known the town.
One and other are always fertile in models.
By these means, Molière, illustrating his writings,
Might perhaps have carried off the prize of Comedy;
If allied less to the people in his learned portraiture,
He had not often made the faces grimace,
For clowning abandoned the fine and pleasant,
And coupled shamelessly Terence and Tabarin.
In that ridiculous sack where Scapin hides himself,
I can no longer recognise the author of The Misanthrope.

Molière's enemies were all the more eager to denounce any lack of taste or decency as proof of the indissoluble link between comedy and the gutter.

The ideals of the age were nonetheless the yardstick against which Molière measured his work, whatever the style, and however delicate or indelicate the treatment. He reflects contemporary living and engages an expert audience of *honnêtes gens* to judge according to their social ethos. To this audience extravagant conduct was as fascinating as good behaviour was estimable, and the theatre was the exercise where the flawed instance could be examined in practice. The parallel social attitudes of the two brothers in *L'École des maris* are presented almost as an experiment, where Sganarelle's inflexible approach to marriage and to his fiancée is contrasted with the practical wisdom of his brother Ariste, the *honnête homme* in the piece. Sganarelle has few pretensions to *honnêteté*, still less to *galanterie*, and his behaviour offends accepted standards. (The instance was well known enough to be cited and dismissed as 'feeble' by Alceste in *Le Misanthrope*.)[9] Ariste, although the older brother, promotes the idea of a gentle conformity to the sensible and pleasant forms of society, while Sganarelle's rigidity extends from dress to the teaching of morals by means of lock and key. Ariste desires his young bride to learn virtue by practising it in the world, an essentially *honnête* standpoint:

ARISTE

J'ai souffert qu'elle ait vu les belles compagnies,
Les divertissements, les bals, les comédies;
Ce sont choses, pour moi, que je tiens de tous temps

Fort propres à former l'esprit des jeunes gens;
Et l'école du monde, en l'air dont il faut vivre
Instruit mieux, à mon gré, que ne fait aucun livre.

(I, ii, ll. 187–192)[10]

> *ARISTE*
> *I have allowed her to see fine company,*
> *Entertainments, balls, plays;*
> *These are things, as far as I'm concerned, that I have always considered*
> *Most apt to form the minds of young people;*
> *And the school of society, in whose air we must live*
> *Teaches better, to my mind, than any book.*

The play is a moral exemplum: the girl who is shut up misbehaves, and the one who frequents good entertaining society proves dutiful. Moreover, as Ariste insists, attendance at the playhouse is one way in which she learns her good behaviour.

Lock and key reappear in *L'École des femmes* where a character who is apparently better accommodated to the polite world[11] errs in trying to sequester his chosen bride from society where virtues are durable because they are exercised, not memorized as so many precepts. The plays reflect an important characteristic of *honnêteté*: it is a moral code embedded in the real world, where the forms of behaviour aspire to the condition of a moral presentation. If *honnêteté* is most at home in the salon, its practice permeates everywhere, even in the potentially violent oppositions of society, as in duelling, a practice which the state attempted to eradicate. Against this background Molière could make comedy from courteous violence, as in *Le Mariage forcé* where instruction in good behaviour is given to Sganarelle by his fiancée's relatives. As absurd as may be the challenge to a duel delivered with exquisite courtesy, this is followed by the beating which is administered by the gentlemen who are driven reluctantly to regrettable extremes, when their challenge is not taken up.[12] The savour of such a scene is not lost on an audience pursuing refinement in the face of the brutal realities of the age. Madame de Motteville recalls the Marquis de la Trousse, whose civility was undiminished in the duel, where he was wont to pay compliments to his adversary:

> ... lorsqu'il donnait de bons coups à son ennemi, il disait qu'il était fâché, et parmi ces douceurs, il donnait la mort aussi hardiment que le plus brutal des hommes.[13]

> *... when he struck home, he said to his enemy that he was vexed to do so, and among these civilities, he dispensed death as boldly as the most brutal of men.*

Such contradictions are systematically enlarged in Molière where the force of the social ideal is felt in the excesses of the comic subject. We see ignorance or refusal of good standards or practices; or, where these are known, we see the ideal ill-digested or abused, resulting in some mutilated understanding: affectation or obsession. The spectacle of the would-be *honnête* character has a particular charm for the audience whose knowledge of both manners and morals permits a superior perception of the deficiencies they behold. We may recall that the *Lettre sur L'Imposteur* saw in this experience the source of *ridicule*.[14]

In the case of a succession of plays for court festivities from 1668 onwards, Molière treated his audience to creations of extravagant and fantastical ineptitude. Manners of address are expounded by the Monsieur and Madame de Sotenville in *George Dandin*, every inch the provincial snobs:

GEORGE DANDIN

Puisqu'il faut donc parler catégoriquement, je vous dirai, Monsieur de Sotenville, que j'ai lieu de ...

MONSIEUR DE SOTENVILLE

Doucement, mon gendre. Apprenez qu'il n'est pas respectueux d'appeler les gens par leur nom, et qu'à ceux qui sont au-dessus de nous il faut dire – Monsieur – tout court.

GEORGE DANDIN

Hé bien! Monsieur, tout court, et non plus Monsieur de Sotenville, j'ai à vous dire que ma femme me donne ...

MONSIEUR DE SOTENVILLE

Tout beau! Apprenez aussi que vous ne devez pas dire – ma femme – quand vous parlez de notre fille.

GEORGE DANDIN

J'enrage. Comment? Ma femme n'est pas ma femme?

MADAME DE SOTENVILLE

Oui, notre gendre, elle est votre femme, mais il ne vous est pas permis de l'appeler ainsi ...

(I, iv)[15]

GEORGE DANDIN

Since it is necessary to speak in plain terms, I shall say to you, Monsieur de Sotenville, that I have reason to ...

MONSIEUR DE SOTENVILLE

Steady on, son-in-law. You must learn that it is not respectful to call persons by their names, and to those who are above us we must say – Monsieur – simply.

GEORGE DANDIN

Well! Monsieur, simply, and no longer Monsieur de Sotenville, I have to tell you that my wife gives me ...

MONSIEUR DE SOTENVILLE

Hold on! You must learn also that you must not say – my wife – when you speak of our daughter.

GEORGE DANDIN

This drives me mad. What? My wife is not my wife?

MADAME DE SOTENVILLE

Yes, son-in-law, she is your wife, but you are not permitted to call her so ...

Manners are indeed a matter of class and position, but *honnêteté* eschews overbearing insistence of this kind, and requires both knowledge and discretion. The absurdity of the social climber or the snob is equally risible, claiming those qualities which should be tacit, inherent in manners, dress or conversation. The costume and appearance of Molière's Monsieur de Pourceaugnac in the *comédie-ballet* of 1669 signals his ridiculous position in polite society, and the naïvety which is exploited by the obvious rogue Sbrigani. The newcomer denounces the 'foolish town' which laughs at him and which Sbrigani decries for its lack of consideration for *les honnêtes gens*. Sbrigani's manners are those of the theatre entertainer, sharing the comedy with a complicit audience. His dupe is a social clown incapable of the subtle understanding bred of politeness.

SBRIGANI

Je vous l'ai déjà dit: du moment que je vous ai vu, je me suis senti pour vous de l'inclination.

MONSIEUR DE POURCEAUGNAC

Je vous suis obligé.

182

SBRIGANI

Votre physiognomie m'a plu.

MONSIEUR DE POURCEAUGNAC

Ce m'est beaucoup d'honneur.

SBRIGANI

J'y ai vu quelque chose d'honnête.

MONSIEUR DE POURCEAUGNAC

Je suis votre serviteur.

SBRIGANI

Quelque chose d'admirable.

MONSIEUR DE POURCEAUGNAC

Ah! Ah!

(I, iv)[16]

SBRIGANI

I have said already: from the moment that I saw you, I felt myself drawn to you.

MONSIEUR DE POURCEAUGNAC

I am much obliged.

SBRIGANI

I liked your physiognomy.

MONSIEUR DE POURCEAUGNAC

You do me too much honour.

SBRIGANI

I saw in your features a certain gentility.

MONSIEUR DE POURCEAUGNAC

I am your servant.

SBRIGANI

Something admirable.

MONSIEUR DE POURCEAUGNAC

Ah! Ah!

The absurd inventory of Pourceaugnac's *honnête* characteristics provokes wordless, and senseless, gasps of pleasure, the inverse of social accomplishment. The appeal to the court audience culminates in the reference to the Louvre and the King. Pourceaugnac has dressed *à la mode de la cour*:

183

SBRIGANI

Ma foi! cela vous va mieux qu'à tous nos courtisans.

MONSIEUR DE POURCEAUGNAC

C'est ce que m'a dit mon tailleur: l'habit est propre et riche,
et il fera du bruit ici.

SBRIGANI

Sans doute. N'irez-vous pas au Louvre?

MONSIEUR DE POURCEAUGNAC

Il faudra bien aller faire ma cour.

SBRIGANI

Le Roi sera ravi de vous voir.

MONSIEUR DE POURCEAUGNAC

Je le crois.

(I, iv) [17]

SBRIGANI

My word! That suits you better than any of our courtiers.

MONSIEUR DE POURCEAUGNAC

*That is what my tailor said: the costume is choice and richly made,
and will cause a stir here.*

SBRIGANI

No doubt of it. Will you not go to the Louvre?

MONSIEUR DE POURCEAUGNAC

I must indeed go and pay court.

SBRIGANI

The King will be enchanted to see you.

MONSIEUR DE POURCEAUGNAC

I think he will.

For the audience of *La Comtesse d'Escarbagnas* the pleasure of the
ballet is framed by the comedy of provincial suitors competing for
the hand of the unlikely 'comtesse', with an *honnête homme*, le
Vicomte, who, unknown to all, arranges the dancing for the forbid-
den, but *honnête*, Julie. As in *Le Bourgeois gentilhomme* the ignorance
of the upstart is the opportunity for a superior to press his own suit.
This deception is a falling away from even a pragmatic *honnêteté*,
but is on the other hand the theatrical means of locating the

courtly ballet amusingly in the context of a bourgeois or provincial assembly. The stratagem of the aristocratic deceiver leads the revels to a happy consummation in marriage or ennoblement, and to the ballet which brings the courtly spectator into the embrace of the fantasy.

The significance of *honnêteté* on Molière's stage lies in the blending of elements whose integration is manifest in a style of behaviour, where a guiding sense transcends particular social practices. Style expressed the condition of coherence and meaning which lay in the proper and seemingly effortless integration of elements whether in conversation, or dancing, or the composition of a sonnet. We may recall how important it is for an Oronte as the *honnête homme* to establish that the fruit of his genius has been picked at moments of occasional leisure. Trissotin, the salon hack of *Les Femmes savantes* has rather more of the pedant about him, like his admirers who cannot wear their learning lightly. Molière reduces the affected, and modish, speech of the ladies to a farmyard cackle.

PHILAMINTE

On se sent à ces vers, jusques au fond de l'âme
Couler je ne sais quoi qui fait que l'on se pâme.

ARMANDE

'Faites-la sortir, quoi qu'on die,
De votre riche appartement.'
Que 'riche appartement' est joliment dit!
Et que la métaphore est mis avec esprit!

PHILAMINTE

'Faites-la sortir, quoi qu'on die',
Ah! que ce 'quoi qu'on die' est d'un goût admirable!
C'est, à mon sentiment, un endroit impayable!

ARMANDE

De 'quoi qu'on die' aussi mon coeur est amoureux.

BELISE

Je suis de votre avis, quoi 'qu'on die' est heureux.

ARMANDE

Je voudrais l'avoir fait.

BELISE

Il vaut toute une pièce.

185

PHILAMINTE

Mais comprend-on bien, comme moi, la finesse?

ARMANDE ET BELISE

Oh, oh!

(III, ii, ll. 778–788)[18]

PHILAMINTE

One feels, to hear these verses, flowing down to the depths of the soul
A certain je ne sais quoi *that brings me close to fainting.*

ARMANDE

'Drive it out, whatever may be said,
From your rich lodging.'
How 'rich lodging' is prettily said!
And how the metaphor is wittily turned!

PHILAMINTE

'Drive it out, whatever may be said',
Ah! that 'whatever may be said' is in admirable taste
It is, to my mind, a priceless passage!

ARMANDE

My heart too is in love with 'whatever may be said'.

BELISE

I am of your view, 'whatever may be said' is happy.

ARMANDE

I would I had written it.

BELISE

It is worth a whole play.

PHILAMINTE

But do you understand, as I do, its subtlety?

ARMANDE ET BELISE

Oh, oh!

The refinement which the three *femmes savantes* seek is something
understood, a sense of the subtle blending of these literary elements
into the indefinable *je ne sais quoi* which constitutes the essence of
style. Molière's comedy ruthlessly disaggregates the whole in a parody of *honnête* responses, and exposes the absurd and affected conceits
of the poetaster and his acolytes. Style as the condition of coherence

explains some of Molière's most distinctive comedy, where matter and manner are at odds: the absurd inelegance of Alceste's love for the worldly Célimène, the pomposity of the masterful Arnolphe, the dangerous insinuation of the theological image in Tartuffe's pursuit of Elmire, or the vain *amour-propre* of Dom Juan's defiance of God.

In his more rumbustious moments Molière uses the comic contrast of style between characters of different classes to dismantle notions of good behaviour. The parallelism of the sets of lovers in *Le Malade imaginaire* is a case in point, as in *Le Dépit amoureux*, where Gros-René presses his suit in a pastiche of *galanterie*. In *L'École des femmes* the servants' expressive but unseemly metaphors of 'soup' and 'fingers' parallel the bogus heroics of Arnolphe's pursuit of his bourgeois honour. Faced with the extravagant behaviour of Arnolphe, his servants struggle to master the niceties of behaviour, in particular the delicate question of sexual jealousy, which is far from *galant* in the explanations that Alain gives Georgette:

ALAIN

C'est que la jalousie … entends-tu bien, Georgette,
Est une chose … là … qui fait qu'on s'inquiète …
Et qui chasse les gens d'autour d'une maison.
Je m'en vais te bailler une comparaison,
Afin de concevoir la chose davantage.
Dis-moi, n'est-il pas vrai, quand tu tiens ton potage,
Que si quelque affamé venait pour en manger,
Tu serais en colère, et voudrais le charger?

GEORGETTE

Oui, je comprends cela.

ALAIN

C'est justement tout comme:
La femme est en effet le potage de l'homme;
Et quand un homme voit d'autres hommes parfois
Qui veulent dans sa soupe aller tremper leurs doigts,
Il en montre aussitôt une colère extrême.

GEORGETTE

Oui; mais pourquoi chacun n'en fait-il pas de même,
Et que nous en voyons qui paraissent joyeux
Lorsque leurs femmes sont avec les biaux Monsieur.

(II, iii, ll. 427–442)[19]

ALAIN

The reason is that jealousy ... now, understand this well,
Georgette,
Is such a thing ... you see ... that makes a person edgy.
It chases away the folks from round about the house.
I am going to give you a comparison,
So you may better get the hang of the thing.
Tell me, is it not true, when you are holding your soup,
That if some hungry chap came along and tried to eat it,
You would get angry, and like to thump him?

GEORGETTE

Yes, I understand that.

ALAIN

This is just the same thing:
Basically the woman is the man's bowl of soup;
And when a man at times sees other men
Who mean to dip their fingers in his soup
Upon the spot he gets extremely angry.

GEORGETTE

Yes, but why does everyone not do the same
For we do see plenty who seem quite happy
When their ladies go off with the handsome gents.

Such rude observations on the nature and practice of sexual love serve to confirm the position of the worldly audience which laughs at the clumsy but morally aware debates of the menials. The scenes between Charlotte and Pierrot in *Dom Juan* turn on the contrast of style in behaviour between these lovers, with the boy complaining of the absence in the cow-shed of love-play appropriate to true feeling, and the nobleman adopting a veneer of style to seduce the naïve Charlotte.

DOM JUAN

Haussez un peu la tête, de grâce. Ah! que ce visage est mignon! Ouvrez vos yeux entièrement. Ah! qu'ils sont-beaux! Que je vois un peu vos dents, je vous prie. Ah! qu'elles sont amoureuses, et ces lèvres appétissantes. Pour moi, je suis ravi, et je n'ai jamais vu une si charmante personne.

CHARLOTTE

Monsieur, cela vous plaît à dire, et je ne sais pas si c'est pour vous railler de moi.

DOM JUAN

Moi, me railler de vous? Dieu m'en garde! Je vous aime trop pour cela, et c'est du fond du coeur que je vous parle.

(II, ii)[20]

DOM JUAN

Lift your head a little, if you please. Ah! What a dear little face! Open your eyes, wide. Ah! Beautiful! Let me see your teeth, I beg you. Ah! how full of love, and the lips, so appetising! I am overcome, and I have never seen such a charming creature.

CHARLOTTE

Sir, if it please you to say so. But I don't know if you're making fun of me.

DOM JUAN

Make fun of you? Heaven forbid! I love you too much, and I speak from the bottom of my heart.

The lord treats the girl like a beast at market, for all his superiority. The more the Dom departs from the grounds of *honnêteté* and the greater the discrepancies of style and moral standards, the greater the *ridicule* of the lord's wickedness and the victim's gullibility. As he deals with the peasant girls in Molière's inverted *pastorale*, so does the Dom mislead Monsieur Dimanche, his tradesman, in a study of urban politeness. Playing upon *honnête* conceits of honourable servitude to an esteemed person, he cruelly avoids the reality of the subjection of the merchant who cannot elude the forms of politeness and ask for the money he is owed. Style is appropriated to mask deceit, and the outrageous comedy is felt through the formal incoherence, the *forme extérieure et sensible*, of what purports to be *honnête*. Indeed *Dom Juan* is almost as remarkable for social as for theological outrage.

Less dangerous are the subjects where the appropriation of style in manners and dress betrays an obsession with its importance as a marker of status and pedigree. Such are the displays of the *petit marquis*, and to an audience aware of the ideals of *honnêteté* they are clear for what they are: an imperfect and overblown assimilation of fashions. Just as much as the displays of the 'false marquis', the servants in *Les Précieuses ridicules*, they demonstrate a superficial response to the way persons look without any knowledge of the inner content: study without knowledge, that is to say affectation.

Molière's various studies of excess have frequently been seen as satirical, implying an element of moral outrage in the writer and a certain corrective vocation, but the discipline of *honnêteté* works in another direction. For while it is possible to identify the elements in the comic subject which are morally wrong, the plays and the social codes of the time take us further into the study of how behaviour should be constructed and how familiar human errors are manifested and understood in terms of a theory. If one were to see his plays as so many *écoles*, it would be because they are the occasion for dramatic study and understanding, not for the inculcation of a simple moral doctrine. Aberrations stand out against a supple principle of behaviour in characteristic ways. There are those characters who are *fâcheux*, tiresome because they misunderstand. Other characters are more dangerous: they try too hard to get part of the picture right, or may try to redefine what is right. One might term these characters *bricoleurs*, do-it-yourself moralists, contemptuous or ignorant of the shared wisdom of society. There are also those who prey on ignorance and naïvety, with varying degrees of malice or mischief, from Tartuffe to the entourage of Monsieur Jourdain. These are the rogues or *fourbes* whom Molière found in the comic tradition and whom he placed with care in a theatrical and social environment.

Like Arnolphe, who is an *honnête homme* in certain matters, so too is Orgon (while it is Madame Pernelle who is *fâcheuse*). Both pursue a *bricolage* which attempts a re-interpretation of the ethics which underlie accepted behaviour. For Orgon to regard friends and family, in other words, good society, as so much manure, is a poor advertisement for religion and abuses its deeper principles. This is the source of a serious and dangerous comedy, most evident when religion enters into the social scheme. *Dom Juan* the *grand seigneur méchant homme* is the most appalling type of *fourbe*, taking moral qualities and abusing them: the search for independence; libertarianism; a courageous, philosophical approach to life. Molière's hero subverts the forms of decent behaviour, promoting judgment of the distortions which underlie his *fourberies*. These are imagined, abstract reflections of life and not, as Uranie says in the *Critique*, a criticism of individuals. When an audience engages in a playful moral exercise, the recognition which results is of the forms of social life, and only by subsequent reflection may this to be brought to bear upon actual cases.

The notion of *honnêteté* and its powerful role in contemporary culture marks out Molière's audience as one unusually sensitive to the possibilities of drama. To the theatricality of social living was added a practical philosophy which excited men and women to questions of moral integrity, and to the pleasing integration of human capacities in the personality and their expression in the social world. Méré's advice to Madame de Lesdiguières addresses this question in his advocacy of *le bon ordre* in conduct. He chooses as his example a young man incapable of executing a certain dance if he might not approach it as part of a sequence. Méré insists that a performer cannot allow the ordering of physical form to usurp the independence of the integrated personality, for 'l'indépendance est agréable, même dans les exercices (*independence is pleasing, even in the exercise of the dance*)'.[21]

The practices whereby the dancer disciplines and orders the elements of the performance should be, as in all performances in society, so perfectly integrated that they cohere internally, with no expression of effort, nor any obsession with minutiae.

> [Il faut] garder en toutes les choses dont nous disposons un ordre secret et naturel qui les démêle, qui les distingue, et qui les fasse paraître si à propos et si bien placées, que ce soit toujours dans le temps et de la manière qu'on le peut souhaiter.[22]
>
> {*We must*} *keep in all those things in which we engage a secret and natural order, which unfolds them, distinguishes them, and makes them appear so fitting and so well placed that they may be always at the desired time and in the desired manner.*

The striking unification of ethics and pleasure is typical of the culture, and its sensitivity to performance. Moral observance is insufficient unless manifested in the actual world, where the individual undertakes what is fitting, and the world beholds those delightful qualities of apparently unstudied and effortless manners. Méré shrewdly ridicules the man who makes his way in the world by shutting himself in his oratory while the King is at the theatre.

> C'est un moyen bien détourné de faire sa fortune, que de s'enfermer dans un oratoire pendant que le Prince est à la comédie.[23]
>
> *It is a strange way to make a man's fortune, to shut oneself in a chapel, while one's prince is in the playhouse.*

Virtue must be embodied without studied protestations or anything resembling fanaticism. Lest this appear an endorsement of the performance of a Tartuffe, it must be remembered that the King is *ipso facto* a model of *honnêteté*.

We can recognize in this worldly ethic something of the ideas which inform Molière's comedy, but also the principles of behaviour behind his use of the actor and the construction of the individual role. *Bienséance* or propriety, and *agrément*, the pleasing appearance of person or performance, link the inner coherence of performance with the moral and aesthetic expectations and character of the outside world. If, according to Méré, a pretty lady weeps when she is abandoned by a fool, she may do so with *agrément*, but not with *bienséance*. *Honnêteté* prescribes a state of integratedness rather than a prescription of certain rules: whether on the stage or in the salon it calls for the integration of the role within the person of the actor, rather than the playing out of a set of signalled characteristics. An audience which understood and appreciated these matters was vital to Molière, and he wrote for it *Le Misanthrope*, the comedy which embodied the discord of *bienséance* and *agrément*.

12

BEHAVIOUR REVIEWED:

Le Misanthrope at the Palais-Royal

In *Le Misanthrope* Molière invites the judgement of *les honnêtes gens* upon their own standards and principles of behaviour in society, in a play set in the urban world of the minor nobility, easily recognizable to his audience. Despite the technical capacity of the Palais-Royal, which had engineered the scenic transformations of *Dom Juan* in the previous 1665 season, he employed a simple scene representing the interior of Célimène's residence. This was a suitably painted 'salon' where she queens it over her four admirers who, after their different fashions, play court to her, while in the background is the larger stage of the Louvre, to which one or other repairs and where their fortunes are ultimately adjudicated. The attractions for the eye lay in fashionable costume, with Molière playing Alceste in his coat with 'green ribbons' and, more importantly, in the persons and deportment of the players. For the town audience, conscious of its quality and socially ambitious, here was a play where the problems of society and behaviour were teasingly combined in a comedy of rare subtlety. From the outset it was a play which contrived to be both 'serious' and 'amusing', but its success was far from immediate. This has never been the play to raise a belly laugh, requiring a knowledge of both manners and morals for a clear perception of their comic misunderstanding. As the *Lettre sur l'Imposteur* makes clear, a knowledge of reasonable conduct is the condition for extravagance to manifest itself in *le ridicule*.

The subtitle of the play, *L'Atrabilaire amoureux* (the melancholy lover), promised a tension between mood and desire: what in modern terms would be depression (Alceste suffers from an excess of black bile), and love. There are two contradictory social impulses in the protagonist: towards isolation (Alceste ultimately quits the scene to take refuge in 'the desert', far from the company of the men he detests), and towards the necessary cultivation of the salon where he may meet Célimène whom he loves, albeit with a reluctance which he publicly declares. In the realistic world of the comedy the lover is not given the free access to the beloved so characteristic of the extended scenes of Cornelian or Racinian tragedy. Alceste must wait upon the 'young widow' Célimène in the salon where it pleases her to receive his rivals. For the only time in Molière's plays the young woman escapes the domination of a father or a husband, and is placed like a queen in her court.[1] It is a busy place, and the restrictions of the stage, spectators and all, and the visible auditorium, combine to emphasize the public nature of the role which Alceste is obliged to play.

Molière gives himself an absorbing dramatic problem: how to play an exaggerated *honnêteté* perversely at odds with the world, in a character obliged to court a woman who epitomizes the practices of the polite society that he simultaneously criticizes. Thus Molière's grouch shuns the world only at the final moment of the play, unlike, say, Orgon, who is able to sustain his tyrannical obsessions in the protected world of his home. Alceste is firmly implicated in society both by the strength of his own philosophy of life, and as an *amant malgré lui*, a lover in spite of himself. In both senses he is obliged to participate in a world of men whom he declares he hates. Rather than disdain society and simply reject his role as lover, he surpasses it. In his own eyes, he is an *amant magnifique*.

Alceste's criticisms of the world are sustained by moral superiority: a pursuit of sincerity and a passion for honourable conduct. Joined to constancy in love, these qualities might seem to define the complete gentleman, were it not for a distorted idealism derived from the very values of decency and politeness which underscore the less obsessive social behaviour of others. Molière's man-hater aspires to correct the *honnête* world in which he lives. Here the *extravagant* threatens to replace in the audience's mind the discreet pragmatism of society with a cult of frankness, for what can be more laudable than the pursuit of sincerity? The role tests the given parameters by exposing the values of social living to an ethical onslaught where the individual is the ultimate arbiter. Molière knew his audience; or did he here overestimate its discrimination? Louis Racine suggests a slow success, describing how his father was informed of the 'failure' of the play.[2] We shall see below what a contemporary reviewer thought of the audience response, and it suggests a modest start to a brilliant work. It required discernment, not alone in the perception of social morality, but also in sensitivity to acting. It was a play which Molière rarely played at court, and we may well speculate that it was written with the town theatre exclusively in mind.[3] The theatrical display is minimal, the style of playing and the range of characterization is restrained, holding the mirror up to the cultivated stratum of town society which must have supplied the most important part of the audience.

The reaction to *Le Misanthrope* may well have hastened the writing of *Le Médecin malgré lui* to support the repertoire and give a possible double bill. Although Grimarest, Molière's biographer, may mistake his dates, there is more than one opinion that the two plays together were intended to cover a range of tastes in the audience. We should not, however, assume that the bourgeois of the rue Saint-Denis found more difficulty than the marquises in appreciating the subtleties of Alceste's social morality:

> At the fourth performance of *Le Misanthrope*, he gave *Le Fagotier* (*The Woodcutter*) [*Le Médecin malgré lui*], which raised the laughter of the bourgeois in the rue Saint-Denis. *Le Misanthrope* was judged to be better, and slowly but surely it was judged to be one of the best comedies that had ever appeared. And *Le Misanthrope* and *Le Médecin malgré lui*, played together, brought in the commoners of Paris as well as the connoisseurs.[4]

The closeness of stage and society, the familiar difficulty Molière alleged for his art, was a source of well documented satisfaction for his audience, who saw in Alceste another entertaining *fâcheux* for which a model could be discovered in good society. Nor was it lacking.[5] After the success of the play in town, opinion had it that the cap fitted Monsieur de Montausier, the *gouverneur* (rather more than a tutor) of Monseigneur the Dauphin.

> When *The Misanthrope* was played, the abbé Cotin and Ménage were at the first performance and both, on leaving the performance, went to sound the alarm at the Hôtel de Rambouillet, saying that Molière was openly imitating the duc de Montausier, whose austere and inflexible virtues were indeed viewed severely on certain sides because they leaned too greatly towards misanthropy.[6]

Learning the gossip in Paris, Monsieur de Montausier declared publicly that he was being lampooned and threatened Molière with a beating and even death. There then followed a choice scene, according to Saint-Simon, when the *gouverneur* attended on his charge, the latter being of an age to follow his father to a performance of the play at Saint-Germain. (Other accounts differ: Montausier was at the first performance or had even read the play at Molière's invitation.) At all events the 'victim', having attended the performance, pronounced himself deeply satisfied by the character, declared the play to be good, and invited the playwright to supper.

Donneau de Visé, in the past a hostile critic, saw the production and reviewed it in the form of a letter to a courtier anxious to know about the town play, and managed to have his *Lettre sur le Misanthrope* annexed by the printer to the edition that Molière got out some time after the *privilège* was granted in June 1666. The journalist thus enjoyed some reflected esteem, and consolidated relations with Molière, the actor he had calumnied in the quarrel over *L'École des femmes* three years before. In a pedestrian narrative of the play's fine scenes, and conscious of the compliment paid to the dramatist, the reviewer insists on the delicate taste required to appreciate the play's beauties. The design of the play is praised for the brilliance of its representation of society and its manners, including behaviour which is *assez ordinaire*, such as the flirtatious, backbiting young widow in her salon, daringly matched with the lover who hates mankind.

> En vérité, l'adresse de cet auteur est admirable: ce sont là de ces choses que tout le monde ne remarque pas, et qui sont faites avec beaucoup de jugement. Le Misanthrope seul n'aurait pu parler contre tous les hommes; mais en trouvant le moyen de le faire aider d'une médisante, c'est avoir trouvé en même temps celui de mettre, dans une seule pièce, la dernière main au portrait du siècle. Il y est tout entier, puisque nous voyons encore une femme qui veut paraître prude opposée à une coquette, et des marquis qui représentent la cour: tellement qu'on peut s'assurer que dans cette comédie, l'on voit tout ce qu'on peut dire contre les moeurs du siècle.[7]

> *Truly, the skill of this author is admirable: for there are things here which not everyone notices, and which are done with great discretion. The Misanthrope himself alone could not speak out against all men; but to find the device of seconding him with a slanderous woman is to have found at the same time the means of putting the last touch to the portrait of our time. It is there complete, since we see also a woman who would wish to appear a prude opposed to a flirt,*

*and marquises who represent the court: so much that you may be
assured that, in this play, you can see all that may be said against
the manners of our age.*

There is no suggestion that it is the age which is at fault, but rather
that society presents just such an amusing spectacle of boorishness,
calumny, false modesty and affectation, which are pleasingly judged
by persons of taste and understanding, a view which animates Uranie
in *La Critique de l'École des femmes*.

URANIE

La délicatesse est trop grande, de ne pouvoir souffrir que des
gens triés.

ÉLISE

Et la complaisance est trop générale, de souffrir indifférem-
ment toutes sortes de personnes.

URANIE

Je goûte ceux qui sont raisonnables et je me divertis des
extravagants.

(Sc. i)[8]

URANIE

You are too nice, if you will tolerate only a select few.

ÉLISE

*And it is too general an indulgence to tolerate all sorts of persons
without differentiation.*

URANIE

*I enjoy those who are reasonable and I find the extravagant ones
amusing.*

Nonetheless Donneau de Visé, in admiring the worldly style of the
play, and praising its delicate accordance with the best taste of the
time, is somewhat unsure where to take a position vis-à-vis the social
criticism which he finds. In particular, he is disoriented by the qualities he sees in the role of Alceste, clearly an *honnête homme* and most
unlike the expected protagonists of comedy.

... le héros en est le plaisant sans être trop ridicule, et [...] il
fait rire les honnêtes gens sans dire des plaisanteries fades et
basses, comme l'on a accoutumé de voir dans les pièces

comiques. Celles de cette nature me semblent plus divertis-
santes, encore que l'on y rie moins haut; et je crois qu'elles
divertissent davantage, qu'elles attachent, et qu'elles font
continuellement rire dans l'âme. Le Misanthrope, malgré sa
folie, si l'on peut ainsi appeler son humeur, a le caractère
d'un honnête homme, et beaucoup de fermeté, comme l'on
peut connaître dans l'affaire du sonnet [...] ... ce qui est
admirable est que, bien qu'il paraisse en quelque façon
ridicule, il dit des choses fort justes.[9]

> ... the hero is amusing without being too ridiculous, and ... makes
> polite persons {honnêtes gens} laugh without stale or vulgar jokes,
> such as we have been used to experience in comic plays. Those of this
> kind seem to me more entertaining, for all that we laugh less loudly;
> and I believe that they entertain better, that they capture our inter-
> est, and that they make us continually laugh in our hearts. The
> Misanthrope, despite his folly, if I may thus term his humour, has
> the character of a gentleman {honnête homme}, and much firmness,
> as can be seen in the affair of the sonnet ... what is so admirable is
> that, while he appears in some way comic, he says things which are
> correct.

Donneau de Visé was almost certainly one of those whose criticism of
Arnolphe is repeated in La Critique de L'École des femmes, and who
found the role too comic for a gentleman. Then, he was of the party
which eagerly sought out anything resembling an indecency; here,
he was glad to point out the way the new play was in harmony with
good taste. Nobody, claimed the reviewer, could fail to appreciate the
play without appearing unschooled in good society: 'que l'on ignore
la manière de vivre de la cour et celle des plus illustres personnes de
la ville (that one is unaware of the way of life at the court and among the
most illustrious persons of the town)'.[10]

Acting style is the key to the role. In Alceste, Molière compresses
the demands he made on himself as an actor. Alceste is the principal
fâcheux of the play, the furious critic of his immediate social circle,
yet a participant, meddling in the society that irritates him, and self-
tormenting under Célimène's heedless goading. The structure of the
role resembles the double identity of Arnolphe/Monsieur de la
Souche, or the double acts Molière played with La Grange and du
Croisy in Dom Juan and Tartuffe. The internal contradictions of the
splenetic philosopher and truculent lover produce naturally a physical comedy fitfully regulated by everyday salon behaviour.

Donneau de Visé's review stresses the fertility of the writer's imagination, but regrettably fails to discuss the qualities in the acting which he enjoyed. We may however judge that Molière's performance managed both the style of the gentleman and the excesses of the *fâcheux*. One remark makes this explicit:

> Cette ingénieuse et admirable comédie commence par le Misanthrope qui, par son action, fait connaître à tout le monde que c'est lui, avant même d'ouvrir la bouche: ce qui fait juger qu'il soutiendra bien son caractère, puisqu'il commence si bien de le faire remarquer.[11]

> *This ingenious and admirable play begins with the Misanthrope who, by his actions, makes clear to all that it is he, before even opening his mouth: which makes us judge that he will sustain this character, since he begins to make it stand out so well.*

If the function of a *fâcheux* is to disrupt the balanced rhythms of polite living, then Alceste's entrance does not disappoint, with his demand that Philinte hang himself. Like *Tartuffe*, the play begins with the abrupt gesture of the *fâcheux*, followed by an inquisition. In *Le Misanthrope*, a progressive rhythmic integration of the two performers allows a shared enquiry into a possible theory of living, unlike the cameo Madame Pernelle, who condemns the obviously *honnête* life in the house without entering into any examination of the reasonable morality it represents. She does the portrait of each member of the house before sweeping off with the luckless Flipote. In *Le Misanthrope* again Molière uses the technique of the salon portrait in order to propose various possibilities of living which then are quickly examined in the light of Alceste's inflexible philosophy. His eccentric image of perfect *honnêteté* is worked out against a series of absent cases and hypothetical problems. In the abstract, an inflated attachment to his one-sided virtue assures Alceste that he can deal with the world however it actually exists beyond his obsessions.

Philinte, the practised man of the world, introduces the dramatic hypothesis of the play that a man who is melancholy should not fall in love with a skittish, gregarious and beautiful young woman. Alceste, confessing his weakness for the problematical Célimène, recognizes her blemished *honnêteté*, the gift of pleasing in society:

> Je confesse mon faible, elle a l'art de me plaire:
> J'ai beau voir ses défauts, et j'ai beau l'en blâmer,

En dépit qu'on en ait, elle se fait aimer;
Sa grâce est la plus forte ...

(I, i, ll. 230–233)[12]

I confess my weakness, she knows the art of pleasing me:
In vain I see her faults, in vain I scold her for them,
In spite of everything, she makes one love her;
Her graces are the stronger ...

Donneau de Visé notes the impossible proposition. Célimène, by the power of the *art de plaire*, so vital to true *honnêteté*, pleases a man who violently disapproves of the worldly manners she represents.

While in the opening scene, Alceste's doctrine of candour is measured against abstract portraits, in the second we have the dramatic realization of one such, the literary bore. An invitation to give approval is not a request for serious literary criticism. The first is a familiar social gesture, the second a professional exercise, and the *honnête homme* is not a professional. To mistake one for the other is to fail to understand the forms of courtesy that allow a society to practise its daily arts of good behaviour. The exercise of literary gifts is a salon accomplishment, and the performances of occasional verses in the plays of Molière are to be seen as part of a display of taste, elegance and talent, rather than professional skill which few, and certainly no gentleman such as Oronte, would dream of claiming. The occasional verses he offers to recite allow the mutual expression of esteem and social regard, where the listener profits as much as the amateur versifier.

The recitation of Oronte's sonnet occasions a performance-within-the-performance of a kind Molière often exploits, here (rather as in *Les Précieuses ridicules* or *Les Femmes savantes*) to explore the response of the audience within the play. The *honnête homme* should disclaim effort, as does Oronte, but the performance should be coherent and modest as well as pleasing and effective. Such a performance should engender another as the listener delivers a well turned compliment. Here Molière disintegrates the elements of the social occasion with Oronte's absurd interpolations, inviting a response which Alceste withholds, and which is ultimately supplied instead by Philinte, who is rebuked *sotto voce* by Alceste.

ORONTE

Sonnet ... C'est un sonnet. L'espoir ... C'est une dame
Qui de quelque espérance avait flatté ma flamme.

200

L'espoir ... Ce ne sont point de grands vers pompeux,
Mais de petits vers doux, tendres et langoureux.
(À toutes ces intérruptions il regarde Alceste).

ALCESTE

Nous verrons bien.

(I, ii)[13]

ORONTE

Sonnet ... *It's a sonnet.* Hope ... *It's a lady*
Who had rewarded my passion with some hope.
Hope ... *There is nothing high-flown in the lines,*
They are rather sweet, tender, languorous.
(At each interruption he looks to Alceste.)

ALCESTE

We shall soon see.

The review noted that the comedy of unwise judgement extended to some members of the original public. The closeness of the play to the tastes of its audience meant that the very practices of the spectators of the day were actively examined in the sonnet scene, and some made evident too soon their appreciation of its merit.

> Le sonnet n'est point méchant, selon la manière d'écrire d'aujourd'hui. {...} J'en vis même à la première représentation de cette pièce, qui se firent jouer pendant qu'on représentait cette scène; car ils crièrent que le sonnet était bon, avant que le Misanthrope en fit la critique, et demeurèrent ensuite tout confus.[14]

> *The sonnet is not bad, by the standards of what is written today.*
> *{...} I even saw at the first night some who made fools of themselves*
> *while the play was acted on the stage; for they cried aloud that the*
> *sonnet was good, before the Misanthrope made his criticisms known,*
> *and then they were left in a state of confusion.*

This scene has a clear physical character, indeed it has been likened to a dance. The alternating gather and scatter of the playing, as the vector of attention and action repeatedly changes, involves the actor in growing bodily tensions which erupt finally when Alceste exclaims that the sonnet should be thrown in the privy. Those who have been tempted to see good sense in Alceste's sincerity overlook

201

the incoherence which Molière builds into such a scene, through its sustained repetitions and the cumulative tensions in the actors, thanklessly moderated by the third, playing the tractable *honnête homme*, Philinte. The actor playing Alceste must cope with the rapid alternation of actions whose direction is reversed and contradicted. It is exhausting, and exasperating, to be required to do something and then affirm that you do not do it. Thus the sonnet scene creates a progressive growth of tension as a promised performance is solicited but not delivered. This is fully appreciated only within the physical rhythms of the actor, realized empathically in the shared experience of the audience. The superior philosophy which permits Alceste to criticize the *honnête* world is put to a physical test in the actual conditions of society, and in reading the play we must go beyond the misanthrope's remarks and sense the form in which they are embedded. The famous 'je ne dis pas cela' (*I don't say that*) of the sonnet scene has the quality of a refrain, but its effect is a repeated denial racking the actor. We await the performance drafted in Alceste's social manifesto, but we experience only the strangled failure to engage with the given moral exercise.

The play rings the changes on this tenuous grasp of physical composure and moral integrity, and what might be a free and well expressed science of life, even if characterized by an austere sincerity, is found wanting. Despite the numbers of persons who surround him, someone who advocates uninhibited exchange with society achieves nothing of the sort. In other scenes he is faced with the refusal of Célimène, his potential ally, to acquiesce in the adulterated forms of his social scheme, and again Molière develops the conflict within the opposed tensions of Alceste's bilious character. What would now be seen as psychopathology, the seventeenth century identifies with physical dysfunction. Rigid sincerity, an uncomfortable but credible social philosophy, becomes an emanation of a powerful physical state of melancholic self-obsession and ill-temper. The old medical scheme contained an intuition of the way thought may be embedded in physical processes; thinking was seen to be directed by passion, itself a result of an imbalance of the bodily humours. Many of the accounts of Molière's acting, given the praise which is heaped on it for its naturalness, still stress distortion: the facial grimaces, the bodily postures, and the variety of passions which are physically conveyed.[15] Donneau de Visé identifies qualities that might seem to belong to a primitive psychology, but his discussion is linked to the way states are manifest to the audience in action, rather than presumed to be felt within the characters.

The design of the play promotes pleasing illusions of personality, all
the more where the characters are drawn in sharp contradistinction:

> Il y a, dans le même acte, une scène entre deux femmes, que
> l'on trouvera d'autant plus belle que leurs caractères sont
> tout à faits opposés et se font ainsi paraître l'un l'autre.[16]

> *In the same act there is a scene between two women, which will be
> found all the more beautiful for the fact that their characters are
> quite opposite and thus make each other the clearer.*

The play is praised for the way in which a well designed proposition
as to behaviour in society is sustained by ideas. The role is the set of
attitudes and behaviours appropriate to an element in the proposition, and any notion of individual experience being the key to
'character' is quite foreign to this view of society and the stage.
When reviewing the Arsinoé–Célimène scene, Donneau de Visé
observes 'how there are two sorts of character in women', and pauses
only to allow of variations:

> L'on peut assurer que l'on voit dans cette scène tout ce que
> l'on peut dire de toutes les femmes, puisqu'elles sont toutes
> de l'un ou de l'autre caractère, ou que, si elles ont quelque
> chose de plus ou de moins, ce qu'elles ont a toujours du rap-
> port à l'un ou à l'autre.[17]

> *You may be assured that one sees in this scene everything that one
> may say of women in general, since they are all of one or the other
> character, or that, if they have something more or less, what they
> have is always connected with one or the other.*

The play, and the playing, manage to convince him of two life-like
types which are observed in a consciously schematic fashion. The contrasted figures of *coquette* and *prude* adopt and exaggerate the necessary
forms of polite exchange which make social intercourse tolerable, or
possible. Célimène sets the scene before the arrival of the lady:

CÉLIMÈNE
Cependant un amant plairait fort à la dame,
Et même pour Alceste elle a tendresse d'âme.
Ce qu'il me rend de soins outrage ses attraits,
Elle veut que ce soit un vol que je lui fais;

Et son jaloux dépit, qu'avec peine elle cache,
En tous endroits, sous main, contre moi se détache.
Enfin je n'ai rien vu de si sot à mon gré,
Elle est impertinente au suprême degré,
Et …

Scène iv
ARISINOÉ, CÉLIMÈNE

CÉLIMÈNE

Ah! quel heureux sort en ce lieu vous amène?
Madame, sans mentir, j'étais de vous en peine.

ARISINOÉ

Je viens pour quelque avis que j'ai cru vous devoir.

CÉLIMÈNE

Ah! mon Dieu! que je suis contente de vous voir!

ARISINOÉ

Leur départ ne pouvait plus à propos se faire.

CÉLIMÈNE

Voulons-nous nous asseoir?

ARISINOÉ

                        Il n'est pas nécessaire,
Madame. L'amitié doit surtout éclater
Aux choses qui le plus nous peuvent importer;
Et comme il n'en est point de plus grande importance
Que celles de l'honneur et de la bienséance,
Je viens, par un avis qui touche votre honneur,
Témoigner l'amitié que pour vous a mon coeur.

(III, iii–iv, ll. 865–880)[18]

CÉLIMÈNE

However, a lover would please the lady well,
Even for Alceste her heart is tender.
The devotion he offers me is an outrage to her attractions,
She will have it that I steal something that is hers;
And her jealous spite, which she scarcely conceals,
Everywhere, but underhand, is unleashed against me.
But then, by my life, I have seen nothing so foolish,
She is impertinent to the last degree,
And …

Scene iv
CÉLIMÈNE, ARSINOÉ

ARISINOÉ

Ah! what happy chance brings you here?
Madam, truly, I was missing you.

ARISINOÉ

I have come to offer a word of advice I think I owe you.

CÉLIMÈNE

Ah! heavens! how happy I am to see you!

ARISINOÉ

Their leaving could not be more convenient.

CÉLIMÈNE

Shall we sit down?

ARISINOÉ

That will not be necessary,
Madam. Friendship must show itself
In those matters which most importantly concern us;
And since there is none of greater importance
Than those of honour and propriety,
I come to warn you of something which touches on your honour,
And prove the friendship my heart holds for you.

The spectacle of the forms of behaviour taxed by insincerity and malice delighted an audience used to managing thoughts and feelings,
and preserving appearances.[19] Donneau de Visé particularly admires
the construction of a scene that mirrors his world and that of his *honnête* audience, and he repeatedly praises Molière's ability to fill the
scenes with new things 'to be said', with dialogue which renews the
initial proposition of the play. He judges it much as he might appreciate, journalist that he was, an elegant or scandalous event in society
where wit, judgement and reputation were the issues.

Molière's art and method went deeper into the sensibility of his
age and its affinity with the theatre. Some modern observers confuse
the ethical sense of *Le Misanthrope* with a concern for individualism
and sympathy for the idealist at odds with society. On the page such
a reader may find statements to admire or deplore, divorced from any
context of enactment. In performance comes the realization that the
comedy depends on the management of mind and body to which the
text is the key,[20] and not the prosecution of particular philosophies.

Equally, such a pursuit of an all-embracing integration, a physical and moral wholeness, is the object of *honnêteté* in the social world from which Molière draws his inspiration.

Molière's enemies would have been loath to characterize him as *honnête*, and yet he was the supreme entertainer of polite company. Comedy always strains contemporary forms towards distortion, or beyond into the grotesque. The close integration and the determined self-confidence of contemporary society gave Molière an audience schooled in the behaviour which he studies as an actor. Good behaviour resonated a principle of inner coherence which extended to every aspect of living. Nothing escaped this simple requirement. No ideal, no moral scheme could be promoted beyond the supreme social achievement, which was composure. Small wonder that the comic exploitation of *honnête* sensibility leads to the ruthless exposure of a spectrum of extravagance, and to such a dangerous backlash. Gossip tried to identify the supposed originals of Molière's characters, and powerful interests characterized his purposes as being envious, malicious or subversive. In *L'Impromptu de Versailles*, Molière protests that he is concerned with the form or design of moral propositions, presented as *personnages en l'air*, notions of personality embodied in the actor.

Clearly *honnête* more than critical, Molière, as actor and dramatist, experiments with forms of behaviour which deviate from an ideal of the integrated moral and social being. There is rarely a satirical agenda, and certainly no prescriptive morality against which comic excess is to be measured. Comedy reaches below the injunctions of any ethical system, or personal animosity, and stirs the moral sense and integrity of the human organism as social agent and individual personality. When the organic requirement for coherence cannot be satisfied, comedy itself is part of the systemic effect of self-regulation in mind and body which restores a necessary homeostasis.

The exercise of comedy is natural to a system in which coherence embraces consciousness of self and society, and where the proper balance between the two supplies the grounds of judgement. So deep-rooted is this sensibility that, while its abstractions will often be thought to imply specific bolts aimed at identifiable targets, the focus is necessarily upon absurd and playful hypotheses. In all of Molière's work the most clearly personal note may be that struck in the ingenuous letter written by Agnès in *L'École des femmes*. This may appear to reflect Molière's own sentiment because of the simplicity of human potential under threat by folly. There is no thesis here, and Agnès is essentially no more commendable than Célimène, her thoroughly worldly sister. Innocence and sophistication are circumstances which are properly examined in the pleasant abstractions of the comedy, whose moral value lies in its natural, unpremeditated function as the regulator of the system. Any *a priori* moral judgement is therefore foreign to the comic dramatist, and equally any excess whatsoever is open to examination. The fact that criticism is an inevitable consequence of the pleasure of comedy is in itself a problem for the management of polite entertainment, lest it become the occasion of bias, exaggeration and disorder.

Donneau's somewhat earthbound criticism of the progress of Molière's *Le Misanthrope* leaves us still in no doubt that what he and his fellows identified in the play was resemblance, the forms of society imaginatively removed from the plane of mere observation.

> C'est faire voir ce que peut l'amour sur le coeur de tous les hommes, et faire connaître en même temps, par une adresse que l'on ne peut pas trop admirer, ce que peuvent les femmes sur leurs amants, en changeant seulement le ton de leurs voix, et prenant un air qui paraît ensemble fier et attirant. Pour moi, je ne puis assez m'étonner, quand je vois une coquette ramener, avant que s'être justifiée, non pas un amant soumis et languissant, mais un misanthrope, et l'obliger non seulement à la prière de se justifier, mais encore à des protestations d'amour, qui n'ont pour but que le bien de l'objet aimé {...} et ne le point éclaircir, pour avoir le plaisir de s'applaudir d'un plein triomphe. Voilà ce qui s'appelle manier des scènes, voilà ce qui s'appelle travailler avec art, et représenter avec des traits délicats ce qui se passe tous les jours dans le monde. Je ne crois pas que les beautés de cette scène soient connues de tous ceux qui l'ont vu représenter: elle est trop délicatement traitée; mais je peux assurer que tout le monde a remarqué qu'elle était bien écrite, et que les personnes d'esprit en ont bien su connoître les finesses.[21]

> *This serves to make clear what power love has over the hearts of all men, and to make known at the same time, with a skill which cannot be too much admired, what effect women may have on their lovers, by changing merely the tone of voice, and by taking airs which seem at the same time both proud and seductive. For myself, my astonishment knows no bounds when I see a coquette bring to heel, before ever she justifies her behaviour, not a submissive, pining*

lover, but a man-hater, and oblige him, not only to beg of her some self-justification, but even further to protest his love, with no objective but the well-being of the beloved; and yet to remain firm, having brought him to this pass {...} and give him no enlightenment, to have the pleasure of congratulating herself on an absolute triumph. This is what we call managing a scene, this is what is termed working with art, and representing with delicate touches what passes daily in the world. I do not think that the beauties of this scene were understood by all those who saw it played: it is too delicately handled; but I may affirm that all noticed that it was well written, and that persons of understanding were well able to appreciate its fine quality.

Molière claimed great difficulties for his art, and here we see them. To represent extravagance while preserving a balance in the play was the challenge. The achievement was to create a theatre where the best values of his society were given recognizable expression in physical form. The manifestation of those ideals was the business of the *honnête comédien*, the model of behaviour.

CONCLUSION

There is no neat chronology to the career of Molière and certainly no orderly line of development for the literary historian to follow. Molière's response to the changing theatrical culture of the day took different forms: his own *comédie-ballet*, which we may suppose took the playwright's fancy, and opera, which manifestly did not. His brief involvement with literary models, and chiefly the example of Corneille's tragi-comedy, was abortive, and it was the practice of actors rather than writers that he was to follow as a dramatist. We see a resurrection of the cruder structures of the farce at moments when a tidy chronology would show Molière's genius to be at the height of its powers, concentrated on the works which now dominate the canon, and which he wrote for the means and tastes of the town theatre. The 'great' five-act works emerged, as we have seen, from the methods of the old farce and a professional practice which extended the potential of comic acting into hitherto unsuspected areas of dramatic interest.

Whatever Molière's own estimate of his different works might have been, he never called in question the theatrical and dramatic importance of even his shorter plays, the *divertissements* or *petites comédies* which first secured his position with the Parisian audience and sustained his popularity at court. These can be more episodic in structure, perhaps because of their brevity or the place accorded to music and dance, and in the past they have challenged critical assumptions about the genius of the writer. We should not be misled by the way Molière appears to excuse insubstantial works by citing the occasion which led to their creation or the tiresome pirates who would steal slight plays he did not publish himself. In his phrases one might wrongly see *le théâtre* as being the ornament which shields the inadequacy of the slight play. Is it not nearer the mark to suggest that Molière's requirement is that we see that the text is meant purely for the purposes of playing? And that, say, *Les Précieuses ridicules* is only conceivable when its acting is understood?

When we read Molière's defence of comedy in the *Critique de L'École des femmes*, we encounter Dorante's claim for its remarkable ability to create laughter in a judicious audience. Not those predisposed to the belly-laugh, nor tickled by mere oddity or idiosyncrasy, but accustomed to see, understand and judge behaviour in polite society. Such laughter, 'strange' as it is, must be moved by the actor. How then can any text, Molière argues, present the essential experience of the play: the performance of the actor? From time to time critics will observe the level of theatrical activity within the action of Molière's plays, his *play within the play*, or the disguise scene played out in the farce or the *comédie-ballet*. What is this but a veritable obsession with the means and practices of the theatre, and in particular the art of the actor?

If we follow the line of Molière's own interests and assess those which predominate, it is always the stage and playing which are to the fore, not the fate of society or the morals of his fellow men and women. If the focus of this book has been upon one thing it is on the medium of drama as Molière conceived it and the way in which he exploits and highlights its primary characteristics. He possibly encountered it first as a means of conducting business in the open street, and of handling the information needed to get a sale. There was in this no disposition to see the stage as descriptive of the world nor the actor as the credible simulacrum of the persons it contains. We have seen how acting on such a stage was a means of abstracting and clarifying certain key actions which could be developed in accordance with fancy rather than everyday probability. Acting here was a trigger for the mind. The salesman does not wish any reference back to the awkward detail of everyday living, but proposes to share a fantasy of life in which the desires of the customer may for a fleeting moment be satisfied.

The use of actors in the commerce of the street was a powerful tool in directing the thought of the audience in entertaining and profitable directions. Part of the challenge, as with modern television advertising, was to recognize the character of the human mind and what one might term its creative inattention, its tendency to slip from one focus of attention to another, and compound its understanding out of a series of fleeting experiences. For the screen medium today even the languorous sexual rhythms in which the model girl presents the attractions of the family saloon car will be subject to multiple jump cuts, sometimes witty in their reference to the very 'sell' which is attempted. From the unmoving stage of Molière's Paris streets, the actors who would secure the attention of the passing trade naturally employed the forms of playing most apt to ensnare this faculty of mind, those of comedy and its surprising shifts of action and attention.

Is it not possible to see in Molière the *farceur*, one whose stock-in-trade is the mental athleticism of actor and audience which is procured in playful situations for its own inherent delight? Such mental exercise will hardly be pointless, and still less thoughtless. A shallow involvement with the stimuli which we encounter in life will undermine the recognition which the game of drama requires. Nor can the dramatist cheat attentive minds by falsifying the nature of social interactions. On the other hand, given a sound instinct for the concerns and drives of his audience, the dramatist will set out on the stage the terms for the audience and the actor to meet in a playground of thought and feeling. The question which arises as we consider our present-day experience and practice of the texts left us by a seventeenth-century French actor is one of the interaction of playing and the experience and knowledge of the play-goers and their society.

Much fine twentieth-century production of Molière has created stagings and interpretations of the plays which are alert to the different contexts of theatrical meaning. As Carmody has argued,[1] the modern mise-en-scène resolves numerous questions of theatrical, cultural and intellectual context at the moment of its staging at the hands of the director. It seems right to argue that notions of 'fidelity' to Molière's text are problematic, inasmuch as any dramatic text is unrealized until a moment of performance, and therefore that all performance must decide on or discover the significant power of any text for the audience of a later age. Those that are classics, transmitted from an irrecoverable past, cannot be realized in terms of their original vanished context. Carmody uses a terminology which identifies 'readings' to which a text can give rise in altered circumstances of playing: a process of 'recoding Molière'. His method in that study is in conformity with critical practices which problematize meanings and see the work of the modern stage as being one of adaptation of works, in Anne Ubersfeld's phrase, 'for our ears'. Carmody explains the purpose of his study in terms which state both the achievement and the problem of the director:

> Though each director claimed a certain degree of authenticity in his interpretation, he in fact staged his own ideas about the text and the socio-historical context. Indeed, following Dort and Ubersfeld, I shall be arguing that the

director can only stage ideas *about* the classic text. Rather than investigate how closely individual directors hew to Molière's intentions, I shall be looking at how directors have adapted Molière's classic text to their own needs as twentieth-century theatre artists.[2]

Stated in this fashion we may see an epistemological problem. Carmody rightly identifies a process which at least foregrounds the 'staging of ideas about' the play, and which derives from the culture and practices of the stage in the last century. Postmodern criticism reinforces the argument for the director engaging in a momentary stabilization of the text amid its multiple and changing contexts of meaning.

This book has argued a somewhat different conclusion, albeit far from the 'humanist' view of the eternal classic that Carmody reproves. In the modern exercise of 'staging', there appears to me to be an epistemological lacuna which arises as the actor plays the play in which the director stages his ideas. For the actor, experience is governed by dramatic form, while for the director the vehicle for the expression of meaning is the manipulation of theatrical presentation. While for all practical purposes there may be no necessary conflict of method, there remains the question of the knowledge of the actor of the forms which he or she inhabits within the staging of the play. If we accept the argument which I trust derives from the practice and the precepts of Molière, then the premise must be that meaning resides at the outset in the embodiment of forms created or adumbrated in the notation of the composer of the work. While again, for all practical purposes readers and directors derive their understanding from an analogous physical engagement with the text which may be compared with the embedded rehearsal undertaken by the actor, the only transaction of the reader's or director's experience can be in some discursive and extra-dramatic examination. For the actor, the embodied playing of the comedy in the presence of and with the complicity of the audience is the sole moment of its realization. For the director, there is the realization of the 'reading' which is brought from the study to the stage, and (if we assume no cutting or alteration of the text) which must be invested in the signifying apparatus of the mise-en-scène. Where these reflections on the text go further, and require of the actor a *particular* understanding and inflection of the playing, then we see the stultifying effect on the actor of indicating this in performance. Meanings cannot be chosen. They arise from action.

Molière's dramatic invention will naturally and organically stimulate thoughts about the structures and contexts of our lives. Were it otherwise, the implications of the playing would be unnoticed firstly by the actor, and thereafter the requirement of recognition in the spectator, advanced by Molière, would be lost. But this recognition is a necessary condition, as the *Critique* and the *Lettre sur l'Imposteur* argue, and not the end of playing. The question, then, of the specificity of recognition arises, and the degree to which this should be established or argued by any mise-en-scène. Molière's thought and practice leads us to see acting as a process to be engaged without any particular conclusion being premeditated.

We might suggest that the experience of Molière in performance is systemic in nature. The greatness of the works, and their perennial appeal to *actors*, lies in their ability to mobilize the human capacity to embody a symbolic experience of physical forms and associated rhythms of thought. Ultimately, the pleasure which Molière *did* see as the end of playing lies in the stimulation of the nervous system and in the integrated experience of mind and body.

In this condition, then, the quality of the experience is bound up with the forms of living and learning, and dramatic performance presupposes the individualized and accultured nature of any specific response. The meanings of drama reside for the individual, actor or spectator, in the experience of the self and its exchanges with others and with the world. In the *Lettre sur l'Imposteur* there is the pious argument that the lady who is struck by the *ridicule* of the zealot attempting to seduce his friend's wife will be predisposed to find such behaviour laughable should she encounter it in her everyday life. We may see this as a weak defence of the moral utility of comedy by a dramatist desperate to find justification for a pleasing and licentious work. On the other hand, it can be seen as an expression of a view of the phenomenon of embedded knowledge and its functioning in the human system. Dramatic experience involves direct unmediated knowledge of the physical life of the actor arising in the spectator. Such experience is subject to discursive examination subsequent to performance, but at the time it is unpremeditated and unreflected, save in the terms and conditions which are achieved in the drama. If we do not stress the general context of living which attaches to spectator response we do not neglect it. We only point to its general character. Our society is not the society of Molière's day, but we might suppose that our bodies are substantially the same. 'Que fait là votre main?' is for all time, even if the role of the *directeur de conscience* is something we must deduce from the given circumstances of the play.

Molière, like all great dramatists, is preoccupied with means rather than ends. The means he uses are the embodiment of the difficult processes of social and moral life as they are generally and systemically experienced; and his imaginative response to these, actor that he was, was hypothetical and playful, and not prescriptive. For subsequent generations the adventure of mind which is promoted by his plays can be shared, and its mystery is not a question of the gulf which separates our society from his. The strangeness of the experience of Molière's comedy is one which he noted himself, and it arises from the actor entering into *le ridicule des hommes*, which is a matter of form. This was, Molière noted, a matter of the general experience, and not what we would now term particular 'socio-historical' conditions. The task of the actor was to embody in a particular performance the general qualities of humanity, *rendre agréablement sur le théâtre les défauts de tout le monde*. W.G. Moore was right when he suggested that the most important thing about Molière was that he was 'just' an actor, for the actor is aware that his art always requires the highly specific qualities and capacities of the individual being witnessed by the mass of his fellows. As a dramatist, his achievement was to define with extraordinary incisiveness the elements of performance as they are to be assembled on specific occasions by specific performers. His legacy is his teaching of the art of the actor in the embodiment of his comic roles.

1

NOTES

PREFACE

1 W.G. Moore, *Molière: A New Criticism* (Oxford: Clarendon Press, 1949).
2 L. Jouvet, *Molière et la comédie classique, extraits des cours de Jouvet au Conservatoire (1939–1940)* (Paris: Gallimard, 1965).
3 M. Jurgens and E. Maxfield-Miller, *Cent ans de recherches sur Molière, sa famille et sur les comédiens de sa troupe* (Paris: Imprimerie nationale, 1963)
4 G. Mongrédien, *Receuil des textes et des documents du xviie siècle relatifs à Molière* (Paris: CNRS, 1965), 2 vols.
5 S. Chevalley, *Molière en son temps* (Paris/Geneva, Minkoff, 1973)
6 Moore, p. 30.
7 G. Lanson, 'Molière et la farce', *Revue de Paris* (1901), pp. 129–53.
8 I discuss Jouvet's teaching at the Conservatoire in 'Jouvet and the playing of Molière' in *Nottingham French Studies*, vol. 33, No. 2 (Autumn, 1994), pp. 1–9.

INTRODUCTION

1 René Bray, *Molière, homme de théâtre* (Paris: Mercure de France, 1954).
2 Il faut finir par la Béjart. Je ne l'ai jamais vu jouer; mais on dit que c'est la meilleure actrice de toutes. Elle est dans une troupe de campagne; elle a joué à Paris, mais ça a été dans une troisième troupe qui n'y fut que quelque temps. Son chef-d'oeuvre, c'était le personnage d'Épicharis, à qui Néron venait de faire donner la question.
Historiettes (ed.) 1932–1934, vol. VII, quoted from Mongrédien, p. 102.
3 Un garçon, nommé Molière, quitta les bancs de la Sorbonne pour la suivre; il en fut longtemps amoureux, donnait des airs à la troupe, et enfin s'en mit et l'épousa. Il fait des pièces où il y a de l'esprit. Ce n'est pas un merveilleux acteur, si ce n'est pour le ridicule. Il n'y a que sa troupe qui joue ses pièces; elles sont comiques.
Ibid.

CHAPTER 1

1 After the ending of the Wars of Religion and with the coronation of Henri IV, the city had experienced a new vitality and a period of expansion and growth. The Pont Neuf, begun in 1578, was completed in 1606 and thereafter the Place

Dauphine was constructed at the western end of the Île de la Cité. In the east the Place Royale was created as a residential square, the present-day Place des Vosges, in which all classes would be admitted to the elegant garden promenade. Further north within the old wall an elegant semicircular Place de France was planned as an entrance into Paris of suitable magnificence. Both are designed to impress the eye, but also to contain spaces for the staging of public events, particularly the royal *entrée*.

2 *Lettres* (Paris: 1682), vol. III, p. 246.

3 G. Couton (ed.), *Molière, Oeuvres completes* (Paris: Gallimard, 1971), vol. I, p. 13.

4 Couton, vol. II, p. 111.

5 Couton, vol. II, p. 1238.

6 Couton, vol. I, p. 1272.

7 Couton, vol. II, p. 1273.

8 The connection can be confirmed in the case of the great actress La du Parc, who joined Molière's touring company in Lyon, where her father, the *opérateur* Jacomo de Gorla, maintained a licensed theatre on the Place des Jacobins.

9 Skippon (1667), quoted from J. Lough, *France Observed in the Seventeenth Century by British Travellers* (Stocksfield, UK; Boston; Melbourne: Oriel Press, 1984), p. 117.

10 '... tant en comédie que ballets', in M. Jurgens and E. Maxfield-Miller, p. 241.

11 The French rope-dancers were known abroad, certainly in the Low Countries and perhaps even in England where they are mentioned in Middleton's *Women Beware Women*.

SORDIDO

Never went Frenchman righter upon ropes
Than she on Florentine rushes.

(III, iii, ll. 117–118)

CHAPTER 2

1 In J. Wildeblood, *The Polite World* (London: Davis-Poynter, 1965), p. 101.

2 Jean Gailhard: *The Compleat Gentleman* in Wildeblood, p. 93.

3 Couton, vol. I, p. 579.

4 ... pour bien faire tenir le corps, le maître posera lui-même l'écolier dans la posture qu'il doit tenir et chaque membre à l'endroit où il doit être et quand il les verra changer de posture, il aura soin de les y remettre.
(from R. Chartier, *L'Education en France du 16ᵉ au 18ᵉ siècles* (Paris: Societé d'enseignment superieur, 1976), p. 133)

5 Couton, vol. I, p. 581.

6 C'est une chose humainement divine et divinement humaine de savoir digne-ment manier d'esprit et de langue un subject, le concevoir dans l'âme avec de belles et judicieuses pensées, ranger ses pensées d'une sage ordonnance, les reve-stir d'un riche langage, et les porter à l'oreille de l'Auditeur avec une mémoire ferme, une voix vivement esclattante, et doucement penetrante, et d'une pareille séance de tout le corps, se faire efficacement entendre; planter de nou-velles opinions et nouveaux désirs es coeurs et en arracher les vieux; fleschir et plier les volontez roidies; s'addresser et roidir les tortues et lasches: et victo-rieusement persuader et dissuader ce qu'on veut.
(*L'Académie d'honneur sur l'humilité*, vol. II, p. 648, cited by F. de Dainville, in J. Jacquot, *Dramaturgie et société* (Paris: CNRS, 1968), vol. II, p. 433.)

7 Couton, vol. I, p. 191.

8 Couton, vol. I, p. 942.

9 Couton, vol. I, p. 943.

10 Couton, vol. I, p. 944.

11 Les exercices de diction se transforment en de véritables pièces au détriment des études ... L'art oratoire est négligé au profit de la tragédie.
In F. de Dainville, quoted in J. Jacquot, p. 433.

12 Nevertheless, Racine's return to the theatre in the 1690s was occasioned by the patronage of Louis's pious companion. *Esther and Athalie* were played by the young ladies of the academy at St. Cyr, founded by Madame de Maintenon.

13 Dans ce genre, nous sommes ordinairement maladroits et ridicules. En outre, nos règles s'y opposent et veulent que nos exercices servent à perfectionner la jeunesse dans la langue latine. Nos spectacles ne doivent pas procurer un plaisir quelconque, mais un plaisir digne d'hommes instruits et de spectateurs d'élite. Les produits merveilleux de l'art s'avillissent quand le poète se préoccupe de flatter le goût de la multitude ignorante.
(from E. Boysse, *Le Théâtre des Jésuits* (Geneva: Skatline, 1970), p. 28.)

14 Loret, *Muse historique*, in Boysse, p. 141.

15 ibid.

16 Il n'y eut maison religieuse qui n'ornât ses murailles de chandelles. Les Jésuites, après leurs dévotions particulières et publiques, outre près de mille flambeaux dont ils tapissèrent les murs, le 5 et 6, firent le 7 un ingénieux feu d'artifice dans leur cour qu'un dauphin alluma entre plus de deux mille autres lumières qui éclairaient un ballet et comédie sur le meme sujet, représenté par leurs écoliers qui firent en maîtres.
(from M. McGowan in J. Jacquot (ed.), *Le lieu théàtrale à la Renaissance* (Paris: CNRS, 1964), p. 226.)

17 ibid.

18 Au collège de Clermont, où se fait tous les ans une grande tragédie, on lie le plus souvent le sujet du ballet à celui de la tragédie. Ainsi à la tragédie ayant pour sujet la Ruine de l'empire des Assyriens, on choisit pour sujet de ballet les Songes, parce que cette ruine avoit été prédite par plusieurs songes ...
(Boysse, p. 53.)

19 Il ne suffit pas que ces mouvements et ces gestes soient composés, élégants, harmonieux, agréables à voir; s'ils n'ont un sens déterminé, une signification précise, ils n'offriront qu'une danse vaine et futile, et ne mériteront pas le nom de ballet dramatique, lequel a pour but l'imitation. Il faut donc que les gestes et les pas soient la représentation des actions que l'on interprète et les mettent sous les yeux des spectateurs, de telle sorte que celui-ci n'ait pas besoin d'un commentataire explicatif et comprenne le langage muet du danseur.
(Boysse, p. 54.)

20 We shall return to this with the consideration of Molière's *Le Misanthrope*. Alceste refuses to make any approach to judges or influential persons in the pursuit of his action in law. He believes in the abstract value of justice. Boileau satirizes the lack of just proportion between merit and fortune in his first satire. One example is Francois de Cassandre whose 'villainous and wild temperament, which rendered him unfit for any society, caused him to lose all the advantages that fortune brought him; in such a way that he lived in a manner most obscure and most wretched'. (... *son humeur bourrue et farouche, qui le rendoit incapable de toute société, lui*

fit perdre tous les avantages que la fortune lui fit présenter: de sorte qu'il vécut d'une manière fort obscure et fort misérable.)
(from A. Adam (ed.), Boileau, *Oeuvres completes* (Paris: Gallimard–Pléiade, 1966), p. 875, n.1.)

21 ... elle va jusqu'à exprimer la Nature des choses, et les habitudes de l'âme, qui ne peuvent tomber sous les sens que par les mouvements.
(from M. McGowan, *L'Art du ballet de cour en France 1581–1643* (Paris: CNRS, 1963), p. 226)

CHAPTER 3

1 Austin Gill raised the question of a possible evolution of the farce acting into a newer Italianate form of literary comedy, but the evidence for this is slight. The actors' material was traditional, coming as Barbara Bowen has demonstrated, from the old plays of the sixteenth century, and incorporating material from the brilliant and popular humanism of Rabelais.

2 See S.W. Deierkauf-Holboer, *Le Théâtre du Marais* (Paris: Nizet, 1954), p. 39. He is partnered almost certainly by his wife La Lenoir. She was one of the attractions of the day, but does not warrant identification in this illustration of the farce.

3 It seems possible that in the Bosse engravings we see elements of the set for the earlier tragedy, although the upper windows are perhaps inappropriate. However, a scene overheard is a device used in an early tragedy at the Bourgogne, imitated later by Racine in *Britannicus*.

4 The stock-in-trade of the actor. His stock character.

5 L'Estoile, quoted by P.-L. Duchartre, (trans.) R.T. Weaver, *The Italian Comedy* (New York; Dover, 1966), p. 88.

6 Duchartre, p. 94.

7 Duchartre, p. 32.

8 Président de Brosses, 'Lettres familières écrites d'Italie en 1739 et 1730' (Paris: Garnier), quoted from Duchartre, p. 34.

9 Duchartre, p. 245.

CHAPTER 4

1 La Grange and Vivot, Preface (1682); quoted from Mongrédien, p. 102.

2 J. Grimarest, *Vie de Molière* (Paris: Jaques Lefebvre, 1705), pp. 45–46, in Mongrédien, p. 103.

3 A letter of 19 May 1658 from Thomas to the abbé de Pure indicates the shifts of position going on behind the scenes. Corneille writes of his hopes that the 'the troupe of Molière and Madeleine Béjart' might be persuaded to contract an alliance with the Marais actors, 'whose destiny they might change'.

4 Corneille had followed the fashion with *Andromède*, played in 1650 at the Marais, where, after its re-fitting, the company earned a reputation for *pièces à machines*, machine plays with changeable scenery and elaborate effects.

5 The company returned a second night to play *L'Étourdi*. This adaptation of an Italian source must have pleased at least the English visitors at court, for it engendered a *Sir Martin Mar-all* in London in 1668.) Mascarille appears in the 1663 edition of the play and would hardly have been renamed after the play was first performed in Lyon in 1655.

6 Préface to *Les Précieuses ridicules* (Couton, vol. I, p. 263).

7 Couton, vol. II, p. 95.

8 Couton, vol. I., p. 13.

9 Couton, vol. I., p. 21.

10 Couton, vol. I, p. 22–23.

11 Couton, vol. I, p. 23.

12 Couton, vol. I, p. 23–24.

13 Rather as Sganarelle cannot sustain speech in *Dom Juan* without some physical interruption. (III, ii; Couton, vol. II, p. 58)

14 Couton, vol. I, p. 14.

15 Quand le Docteur parle l'on doute
Si c'est latin ou bas breton
Et souvent celuy qui l'escoute
L'interrompt à coups de baston
(Duchartre, p. 199).

16 This would form the basis of *Le Médecin malgré lui* and the techniques would still be in Molière's repertoire in February 1673 with the first performance of *Le Malade imaginaire*.

17 Couton, vol. I, p. 34.

18 Couton, vol. II, p. 1162.

19 Couton, vol. I, p. 34.

20 Couton, vol I, p. 35.

21 Couton, vol I, p. 43.

22 Préface, Couton vol. 1, p. 264.

23 Couton, vol. I, p. 267.

24 Couton, vol. I, p. 281.

25 M. Despréaux ne se lassait point d'admirer Molière, qu'il appelait toujours le Contemplateur. Il disait que la nature semblait lui avoir révélé tous ses secrets, du moins pour ce qui regarde les moeurs et les caractères des hommes. Il regrettait fort qu'on eût perdu sa petite comédie du Docteur amoureux, parce qu'il y a toujours quelque chose de saillant et d'instructif dans ses moindres ouvrages. Selon lui, Molière pensait toujours juste, mais il n'écrivait pas toujours juste, parce qu'il suivait trop l'essor de son premier feu, et qu'il lui était impossible de revenir sur ses ouvrages.

(Mongrédien, p. 103.)

CHAPTER 5

1 For a discussion of the play and the significance of its production, see below, pp. 87–99.

2 The season of 1661–1662 had launched *L'École des maris*, a three-act work which would be programmed with a tragedy, or perhaps the five-act *L'Étourdi*, which remained popular.

3   ORPHISE

Il est si grand comédien qu'il a été contraint de donner le rôle du Prince Jaloux à un autre, parce que l'on ne le pouvait souffrir dans cette comédie qu'il devait mieux jouer que tous les autres, à cause qu'il en est l'auteur.
He is so great an actor that he was compelled to give over to another the role of the Jealous Prince, because none could bear him in that play, which he should have played better than anyone else, being himself its author.

(Donneau de Visé, *Zélinde*, in Couton, p. 1103.)

4 Spanish plays gave the example of the *gracioso* (one that Molière adopted in *La Princesse d'Elide*) and French reworkings created vehicles for players such as Jodelet. But these are really plays of mixed genre, where the comic burlesques the serious. While Corneille responded to Spanish examples, particularly in his *Le Menteur*, Molière remained largely uninspired by this important and well known neighbouring tradition.

5 Frequently the comic action is presented as a challenge to the inventiveness of the artful parasite. Plautus supplied many an example. Cf. *L'École des maris,* ll. 143 ff., where Lisette throws down the gauntlet. Molière's last play, *Les Fourberies de Scapin*, still employs this formula.

6 See Judd D. Hubert, *Molière and the Comedy of Intellect* (Berkeley: University of California Press, 1973).

7 See p. 3.
Ce n'est pas un merveilleux acteur, si ce n'est pour le ridicule.
He is not a marvellous actor except in comic things.

8 *The Portrait of the Painter or the Counter-Criticism of The School for Wives*, re-printed in part in Couton, vol. I, pp. 1015–1142.

9 For this and a detailed discussion of the whole affair see Couton, vol. I, p. 1014.

10 See Couton, vol. I, p. 696.

11 Ce dernier lui devrait faire meilleure mine, et en feignant de le vouloir servir [Horace], lui donner des conseils pour le perdre, ou lui jeter de la crainte dans l'esprit: lui dire qu'on l'épie, et lui faire des raisons pour lui faire abandonner Agnès. C'est ce qu'il fallait faire pour autoriser cette confidence; c'est ce que le théâtre demandait, et c'est ce que tout autre aurait fait à la place d'Arnolphe, qui se contente de se retourner pour faire des grimaces.
(Couton, vol. I, p. 1028.)

12 Couton, vol. I, p. 666.

13 Couton, vol. I, p. 664.

14 Couton, vol. I, p. 588.

15 Couton, vol. I, p. 1029.

16 La scène qu'Arnolphe fait avec Alain et Georgette, lorsqu'il leur demande comment Horace s'est introduit chez lui, est un peu de théâtre qui éblouit, puisqu'il n'est pas vraisemblable que les deux mêmes personnes tombent par symétrie, jusques à six ou sept fois à genoux, aux deux côtés de leur maître. Je veux que la peur leur fasse tomber, mais il est impossible que cela arrive tant de fois, et ce n'est pas une action naturelle.
(Couton, vol. I, pp. 1029–1030.)

17 Il avait les yeux collés sur trois ou quatre personnages de qualité qui marchandaient leurs dentelles, il paraissaît attentif à leurs discours, et il semblait, par le mouvement de ses yeux, qu'il regardait jusques au fond de leurs âmes pour y voir ce qu'elles ne disaient pas; je crois même qu'il avait des tablettes, et qu'à la faveur de son manteau, il a écrit, sans être aperçu, ce qu'elles ont dit de plus remarquable.

ORIANE

[...] Peut-être que c'était un crayon, et qu'il dessinait leurs grimaces, pour les faire représenter au naturel sur son théâtre.

ARGIMONT

[...] S'il ne les a dessinées sur ses tablettes, je ne doute point qu'il ne les ait imprimées dans son imagination. C'est un dangereux personnage ...
(Couton, vol. I, p. 1032.)

18 Couton, vol. I, p. 417.
19 Couton vol. I, p. 545.
20 Couton, vol. I, pp. 546–547.
21 Couton, vol. I, p. 548.
22 Couton, vol. I, p. 546.
23 Couton, vol. I, p. 546.
24 Couton, vol. I, p. 547.
25 Couton, vol. I, p. 550.
26 Couton, vol. I, p. 551.
27 Couton, vol. I, p. 551.
28 Couton, vol. I, p. 552.
29 Couton, vol. I, p. 591.
30 Couton, vol. I, p. 592.

CHAPTER 6

1 Quoted in R.M. Isherwood, *Music in the Service of the King: France in the Seventeenth Century* (Ithaca; London: Cornell University Press, 1973), p.115.
2 Isherwood, p. 115.
3 ibid.
4 M. Ashley, *Louis XIV and the Greatness of France* (London: The English Universities Press Ltd, 1967), p. 7.
5 J. Richardson, *Louis XIV* (London: Weidefeld and Nicholson, 1973), p. 50.
6 It was only in the mid-eighteenth century that the theatre appeared in France as an autonomous public monument.
7 Outre concerts et mélodies,
  Il [Foucquet] leur donna la comédie;
  Savoir *L'École des maris*,
  Charme à présent de tout Paris,
  Pièce nouvelle et fort prisée,
  Que le sieur Molier a composée.
  Sujet si riant et si beau,
  Qu'il fallut qu'à Fontainebleau,
  Cette troupe ayant la pratique
  Du sérieux et du comique,
  Pour reines et roi contenter,
  L'allât encor représenter.

  (Mongrédien, p. 146.)
8 Préface to *Les Fâcheux* (Couton, vol. 1, p. 483).
9 Couton, vol. 1, p. 484.
10 Couton, vol. I, p. 484.
11 When the Italian actors at the Petit-Bourbon found themselves overtaken in 1644 by Mazarin's promotion of the opera, a new music drama with Italian singers and staging, they responded by requesting the Queen Mother to assist in securing for them appropriate new Italian attractions. An Italian dancing master, Gian-Battista Balbi, known as Tasquin, was sent to work with them (presumably because they could not engage the possibly superior French dancers who were in demand at court). In addition, they asked for a vital support in the development of their stage spectacle: an Italian *machiniste*, a stage designer and engineer. In response to the request of the Queen, the Duke of Parma sent an artist capable of

pleasing the crown: Giacomo Torelli, the creator of the superb stage spectacles at the Teatro Novissimo in Venice. The *Finta Pazza* of 1645 represents the range and carefree inconsistency of the delights which resulted.

12 Petit carosse coupé qui a [...] plusieurs ornements. Il sert aux jeunes hommes qui veulent marcher en parade. (Couton, p. 1257, no. 5)

13 Couton, vol. I, p. 489.

14 Tous les sens furent enchantés;
Et le régal eut des beautés
Digne du lieu, dignes du maître,
Et dignes de Leurs Majestés,
Si quelque chose pouvait l'être.
On commença par la promenade. Toute la Cour regarda les eaux avec grand plaisir. Jamais Vaux ne sera plus beau qu'il le fut cette soirée-là ... [...] Il y eut grande contestation entre la Cascade, la Gerbe d'eau, la Fontaine de la Couronne, et les Animaux, à qui plairait davantage; les dames n'en firent pas moins de leur part.
P. Clarac (ed.), La Fontaine *Oeuvers diverses* (Paris: Gallimard, 1948), pp. 522–523.

15 ibid.

16 Couton, vol. I, p. 484.

17 Couton, vol. I, p. 484.

18 Couton, vol. I, p. 485.

19 C'est une forte plaisante chose que de voir accoucher un terme, et danser l'enfant en venant au monde.

20 Couton, vol. I, p, 488.

21 Dans la comédie *les Fâcheux*, qui est une des plus belles de Molière, le Fâcheux chasseur qu'il introduit dans une scène est M. de Soyecourt. Ce fut le Roi lui-même qui lui donna ce sujet, et voici comment. Au sortir de la première représentation de cette comédie qui se fit chez M. Foucquet, le Roi dit à Molière en lui montrant M. de Soyecourt: Voilà un grand original que tu n'as pas encore copié. C'en fut assez de dit, et cette scène où Molière l'introduit sous la figure d'un chasseur, fut faite et apprise par les comédiens en moins de vingt-quatre heures, et le Roi eut le plaisir de la voir en sa place, à la représentation suivante de cette pièce.
(*Menagiana* (1694), in Mongrédien, p. 149.)

CHAPTER 7

1 It must be remembered that the chief project for a court theatre, the *Salle des Machines* at the Tuileries, initiated under Mazarin, and entrusted to the designer Vigarani, was not located in the palaces Louis increasingly occupied, outside Paris.

2 Couton, vol. I, p. 685.

3 Et le soir, Sa Majesté fit représenter, sur l'un de ces théâtres doubles de son salon, que son esprit universel a lui-même inventées, la comédie des Fâcheux, faite par le sieur de Molière, mêlée d'entrées de ballet, et fort ingénieuse.
(Couton, vol. I, p. 827)

4 The text we possess comes from the edition of 1682, and speaks of the setting as the *salle de la comédie,* but this certainly does not mean a permanent theatre and

stage, and such a provision was made only in 1683, in the enlarged South wing of the château.

5 The stage became a conscious meeting place between collaborating minds: the connoisseur patron and the actor eager to *faire sa cour*. In his Remerciement au Roi for a pension granted some time in 1663, their complicity may appear in the description of Molière's Muse approaching the monarch, travestied as the *marquis ridicule* paying court.

6 Couton, vol. I, pp. 709–710.

7 Couton, vol. I, p. 749.

8 Couton, vol. I, p. 751.

9 {...} une comédie nommée Tartuffe que le sieur de Molière avait faite contre les hypocrites. (ibid.)

10 The second version of the play is the one discussed in the *Lettre sur L'Imposteur*, and was first played at the command of the Prince de Condé on 29 November 1664 at Raincy, in honour of the Princess Palatine. The prince commanded performances of the play again in November 1665 and March and September 1666. The final version was played in August, for the King at Saint-Germain, and then for his cousin, la Grande Mademoiselle, at the Luxembourg.

11 Couton, vol. I, pp. 891–892.

12 For a discussion of the possible forms of the *Ur-Tartuffe*, see J. Cairncross, *New Light on Molière: Tartuffe; Elomire hypocondre* (Geneva: Droz, 1956).

13 Couton, vol. I, p. 972.

14 Couton, vol. I, p. 973.

15 Couton, vol. I, pp. 906–907.

16 Couton, vol. I, p. 950.

17 Couton, vol. II, pp. 912–913.

18 Couton, vol. I, pp. 913–914.

19 Couton, vol. I, p. 914.

20 Couton, vol. I, p. 938.

21 Brissart's engraving for the edition of 1669 shows Orgon emerging in view of Tartuffe, which is not the clear indication of the text. As Tartuffe re-enters, Orgon is 'derrière elle', behind Elmire, who has invited him to go back under the table until he is quite sure of Tartuffe's intentions. Does the engraving reflect the artist's experience of an earlier playing of the scene? Or does Molière intend Orgon to emerge on hands and knees and that he is concealed in this position behind his wife's back?

22 Couton, vol. I, p. 962.

23 Couton, vol. I, p. 965.
There is a delightful echo of Orgon's 'C'est un homme ...', his incomplete definition of Tartuffe in Act I, with the break in the rhythm giving the phrase the same form. Tartuffe has no difficulty in completing his phrase. The 'entre nous' is wickedly ironic given the disposition of the actors on Molière's stage.

24 Couton, vol. I, p. 941.

CHAPTER 8

1 The device over a medallion in one of the tapestries woven for the King at the Gobelins and depicting the winter entertainments of his majesty is *Naturam superat*, 'he overcomes nature'. The artist depicts the *Salle des Machines* at the Tuileries and the performance of *Ercole amante* to which we refer below. See J.

Vanuxem, 'Le décor de théâtre sous Louis XIV', in *XVIIe Siècle*, vol. 39 (1958), p. 202.

2 Staged at Versailles only in 1674 (after Molière's death), largely due to the break with Lully. First performed in town with a score by Charpentier.

3 Nonetheless the expenditure for a show such as *Le Bourgeois gentilhomme* was still enormous.

4 Written to a commission by Mazarin for the carnival season of 1648, but postponed because of the young King's illness. It was performed by the Marais theatre in 1654. The vogue for the machine play followed the success of the *Finta Pazza* (played by the Italians at the Petit-Bourbon in 1645), Buti and Rossi's *Orfeo*, at the Palais-Royal in 1647, and *Les Noces de Pélée et Thétis*, again at the Petit-Bourbon in 1654. These were primarily court occasions, and Paris was excited by the accounts of Torelli's triumphant scenes, which made no mention of the *longueurs* of the entertainment remarked by some of those privileged to be present.

5 l'on crut voir effectivement un jardin d'une beauté extraordinaire ... cabinets d'une architecture rustique ... superbe édifice en forme de dôme ... percé de trois portiques ...
(from Despois and Mesnard (eds), *Oeuvres completes de Molière* (Paris: Hachette, 1873–1893), *Editions des Grand Ecrivains de France* (referred to as G.E.: vol. VI, p. 618.))
What is meant by 'cabinet' is unfortunately difficult to establish. The first meaning of the term is a room or office, and this must indicate a small building if it is to be seen from the outside. The rusticity of the architecture would not rule out elegance.

6 Ici la décoration du théâtre se trouve changé dans un instant, et l'on ne peut comprendre comment tant de véritables jets d'eau ne paraissent plus, ni par quel artifice, au lieu de ces cabinets et de ces allées, on ne découvre que de grands rochers entremêlés d'arbres, où l'on voit plusieurs Bergers qui chantent et qui jouent de toutes sortes d'instruments.
(G.E., vol. VI, p. 622.)

7 Equally so the costume for Dandin. The G.E. edition agonizes over the lack of a natural representation of the *paysan*. Should he be seen as a *villageois* or as a *bourgeois campagnard*? The answer to these questions, which mistake the aesthetic of this occasion and come dangerously close to submitting art to the strictures of contemporary agricultural practice, is that 'he' should be seen as a character for the stage. The setting was appropriate to the view to be taken of the action, and a farmyard is not required.

8 Il leur marqua lui-même les endroits où la disposition du lieu pouvait par sa beauté naturelle contribuer davantage à leur décoration; et parce que l'un des plus beaux ornements de cette maison est la quantité des eaux que l'art y a conduites, malgré la nature qui les lui avoit refusées, Sa Majesté leur ordonna de s'en servir, le plus qu'ils pourroit, à l'embellissement de ces lieux, et même leur ouvrit les moyens de les employer et d'en tirer les effets qu'elles peuvent faire.
(G.E., vol. VI, p. 615.)

9 In the earlier version of the play as *La Jalousie du Barbouillé*. See p. 45 ff.

10 Couton, vol. II, p. 605.

11 Or possibly actual trees. See J. Vanuxem, 'Le décor de théâtre sous Louis XIV' in *XVIIe siècle*, No. 39 (1958), pp. 196–217.

12 Je me suis bien gardé de faire rien chanter qui fût nécessaire à l'intelligence de la pièce.

I took great care not to have sung anything which was necessary to the understanding of the play.
(Corneille, H.T. Barnwell (ed.), *Writings on the Theatre* (Oxford: Blackwell, 1965), p. 144.)

13 It fell to Perrin and Cambert to create with the first *privilège* granted by Louis in 1669 an *Académie de Musique* which was devoted to musical drama. Lully took measures two years later to secure sole rights to a form which had succeeded with the Parisian public.

14 Couton, vol. II, p. 452.

15 'il s'est plus attaché aux beautés et à la pompe du spectacle qu'à l'exacte régularité.' Couton, vol. II, p. 821.

16 J'envoie à Madame Royale, de la part du comte de Saint-Aignan, un des livrets du ballet que l'on danse ici [...] nous y demeurâmes cinq heures [...] je n'ai encore rien vu de mieux exécuté ni de plus magnifique et ce sont des choses qui ne se peuvent faire ailleurs à cause de la quantité de maîtres à danser, y en ayant soixante-dix qui dansent ensemble dans la dernière entrée. Ce qui est aussi merveilleux est la quantité des violons, des joueurs d'instruments et des musiciens qui sont plus de trois cents, tous magnifiquement habillés. La salle est superbe, faite exprès, le théâtre spacieux, merveilleusement bien décoré; les machines et changements de scène magnifiques et qui ont bien joué, Vigarani s'étant fait honneur en cette rencontre; mais pour la dernière scène, c'est bien la chose la plus étonnante qui se puisse voir, car l'on voit tout en un instant paraître plus de trois cents personnes suspendues ou dans les nuages ou dans une gloire, et cela fait la plus belle symphonie du monde en violons, théorbes, luths, clavecins, hautbois, flûtes, trompettes et cymbales. L'on voit bien qu'il a fallu qu'ils se soient réduites à suivre en ces sortes de choses les sentiments des Italiens.
    (Mongrédien, vol. I, pp. 386–387. Couton, vol. II, p. 795.)

17 With hindsight it is clear that *Psyché* was one of a number of works which prefigured the emergence of a characteristic French form of opera. Lully returned to the score later. The alexandrines of the text were rewritten by Thomas Corneille in irregular metres and set as recitative. In 1678 *Psyché* was given as an opera.

18 See Jacques Heuzey, 'Notes sur un dessin représentant la Salle des machines au XVIIe siècle', in *Revue d'histoire du théâtre*, vol. I (1954), pp. 60–67.

19 Couton, vol. II, p. 66.

20 Couton, vol. II, p. 715.

21 'de dessous, le théâtre la machine d'un grand arbre chargé de seize faunes.'
    (Couton, vol. I, pp. 818–819.)
    There is no doubt that Vigarani could have done more to vary his scenes had he chosen so to do, and had he secured the collaboration of his writers. Nevertheless, the movement around the garden is a virtue in itself and obviates the temptation to construct machinery in excavations beneath the stage and in structures built above it. The question arises as to precisely what effect he used here for the finale. Did such a large machine actually rise through a trap? Vigarani certainly made a speciality of this type of transformation. It seems to answer an important need to get bands of players and choruses of singers smoothly on and off stage.

22 Couton, vol. II, p. 779.

23 Item, un juste au corps et rheingrave de drap d'Hollande musque avecq une veste de satin de la Chine blanc, les jarretières et bas de soye avecq une garniture de satin, prisé vingt cinq livres, cy... 25 l.

24 Item, une autre boiste où est l'habit de la representation du Tartuffe, concistant en pourpoint, chausse et manteau de Venitienne noire, le manteau doublé de tabis et garny de dentelle d'Angleterre, les jarretieres et rondz de soulliers pareillement garnis, prisé soixante livres, cy… 60 l.

25 Couton, vol. II, p. 595.

26 Anne Hollander, *Seeing Through Clothes*. London, p. 265.

CHAPTER 9

1 Elle [l'héresie] retourne aujourd'hui, comme en triomphe, dans la ville capitale de ce royaume; elle monte avec impudence sur le théâtre; elle enseigne publiquement ses détestables maximes, et répand partout l'horreur du sacrilège et du blasphème.

She {heresy} returns today, as if in triumph, in the capital city of this kingdom; she climbs impudently upon the stage; she teaches publicly her damnable maxims, and spreads everywhere the horror of sacrilege and blasphemy.

(Couton, vol. II, p. 1208.)

2 … un extravagant qui raisonne grotesquement de Dieu, et qui, par une chute affectée, casse le nez à ses arguments; un valet infâme, fait au badinage de son maître, dont toute la créance aboutit au Moine bourru, car pourvu que l'on croie au Moine bourru, tout va bien, le reste n'est que bagatelle; un démon qui se mêle dans toutes les scènes et qui répand sur le théâtre les plus noirs fumées de l'Enfer; et enfin, un Molière, pire que tout cela, habillé en Sganarelle, qui se moque de Dieu et du Diable, qui joue le Ciel et l'Enfer, qui souffle le chaud et le froid, qui confond la vertu et le vice, qui croit et qui ne croit pas, qui pleure et qui rit, qui reprend et qui approuve, qui est censeur et athée, qui est hypocrite et libertin, qui est homme et démon tout ensemble; un diable incarné, comme lui-même se définit.

3 Et où a-t-il trouvé qu'il fût permis de mêler les choses saintes avec les profanes, de confondre la créance des mystères avec celle du Moine bourru, de parler de Dieu en bouffonnant et de faire une farce de la religion?

And where has he found that it is permitted to mingle holy questions with the profane, and to confuse belief in mysteries with that in the bogeyman, to speak of God while clowning and to make a farce out of religion?

(Couton, vol. II, pp. 1205–1206.)

4 Il est vrai qu'il y a quelque chose de galant dans les ouvrages de Molière, et je serais bien fâché de lui ravir l'estime qu'il s'est acquise. Il faut tomber d'accord que, s'il réussit mal à la comédie, il a quelque talent pour la farce; et quoi qu'il n'ait ni les rencontres de Gaultier-Garguille, ni les *impromptus* de Turlupin, ni la bravoure du Capitan, ni la naiveté de Jodelet, ni la panse de Gros-Guillaume, ni la science du Docteur, il ne laisse pas de plaire quelquefois, et de divertir en son genre. Il parle passablement le français; il traduit assez bien l'italien, et ne copie pas mal les auteurs; car il ne se pique pas d'avoir le don d'invention ni le beau génie de la poésie, et ses amis avouent librement que ses pièces sont des jeux de théâtre où le comédien a plus de part que le poète, et dont la beauté consiste presque toute dans l'action. Ce qui fait rire dans sa bouche fait souvent pitié sur papier. […] Je laisse là ces critiques qui trouve à redire à sa voix et à ses gestes, et qui disent qu'il n'y a rien de naturel en lui, que ses postures sont contraintes, et qu'à force d'étudier les grimaces, il fait toujours la même chose.

(Couton, vol. II, p. 1200.)

5 This letter may be by Donneau de Visé who had written a similar letter on *Le Misanthrope* played in 1666. However, the quality and the pertinency of its arguments suggest that Molière either wrote it himself, or had a considerable hand in it.

6 Je suis persuadé que le degré de ridicule où cette pièce ferait paraître tous les entretiens et les raisonnements qui sont les préludes naturels de la galanterie du tête-à-tête, qui est la plus dangereuse, je prétends, dis-je, que ce caractère du ridicule, qui serait inséparablement attaché à ces voies et à ces acheminements de corruption, par cette représentation, serait puissant et assez fort pour contre-balancer l'attrait qui fait donner dans le panneau les trois quarts des femmes qui y donnent.

I am convinced that this play will make appear comical to such a degree all the conversations and persuasions which are the natural preludes to the flirtatious tête-à-tête, which is the most dangerous, I am convinced, I say, that the comical character which would be inseparably attached to those ways and means of corruption by attending this play would be powerful and strong enough to counterbalance the attractions that ensnare three-quarters of the women who engage in them.

(Couton, vol. I, p. 1173.)

7 Couton, vol. I, p. 1174.

8 This section of the letter merits extended quotation. There is more than an echo of Shakespeare's description of acting in Hamlet.

Le ridicule est donc la forme extérieure et sensible que la providence de la nature a attachée à tout ce qui est déraisonnable, pour nous en faire apercevoir, et nous obliger à le fuir. Pour connaître ce ridicule il faut connaître la raison dont il signifie le défaut, et voir en quoi elle consiste. Son caractère n'est autre, dans le fond, que la convenance, et sa marque sensible, la bienséance, c'est-à-dire le fameux quod decet des anciens: de sorte que la bienséance est à l'égard de la convenance ce que les Platoniciens disent que la beauté est à l'égard de la bonté, c'est-à-dire qu'elle en est la fleur, le dehors, le corps et l'apparence extérieure; que la bienséance est la raison apparente, et que la convenance est la raison essentielle.

The comic sense is then the external and sensible form that providential nature has attached to anything which is unreasonable, so that we may remark it, and may by obliged to fly from it. If we are to experience this sense of the comic, we must be acquainted with the reason whose absence is thereby signified. Its nature is none other, in essence, than integrity, and its tangible mark, propriety, that is to say the famous quod decet of the Ancients: in such a fashion that propriety is to integrity what the Platonists say beauty is to goodness, that is to say that it is the flower, the outside, the body and the external appearance; that propriety is reason in appearance, and integrity is reason in essence.

(Couton, vol. I, p. 1174.)

9 Note the enormous popularity of La Bruyère's *Caractères de Théophraste* in which the characteristics of particular (unidentified but sometimes recognisable) persons were anatomised, together with representatives of particular types. Moral deficiencies are to the fore in the exercise. A reflection of this taste is to be found extensively in Molière, where portraits of persons external to the drama are part of its delight. The best example is Célimène's performance for her *petits marquis*, but elsewhere, too, the outside world is characteristically reflected in this fashion. *Les Fâcheux* is constructed as a sort of portrait gallery in which a series of amusing social, and therefore moral, dramatic sketches can be considered.

H. Gaston Hall has coined the useful term 'characterisms' to consider the taste for moral scrutiny of typical persons in literature and the world. See 'Characterisms of vices', in H. Gaston Hall, *Comedy in Context: Essays on Molière* (Jackson: University Press of Mississippi, 1984).

10 Couton, vol. I, p. 676.

11 In Rotrou's *Le Véritable Saint-Genest* of 1649, Genest the Roman actor is converted to Christianity while playing the tragedy of a Christian martyr before the Imperial court. When he is inspired he leaves his text and confuses his fellow players, who are unable to follow him. They call for the one complete text held by the prompter.

12 The modern notion of 'character' as exhibiting particular individualizing marks is quite foreign to Molière's theatre. The description of Molière acting makes clear that it is Molière the player which is being referred to. The character emerges as a generalized proposition, an ethical construct which is given, or better arises from, a particular and individualized performance. This is diametrically the opposite of some tendencies in contemporary acting, where the search for the individualized character as 'another' leads to the attempt to 'recreate' (as if they had existed before) states of being and feeling which are appropriate to that character. The result is often the generalization of the performance into large emotional effects, which show a generalized excitation, but a much less particular form of action.

13 Couton, vol. I, pp. 679–680.

14 Couton, vol. I, p. 680.

15 Couton, vol. I, p. 665.

16 Par exemple, Élomire
    Veut se rendre parfait dans l'art de faire rire:
    Que fait-il, le matois, dans ce hardi dessein?
    Chez le grand Scaramouche il va soir et matin.
    Là, le miroir en main, et ce grand homme en face,
    Il n'est contorsion, posture ni grimace,
    Que ce grand écolier du plus grand des bouffons,
    Ne fasse et ne refasse en cent et cent facons:
    Tantôt pour exprimer les soucis d'un ménage,
    De mille et mille plis il fronce son visage;
    Puis joignant la pâleur à ces rides qu'il fait,
    D'un mari malheureux il est le vrai portrait.
    Après, poussant plus loin cette triste figure,
    D'un cocu, d'un jaloux, il en fait la peinture;
    Tantôt à pas comptés, vous le voyez chercher
    Ce qu'on voit par des yeux qu'il craint de rencontrer;
    Puis s'arrêtant tout court, écumant de colère.
    Vous diriez qu'il surprend une femme adultère,
    Et l'on croit, tant ses yeux peignent bien cet affront,
    Qu'il a la rage au coeur, et les cornes au front.
                              (*Élomire hypocondre*, I, iii: Couton, vol. II, p. 1238.)

17 It is too simple to think of the face-pulling of the popular comic as being an amusing ornamentation of an undemanding if merry intrigue. There is a relationship between internal state and physical form which is clear throughout the tradition of bare-faced comic playing from the seventeenth century to the present day Fernandel, Frankie Howard or Phil Silvers. The relationship is founded in the primacy of the focus of attention in all playing, and above all in comedy, where intellectual structures are crucial to the perceptions of the audience.

18 A question arises as to how the actor makes the face. If this is a calculated procedure, how then, does the actor know which face to pull? How can one think of all
the complex physical indices of engagement of the actor/character in the dramatic
action and its rich consequence? The answer is one must pull the face to know how
one feels. The body must focus the point on the stage where the attention lies for
the actor to know his involvement in his purposes. The contortions of the body
must manifest the bodily tensions which create the resistances to the dramatic
purposes in which you engage. The complexity lies in the definitions of form, the
richness in the actor's experience of the forms. You must pull the face to know how
you feel. You cannot pull a face to show others how you ought to feel at this point.
19 See the English translation of 1734 by John Williams in *A Method to Learn How to
Design the Passions*, (ed.) Alan T. McKenzie (Los Angeles, Augustan Reprint
Society, UCLA, 1980).
20 Le Brun follows Descartes in describing the passions as simple and compound. He
takes up Descartes's notion of the function of the pineal gland in relating the passions to the soul:
But if there be a part, where the soul more immediately exercises her functions, and if it be the part mentioned, in the middle of the brain, we may
conclude that the Face is the part of the body where the Passions more particularly discover themselves.
And as the gland, the middle of the brain, is the image of the Passions; so the
Eyebrow is the only part of the whole face, where the passions make themselves
known; though many have it to be the eyes.
(Antony Levi, *French Moralists and the Theory of the Passions* (Oxford, Clarendon
Press, 1964), pp. 200–201)
21 McKenzie, p. 14.
22 McKenzie, p. 16.
The binary arrangement is reminiscent of the present-day analysis of movement by
Rudolf Laban based on weight, space, time and flow. With allowance made for the
stringency of the latter, both attempt to delineate physical forms in terms of the
relation of the subject to external space and objects.
23 Mignard also painted Louis XIV on horseback, similarly costumed and with a similar martial dignity.
24 Couton, vol. I, p. 685.
25 Couton, vol. I, p. 689.
26 Couton, vol. I, p. 284.
27 Couton, vol. I, p. 495.
28 The tailors were, on the other hand, kept busy. Costume was crucial to the effect of
the play, and of course, no ballet could be meanly dressed.
29 Couton, vol. II, p. 787.
30 Couton, vol. I, p. 650.
31 Couton, vol. II, iv, p. 729.
32 Couton, vol. II, p. 767.

CHAPTER 10

1 Henri Sauval (1623–1676) describes the Palais-Cardinal in his *Antiquités de Paris*,
vol. II, p. 161. See Agne Beijer, *Le Lieu théâtral à la Renaissance* (ed. J. Jacquot)
(Paris: CNRS, 1964), p. 392.

2 I would agree with H. Gaston Hall that the engraving should be taken to represent a composite of elements from performances at the Palais-Cardinal. See Gaston Hall, pp. 41–42, and his further discussion in *Richelieu's Demarets* (Oxford: OUP, 1990).

3 Torelli's professional reputation was supreme but his political position was weak, associated as he was with Mazarin and the Italian influence at court. Torelli's designs for *Les Fâcheux* were his last in France.

4 Philibert Gassot, sieur du Croisy, who created the role of Tartuffe in 1664.

5 Jurgens and Maxfield-Miller, p. 351.

6 See W.L. Schwartz, 'Molière's theatre in 1672–1673: Light from the *Registre d'Hubert*' in PMLA (June, 1941), p. 398.

7 One might also compare the form if not the dimensions of the Salle des Machines, Vigarani's creation at this time, with the adaptation of the Palais Cardinal. It too had an *amphithéâtre* in this same position. The throne was set in the centre on a dais, much as one learns was the case with the performances in Richelieu's hall.

8 There is no lack of references to the composition of the audience in the *parterre*. It certainly included from time to time unruly elements, and there were occasions on which the porters at Molière's doors were subject to attack. These were armed and needed so to be. For most of the tenancy of the Palais-Royal we know that payments were made to soldiers to guard the doors. The picture of the Parisian *parterre* in 1642 in Sorel's *La Maison des jeux* concentrates aspects of the audience which nonetheless can be documented from time to time across the century. The *parterre* comprised mostly 'bourgeois' but there were villains among them.
'The parterre is most uncomfortable because of the crush that one experiences of a thousand bullies among the honest folk, to whom sometimes they want to offer offence, and having quarrelled over nothing, draw a sword and interrupt the play. When they are at their quietest they never cease to speak, to whistle and to shout, and because they have paid nothing at the entrance and come there only for lack of any other occupation, they have no concern to listen to what the actors say. This is a proof that the theatre is infamous.'
(Sorel, *La Maison des jeux* (Paris, 1642, 2 volumes), vol. II, pp. 424–5, quoted in Lough, *Seventeenth Century French Drama*, (ref), p. 84.)

9 *Registre* of Hubert, in Mongrédien, vol. II, p. 426.

10 On one occasion 36 seats were sold for the stage. This was for Donneau de Visé's *Les Maris infidels*, and Schwarz suggests that the numbers were increased in deference to the author. Molière never allowed more than 32 seats to be sold on the stage for a performance of his own plays.

11 The change in taste may be seen in the coming of age of French opera, a spectacular in its scenes and costumes, and where singing and dancing are more easily formalized within the stage design.

12 It is surprising to learn that stage seats were still sold for these performances. One may speculate as to the priorities of those who paid well and did not enjoy the perspective. It was however true that one needed to book early to get a *loge* for a popular play.

13 Dancing had altered somewhat in the movement from the figures of the earlier *ballet de cour*, which stress the movements of the corps of dancers through the space of the hall, to the positioning of fewer dancers against a painted scene. See M. McGowan, *L'Art du ballet de cour en France 1581–1643* (Paris: CNRS, 1963).

14 Invariably the spectators on the stage were men. There is however one recorded instance at the Hôtel de Bourgogne where at a performance of the highly successful

Judith by Boyer there was insufficient room for ladies in the main house and the gentlemen gave up their seats on the stage and stood between the wings. The play was most affecting and contemporaries remarked on the touching sight of so many pocket handkerchiefs.

15 What the cost of *loges* might be at this time is hard to imagine if they were much more than the *demi-louis*. The *écu* was valued at 3 *livres*. When Tallemant wrote this, in the 1640s, the custom of sitting on the stage may have been new enough for prices to be variable. He certainly treats the practice as some appalling new fashion.
   Historiettes. vol. VII, p. 128, quoted in Lough, p. 60.

16 'Critique', Couton, vol. I, p. 653.

17 See the *Registre* of La Grange for 20 January 1663. 'The king honoured us with his presence ...' La Grange specifies that the performance was 'in public'. Nor was the house cleared of other spectators for this visit. There is evidence that there was a box known as the *loge du roi*, presumably the central box in the run of five *loges de fond*.
   ... When the play was over (*L'Avare*), Molière came to the front of the stage in his Tabarin costume, and bowed most civilly to the fine feathers in the Royal Box. I gave him a most polite bow, for I looked him right in the eye, and we are, Heaven be praised, a person of some distinction. But he never looked at me, and you claim after all this, that he has wit?
   (*Araspe et Simandre,* quoted in Mongrédien, vol. II, p. 405.)

18 *Mémoires* (1859), vol. IV, p. 311. Cited by Mongrédien, vol. I, p. 398.

CHAPTER 11

1 Couton, vol. I, p. 677.

2 George Meredith, *An Essay on Comedy*, (ed.) W. Sypher (Baltimore; London: Johns Hopkins University Press, 1980).

3 *Oeuvres posthumes* in M. Magendie, *La Politesse mondaine et les theories de l'honnêteté : en France au xviie siècle* (Paris: F. Alcan, 1925).

4 Mongrédien, vol. II, p. 433.

5 Couton, vol. I, p. 661.

6 In III, iv, (Couton, vol. II, p. 1156).

7 Boursault, *Lettres nouvelles*, vol. I, pp. 119–120. Cited by Mongrédien, vol. II, p. 433.

8 *Art poetique*, Chant III, in *Oeuvres Complètes*, (ed.) F. Escal, Paris, editions de la Pléiade (1966), p. 178.

9 PHILINTE
Ce chagrin philosophe est un peu trop sauvage,
Je ris des noirs accès où je vous envisage,
Et crois voir en nous deux, sous mêmes soins nourris,
Ces deux frères que peint *L'École des maris,*
Dont ...
ALCESTE
Mon Dieu! laissons là vos comparaisons fades.

(I, i, ll. 97–101)

PHILINTE
Your philosophical spleen is a little too fierce,
I have to laugh at the black rages I see you in,

> And I fancy that I see in the two of us, brought up side by side,
> The two brothers of The School for Husbands,
> Whose ...

ALCESTE

> Good God! that's enough of your feeble comparisons.

10 Couton, vol. I, pp. 424–425.

11

DORANTE

Quant à l'argent qu'il donne librement, outre que la lettre de son meilleur ami est une caution suffisante, il n'est pas incompatible qu'une personne soit ridicule en de certaines choses et honnête homme en d'autres.

(La Critique de l'École des femmes, Couton vol. I, p. 666.)

DORANTE

As for the money which he gives so liberally, besides the fact of the letter from his best friend being a sufficient guarantee, it is by no means impossible that a person be comic in certain matters and a gentleman in others.

12 Sganarelle receives a courteous beating in *Le Médecin malgré lui*.

13 *Mémoires* (II, 143).

14 Le ridicule est donc la forme extérieure et sensible que la providence de la nature a attaché à tout ce qui est déraisonnable, pour nous en faire apercevoir, et nous obliger à le fuir. Pour connâitre ce ridicule il faut connaître la raison dont il signifie le défaut, et voir en quoi elle consiste.

The comic sense is then the external sensible form that the providence of nature has attached to whatever is unreasonable, to make us notice it, and to oblige us to run from it. To appreciate this comic sense it is necessary to appreciate the reasonableness whose absence is signified, and see of what it consists.

(Lettre sur la comédie de l'Imposteur, Couton, vol. I, p. 1174.)

15 Couton, vol. II, p. 470.

16 Couton, vol. II, p. 598.

17 Couton, vol. II, p. 599.

18 Couton, vol. II, pp. 1023–24.

19 Couton, vol. I, pp. 566–567.

20 Couton, vol. II, p. 47.

21 Magendie, vol. II, p. 762.

22 Ibid., p. 762.

23 Magendie, vol. II, p. 724.

CHAPTER 12

1 The chevalier de Méré, surveying the position of women in society, points out the good fortune of a woman who finds herself 'a widow and without children' ('veuve et sans enfants'). (*Lettre à Madame. ??? in Lettres* (Paris: 1692), p. 282.)

2 The day after the first performance of *Le Misanthrope*, which was most unfortunate, someone thinking to please my father, hurried to bring him the news, saying: 'The play has flopped, I was there and the reaction could not have been more chilly'. 'You were there, and I was not; however, I don't believe a word of it, for it's impossible that Molière would make a bad play. Go back and look at it better.'
(Louis Racine, *Mémoires,* in Mongrédien, vol. I, p. 265.)

3 Molière's most demanding play was not conceived for the aristocratic audience which customary sycophancy described as the most capable of judgement. Although Molière appealed to the common sense of the court as the jury in the

232

disputes which surrounded many of his works, this play was designed for enjoyment in Paris rather than Versailles. La Grange does not record the performance at Saint-Germain to which reference is made below in the story of Monsieur de Montausier.

4 Grimarest, *Vie de Molière,* in Mongrédien, vol. I, p. 264.
5 This keenness of society to discover and discuss entertaining 'characters' is well demonstrated in the roll-call of eccentrics with which Célimène and her acolytes amuse themselves in Act II, Scene v of *Le Misanthrope.* This sort of portraiture is seen in its full literary form in the *Caractères* of La Bruyère. Each new edition was eagerly received by its salon audience.
6 D'Olivet, *Histoire de l'Académie* (1729), vol. II, p. 158. Cited by Mongrédien, vol. I, p. 265.
7 *Lettre sur le Misanthrope*, Couton, vol. II, p. 132.
8 Couton, vol. I, p. 644.
9 Couton, vol. II, p. 139.
10 Couton, vol. II, p. 140.
11 Couton, vol. II, p. 133.
12 Couton, vol. II, p. 151.
13 Couton, vol. II, pp. 154–155.
14 Couton, vol. II, p. 134.
15 See *Elomire hypocondre*, and the evidence of his 'studying' with Fiorilli the Italian Scaramouche. See p. 146.
16 Couton vol. II, p. 136.
17 Couton, vol. II, p. 136–137.
18 Couton, vol. II, pp. 182–183.
19 Other reviewers make clear that the play must be seen for the performances of three beautiful actresses, Mademoiselle Molière, Mademoiselle Du Parc and Mademoiselle de Brie; that is to say, the actresses who first played the parts of Elmire, Andromaque and Agnès respectively. These women drew an audience.
20 Translations of Molière into English show how a liking for gags and verbal skill can introduce another layer into the text, which perhaps Molière was pleased to avoid. Richard Wilbur uses the couplet (no mean feat) and loads the tags wittily to point up the meanings, but locks the performance into a literary straightjacket. Harrison, on the other hand, often brilliantly combines an easy use of verse with strikingly modern phraseology, and, as with Hampton's unobtrusive text, the rhythms of the body are remarkably well rendered. Surely the key to Molière.
21 Couton, vol. II, pp. 137–138.

CONCLUSION

1 J. Carmody, *Rereading Molière: mise-en-scène from Antoine to Vitez* (Ann Arbor, University of Michigan Press, 1993).
2 Ibid., pp. 20–21.

INDEX